1968

This book may be kept

THE THEORY OF DRAMA

PREFACE

THIS book is in some respects a revised edition of *An Introduction to Dramatic Theory*, published in 1923, but since, in undertaking the revision, I have entirely rewritten the original and at the same time have enlarged it by over half its length, it seemed fitting to put the present volume forward under a new title. The chief additions consist of the section on the theory of drama in general and the section on tragi-comedy.

My principal aim in preparing this work on the theory of drama is to provide a general guide or introduction to the subject. I have tried to eliminate unnecessary detail and confine myself to the major problems, discussing these in the light both of earlier theories and of modern practice. On a subject so vast obviously many volumes might have been penned, but I believed that a single book of this kind might be more useful to the student desirous of embarking on a definite course of study. Further reading is suggested in the two bibliographies presented as an appendix, and an attempt has been made throughout to indicate the chief problems which it is the duty of such a student to analyse, and for which, before he proceeds to criticism of concrete examples, he must find solutions.

I wish to take the opportunity here of thanking my colleague Dr F. E. Budd, who kindly undertook to read the proofs, and of expressing my sense of indebtedness to Mr Barrett H. Clark, whose *European Theories of the Drama* has aided me considerably in the preparation of this volume.

ALLARDYCE NICOLL

CONTENTS

PAGE

I. THE THEORY OF DRAMA

(i) AN HISTORICAL OUTLINE 9

Aristotle and the Greek Drama, *p*. 9. Horace and
the Roman Drama, *p*. 13. Medieval Criticism, *p*. 14.
Renascence and Neo-classic Criticism, *p*. 15. The
Adumbration of New Ideas, *p*. 20. Romantic Criticism, *p*. 21. Modern Criticism, *p*. 23.

(ii) THE MEANING OF DRAMA 24

The Theory of Imitation, *p*. 24. Brunetière's " Law,"
p. 28. Sarcey's Theory and Shaw's Practice, *p*. 30.
The Question of Illusion, *p*. 34. The Basis of the
Dramatic, *p*. 35.

(iii) THE DRAMATIC CONVENTIONS 38

The Three Unities, *p*. 39. The Unity of Action, *p*. 48.
The Unity of Impression, *p*. 56. The Question of
Dramatic Rules, *p*. 57.

(iv) THE JUDGMENT OF DRAMA 60

The Difficulties of Dramatic Theory, *p*. 61. The
Theatre and Drama, *p*. 63. The Question of Moral,
p. 68. The Technique of Drama, *p*. 71. The Style, *p*. 81.

(v) THE FORMS OF DRAMA 84

Tragedy and Comedy, *p*. 85. Melodrama and Farce,
p. 87. The Conflict, *p*. 92. Universality, *p*. 98.

II. TRAGEDY

(i) UNIVERSALITY IN TRAGEDY 103

The Importance of the Hero, *p*. 103. Introduction of
the Supernatural, *p*. 106. The Sense of Fate, *p*. 109.
Tragic Irony, *p*. 111. Pathetic Fallacy, *p*. 112. The
Sub-plot, *p*. 113. Symbolism in the Hero, *p*. 114.
External Symbolism, *p*. 117. Heredity, *p*. 118.

(ii) THE SPIRIT OF TRAGEDY 119

Pity and Terror, *p*. 119. Tragic Relief: (*a*) The Theory of
Katharsis, *p*. 122 ; (*b*) Heroic Grandeur, *p*. 123 ; (*c*) The
Feeling of Nobility, *p*. 124 ; (*d*) The Sense of Universality, *p*. 131 ; (*e*) Poetical Effect, *p*. 132 ; (*f*) Vanity
of Vanities, *p*. 133 ; (*g*) Malicious Pleasure, *p*. 135.

(iii) STYLE 137

The Lyrical Element in Tragedy, *p*. 137. Blank Verse
and Rime, *p*. 139. Blank Verse and Prose, *p*. 140.
Poetic Prose, *p*. 141. The Universality of Rhythm,
p. 143. Verse as a Tragic Relief, *p*. 143.

7

THE THEORY OF DRAMA

PAGE

(iv) THE TRAGIC HERO 145

The Importance of the Hero, *p*. 145. The Tragic Flaw, *p*. 147. Unconscious Error and Thoughtless Folly, *p*. 147. Conscious Error, *p*. 148. Impotence and Ambition of the Hero, *p*. 150. The Flawless Hero, *p*. 150. The Hero swayed by Two Ideals, *p*. 152. The Flaw arising from Circumstances, *p*. 152. The Position of the Hero in the Play, *p*. 153. The Twin Hero, *p*. 153. The Heroless Tragedy, *p*. 154. The Heroine, *p*. 156.

(v) TYPES OF TRAGEDY 158

Features of Greek Tragedy : (*a*) The Chorus and the Unities, *p*. 158 ; (*b*) The Stage, *p*. 159. Early Elizabethan Tragedy, *p*. 161. Marlowe, *p*. 166. Shakespeare, *p*. 170. Heroic Tragedy, *p*. 172. Horror Tragedy, *p*. 173. Domestic Tragedy, *p*. 173.

III. COMEDY

(i) UNIVERSALITY IN COMEDY 175

The Supernatural, *p*. 175. Class Symbolism, *p*. 178. The Sub-plot, *p*. 180. External Symbolism, *p*. 184. Style and Pathetic Fallacy, *p*. 184.

(ii) THE SPIRIT OF COMEDY 185

Classification of Drama, *p*. 185. Distinction between *Drame* and Comedy, *p*. 187. Satire and Comedy, *p*. 190. The Social Aspect of Comedy, *p*. 192. The Sources of the Comic, *p*. 193. Incongruity, *p*. 196. Humour, *p*. 198. Laughter arising from Physical Attributes, *p*. 200. Laughter arising from Character, *p*. 202. Laughter arising from Situation, *p*. 203. Laughter arising from Manners, *p*. 205. Laughter arising from Words, *p*. 207. Wit, *p*. 209. Humour in Comedy, *p*. 210. Satire, *p*. 212.

(iii) TYPES OF COMEDY 213

Farce, *p*. 213. The Comedy of Romance (Comedy of Humour), *p*. 214. The Comedy of ' Humours ' (Comedy of Satire), *p*. 218. The Comedy of Manners (Comedy of Wit), *p*. 222. The Genteel Comedy, *p*. 226. The Comedy of Intrigue, *p*. 228.

IV. TRAGI-COMEDY

Theories regarding Tragi-comedy, *p*. 230. The Admixture of Tragedy and Comedy, *p*. 231. Sentimental Comedy, *p*. 233. The Theory of Sentimental Drama, *p*. 235. The Characteristics of Sentimental Drama, *p*. 237. The Question of Realism, *p*. 239. The Impressions created by the *Drame*, *p*. 239. Conclusion, *p*. 242.

APPENDIX

I. SUGGESTIONS FOR READING IN DRAMATIC THEORY 245
II. SUGGESTIONS FOR READING IN DRAMA 249

INDEX 257

THE THEORY OF DRAMA

I

THE THEORY OF DRAMA

(i) AN HISTORICAL OUTLINE

DRAMATIC theory is a subject which has occupied the minds of many of the most brilliant literary critics and philosophers from the very dawn of European theatrical art in ancient Greece down to our present days. Nor is the reason far to seek. The drama is at once the most peculiar, the most elusive, and the most enthralling of all types of literature. It is so deeply associated with and dependent upon the whole material world of the theatre, with its thronging crowds and its universal appeal; it lies so near to the deeper consciousness of the nation in which it takes its rise; it is capable of addressing itself so widely and so diversely to peoples of far distant ages and of varying climes; it is so social in its aims and in its appreciation; it is so prone to descend to the uttermost depths of buffoonery and of farce, and yet ascends so easily and so gloriously to the most magnificent heights of poetic inspiration, that it stands undoubtedly as the most interesting of all the literary products of the human intelligence. This has been realized in all ages, and all ages have sought to find the secrets of that art which embraces within its sphere the white-faced circus clown and the Prince of Denmark, the most garish provincial booth and the loveliest theatre-temples of antique Athens.

ARISTOTLE AND THE GREEK DRAMA. The fount of all true study of the essential elements of the dramatic form lies, as is well known, in the *Poetics* of Aristotle. All through the ages that work has been taken as a kind of text-book—during the Renascence with uncritical and enthusiastic reverence, critically appreciated and discussed in modern times. Naturally, we are

9

now far beyond the stage when men regarded the Greek philosopher's words as things almost divinely inspired, from which there could be no escape, to which every poet ought to bow. Yet to-day we perhaps have a truer understanding and a deeper admiration for Aristotle's genius than had our fore-fathers, for we are able to appreciate the strength of his thought the more because of our realization of his limitations. These limitations are best revealed by an analysis of the main facts concerning his historical position and the fortunes of the theatre in his own times.

Aristotle was born in the year 384 B.C. At the age of sixty-two he died in 322 B.C. At what precise period of his life he planned and wrote the *Poetics* cannot now be determined with any certainty, but perhaps we may be near the mark if we consider it to have taken final shape about the year 330. By that year Athenian tragedy had risen to its fullest height and was already showing violent signs of that decay which appears inevitable in the growth and development of any species of literature. Æschylus (525–456 B.C.), apparently taking up the rudiments of tragedy left by Arion (*c.* 600 B.C.) and Phrynichus (*fl.* 511–472 B.C.), with a massive strength and a power over character hitherto undisplayed, had laid the definite foundations of Greek tragedy about a century and a half before. In the year 499 he won the tragic prize, and thereafter contributed to the stage some seventy plays, of which only seven are now extant. His successor was Sophocles (495–406 B.C.), a figure more typically Greek, more mellowed and more harmoniously artistic, although lacking the rugged grandeur which had belonged to Æschylus. After Sophocles came Euripides (480–406 B.C.), more humanitarian, not so religious, bringing down tragedy from the heights that hitherto it had kept to the levels of ordinary human existence. Beauty was in all three, but after them this beauty seems to have perished. Writing in 330, therefore, Aristotle had before him the very finest works of tragic inspiration which Greece could offer; but among his contemporaries nothing new or vital was being produced, the old models serving as patterns for the younger poets. Inventiveness here seemed dead, and it looked as if the trio of earlier dramatists had explored every possibility open to the serious playwright. A somewhat different tale has to be told of comedy. Comedy, evidently, was a thing of slower growth, and in the minds of the Athenians was relegated to an inferior position. Omitting the antique Dorian ' mime,' from which, it seems, Aristophanes took many of his tricks, historians are accustomed to divide this comic effort of Greece into three divisions, styled ' old,' ' middle,' and ' new ' respectively. The old comedy, which extended approximately from 470 to 390 B.C., saw its most prominent representative in Aristophanes (born *c.* 448 B.C.). It was largely political in character, and indulged in extravagant, non-realistic types and episodes, the whole a fantasy of the imagination. This gave way to the social comedy of the middle period. The latest form of all, which might almost be styled a comedy of manners, developing its most characteristic features in the hands of Menander, did not come into being until about the year 320 B.C. It flourished until the middle of the third century B.C., and then, like tragedy, vanished.

Aristotle, accordingly, was not fully capable of appreciating the dramatic work of Greece. The date at which he lived prevented him from realizing completely the worth and the possibilities of the comic spirit of his land. As a consequence, the *Poetics* deals most largely with tragedy and with the epic— the two types of literature which Greece had in his time developed finely—and hardly at all with comedy. It is obvious, therefore, that Aristotle's declarations regarding the nature of drama, even when confined and applied to the literature of his own land, can never be looked upon as all-embracing and final.

It is also obvious that, regarded from a still broader stand-point, his judgments must often have a purely topical value. All through the ages till the late eighteenth century his statements were accepted as final and definite, becoming the ' rules ' by which critics judged and dramatists were supposed to write. The topical and temporary nature of his declarations was rarely, if ever, perceived. In practice, of course, men like Shakespeare utterly disregarded both his work and the works of his successors in criticism, but it was not till Ogier's and Dryden's time that critics in theory could be found bold enough to suggest that perhaps Aristotle would have modified his views had he known of the modern developments in the art of drama; and even long after their time this suggestion, important and obvious as it appears to-day, was completely neglected.

In reading the *Poetics*, then, we must always remember that the author of that work lived in the fourth century B.C., that he could have had no idea of the glories of later romantic drama, and that, even in the sphere of Athenian theatrical productivity, he knew nothing of the later comedy of Menander. A still further warning must be given. The *Poetics*, as it has come down to us, is not a book of criticism, as is, let us say, the work of Arnold or of Meredith. Not only are there serious diffi-culties in the text itself, due possibly to corruption, but whole passages have been condemned as spurious interpolations. The possibility is that what we know as the *Poetics* is only part of a very much greater whole, perhaps merely lecture notes of some pupil who had listened to the master in the περίπατοι, ' the shady walks,' of the Lyceum. Remembering this, we may be able to explain to ourselves why such con-siderable parts of this work deal with apparently trivial details. These details—of technique, of scenery, and of plot—might well fit into a huge volume; in the work as we have it they loom disproportionately large.

Aristotle stands majestically alone. In this sphere there is nothing extant from Greek times which approaches his scientific and dispassionately appreciative study of drama and the epic. Literature, of course, is discussed by various writers of that period, but the discussions either are entirely incidental or are related to larger questions of religion and philosophy. Plato's object is thus not that of the critic as such; he is intent upon developing philosophic conceptions, and for him litera-ture is merely a form of man's activity subordinate to the eternal verities it is his object to discover. In the *Republic* the poets are banished because their art, having its own end in view, may run counter to the art of government which, in its ideal state, is conjured forth in his discussion. Various other dialogues contain references to literature and, more particularly, to drama, but in none is there any attempt to establish a literary system such as Aristotle provided in his *Poetics*. Ideas concerning contemporary literature appear also in several plays of Aristophanes, but once more the criticism is indirect and incidental. Aristophanes is concerned with individuals and particulars, not with literary forms and general truths. His mocking allusions to Euripides, valuable as they may be for an understanding of classical Athenian literature, have practically no significance for the study of the theatre and of drama in general. Beyond this, fragments are all we possess. Some ancient material has been preserved in the *Ars grammatica* of Diomedes, and there are some significant judgments from older authors incorporated in the strange *Deipnosophistæ* of Athenæus. Some of these, such as Timocles' explanation of the pleasure we take in witnessing tragedy, must be discussed later.

HORACE AND THE ROMAN DRAMA. After Aristotle there is a long period of silence in dramatic criticism; and when it did arise once more it was destined, for centuries upon centuries, to remain based upon his judgments. In Horace (65–8 B.C.) we see the beginnings of what may be styled neo-classic literary theory. Aristotle's method had been largely analytic. He took play after play, dissected each, and finally gave his opinion as to the main characteristics of all. He laid down the law, it is true, but not in an aggressively didactic manner, and only after careful personal investigation into particular dramatic works. Horace's method is far different. His statements are utterly dogmatic, and, we feel, not often duly considered in the light of fact. In the *Epistle to the Pisos* we find his ideas in their most succinct form. The types of poetry here have been definitely settled; a special metre, it is determined, is appropriate to each. Characters in dramas and in poems alike must be types. There must not be brought " on to the stage what ought to be done behind the scenes "; a play must not " be longer or shorter than five acts "; only three speaking persons must be on the stage at one time; above all, " Let the Greek patterns be never out of our hands by night or day."

Everything is cut and dried; there is little scope for any originality save the originality of new wording. Possibly because of this, Rome did not see so great a drama as did Greece. Of the Roman drama, however, it is exceedingly difficult to judge. Out of the entire works of the trio of once famous playwrights, Ennius (239–169 B.C.), Pacuvius (220–130 B.C.), and Accius (170–86 B.C.), only a few fragments have come down to us, Seneca's ten tragedies alone surviving the shipwreck of Latin serious drama. Plautus (*d.* 184 B.C.) and Terence (*c.* 185–159 B.C.), certainly, wrote then their comedies, but comedy was considered by the critics, again possibly following Aristotle's lead, as a lower species of literary composition.

The importance of Horace as a critic is historical rather than intrinsic. From him the criticism of the Renascence took many of its ideas, and, more important still, it took from him the tendency toward formulation of ' rules,' abandoning thus Aristotle's analytic and almost scientific attitude.

MEDIEVAL CRITICISM. What happened to the older drama during the Middle Ages it is difficult to state with any precision. That something of the Roman stage endured for centuries seems definitely proved, and we may perhaps be justified in believing that all through the medieval period wandering actors (the *histriones*) carried on the traditions of the Roman stage. It was no doubt in an endeavour to counter this that the ecclesiastical authorities, half consciously and half unconsciously, inaugurated the new Christian drama which, starting from mere two- or three-line *tropes*, gradually assumed the vast proportions of the mystery cycles. This drama, however, was purely of the people; it was unliterary, and with it went no new criticism. The Middle Ages, however, did make important contributions (important again historically rather than intrinsically) to the criticism of drama, and for years medieval conceptions are to be seen reappearing in the most unexpected quarters. The early Church was much concerned with the licentiousness of pagan theatrical shows, and with the passionate enthusiasm of the Christian Fathers developed that predominatingly moral attitude which is to be traced into and beyond the Renascence. Prynne's *Histrio-mastix* (1633) packs into its thousand odd pages passages innumerable culled from such sources, and, although the

14

Histriomastix in itself is not a volume of literary criticism, it is obvious that the conceptions which it embodies must have had a considerable influence in the formulating of contemporary ideas concerning dramatic literature. The Fathers of the Church, however, were scholars as well as moralists, and a good Latinity with some came second only to godliness. In the early centuries of the Christian era the schools and the grammarians flourished; these schools and grammarians merged soon into the great educational centres which were the monasteries. Now, Terence and Seneca were masters of Latin style, and accordingly, whatever might be said concerning the iniquity of popular shows, those authors never lost their place on shelves otherwise largely filled with volumes of religious theorizings. Here, however, it must be remembered that neither Terence nor Seneca was regarded as a dramatist in the full sense of the word; they were, in the medieval imagination, poets only, and from the time of Isidore of Seville (seventh century) it was assumed that their works had been recited, by the poet or a friend, from some kind of *pulpitum*. This meant that drama as such became merely part of narrative poetry in general. Now, one of the obvious distinctions between tragedy and comedy was that the one dealt seriously with high characters and the other dealt brightly with ordinary characters. As drama had become indistinguishable from the whole of poetry, this distinction obviously could be made to apply more generally. " Comedy," says Dante in 1318, " beginneth with some adverse circumstances, but its theme hath a happy termination, as doth appear in the comedies of Terence." [1] Hence he has no hesitation in styling his own poem a " divine comedy " (*La Divina Commedia*), since " in its beginning it is horrible and foul, because it is Hell; in its ending, fortunate, desirable, and joyful, because it is Paradise."

RENASCENCE AND NEO-CLASSIC CRITICISM. Then came the Renascence, the rebirth of enthusiasm for things classical, and once more comedy and tragedy were related to the stage, once more a dramatic criticism, distinct from more general poetic

[1] Translated in Barrett H. Clark's *European Theories of the Drama* (1929), p. 47 (copyright 1918 by D. Appleton and Company).

criticism, took its rise. Feverishly men turned to the extant relics of ancient drama, discovering new beauties in those Latin playwrights who had never entirely been lost and finding in the long-forgotten manuscripts of Greek authors treasures greater than could be offered by both the Indies, above all realizing now that these things were not mere poems, but works intended to be performed before an audience by living actors. From the production in semi-classical theatres of plays by Terence and Plautus a step was soon taken to the writing of comedies and tragedies in the vernacular and to the placing of these upon a variety of stages, strangely mingling the medieval with the ancient.   The new drama, the drama which, fused with the medieval, was to lead to Shakespeare, had been born.

Naturally, a fresh interest was taken in Horace, and when the worth of Aristotle was rediscovered many men were inspired to pen critical studies both of the old classical and of the newer drama. During the Middle Ages Aristotle had been all but lost. He was known of vaguely through an abbreviated Arabic version by Averroës, which in its turn served as the basis for a Latin rendering by Hermann in the thirteenth century. Only with the rediscovery of classical manuscript material in the fifteenth century, however, was the true Aristotle given to the world, and even then men still stumbled seriously in their endeavours to elucidate his sentences. In 1498 came the inadequate Latin translation by Giorgio Valla; this served to awaken interest in the philosopher's work, and ensured a certain success both for the first Greek text published by Aldus in 1508 and for the many later versions in Latin and the vernacular, as well as for the innumerable discussions founded on his pronouncements.

Peculiarly enough, in view of the independent creative genius of the Renascence, the critics were inclined toward pedantry and mechanical judgments. The passion for things classical, it seems, made them refuse to recognize as ' nature ' anything except what their imagination conceived of antique art and civilization.   From Vida's *De arte poetica* (1527) onward through a series of critical dissertations in prose and in verse the same cry was reiterated: " Follow the ancients," " Don't try any novelties," " Keep to your five acts," " Imitate Seneca," above all " Keep to the unities." These rules of the neo-classicists, to be discussed in greater detail hereafter, were to be the skeletons in the cupboards of dramatic critics and of dramatists for centuries to come. Some made no endeavour to conceal the dead bones, but treated them with reverence as though they were relics of a saint; others pretended to be free of such impediments in the way of freedom of thought while the spectral rattling within their doors betrayed their secret. A few, it must be confessed, succeeded in escaping, but they were but a handful in all and never had the influence exerted by their opponents.

It must not, of course, be supposed that the whole system of critical thought during this period was based on classical ideas. Men cannot so easily throw off the influence of their environment and of their immediate predecessors; and the Renascence embodied, both in its creative and in its critical activities, a great deal that was medieval. The popular conception of tragedy, as we shall find, was largely based on the ideals of the Middle Ages, while the pronouncements both of the Fathers of the Church and of later schoolmen were eagerly pillaged by the Puritans and elaborately explained by the friends of poetry and the drama. Puritanism, it is true, did not affect the Latin as it did the Germanic races, but the Counter-Reformation played no less important a part among the former than the pure Reformation did among the latter. Through both criticism soon turned to moral problems of which Aristotle was totally ignorant, and the classic ideas became confused with, or were interpreted according to, an entirely alien set of ideas. This moral note is one which has never quite been eradicated; concealed though it may be under a diversity of forms, it still endures after the passing of nearly four centuries.[1]

In France the Italian critics soon established a pre-eminent position. The Parisian Court was in close touch with the houses of Mantua and Florence; Italian was almost the

[1] Thus Benedetto Varchi in 1553 interpreted all literature in the light of religion, and in this he was followed by the greater and more popular Scaliger (1561).

language of politeness; and French authors were frequent visitors to the homes of those transalpine academies which were so instrumental in furthering the scholarly and artistic endeavours of the time. Castelvetro and Scaliger thus became masters in the art of criticism, and Aristotle was taken as the inspired prophet of eternal wisdom. Once more it must be remembered that there were a number of dissentients, but the classical *régime* was almost universally followed and remained to be incorporated in that great school of thought and of creative artistry which flourished in the days of Louis XIV.

The classic ideals, indeed, penetrated everywhere, and the dead bones of Horace and the spurious wraith of Aristotle dominated over and made timorous even the contemporaries of Shakespeare. Charming as Sidney's *Apologie for Poetrie* is, it is wholly under the sway of this artificial theory. Sidney condemns tragi-comedy, which was to be one of the glories of Elizabethan drama; he condemns all those writers who, like Shakespeare, indulged in romantic excess. He speaks of "our Tragedies and Comedies, (not without cause cried out against,) observing rules, neyther of honest civilitie, nor of skilfull Poetrie, excepting *Gorboduck*"[1]—*Gorboduc*, a work which, whatever historical value it may possess, must be admitted but a dull and hopelessly uninspiring piece of variegated rhetoric. After Sidney came Jonson, who tried to put into practice what both he and Sidney preached in theory. Jonson's criticism is fragmentary, being contained mainly in his little volume called *Discoveries*, but his neo-classic tendencies may be seen clearly enough in his two tragedies, *Sejanus* and *Catiline*, obviously written in direct opposition to the romantic plays of Shakespeare. So followed many another critic and dramatist.

Meanwhile the centre of critical activity was shifting from Italy to France. In the former country there is virtually nothing of value from the year 1600 to the year 1700, whereas France can in that period display a liberal-minded Ogier (*d.* 1670), a practical theorist in Molière (1622–73), and a series of " Augustan " rule-givers in Chapelain (1595–1674), La Mesnardière (1610–63), Hédelin (1604–76), Pierre

[1] Ed. E. Arber (1868), p. 63.

Corneille (1606–84), Racine (1639–99), Rapin (1621–87), Boileau (1636–1711), and Saint-Evremond (1610–1703). Quite naturally, they succeeded in strengthening the bonds of the creed which they had inherited from Italy, and their ideas soon took root in seventeenth-century England. As an extreme exponent of the cult stood forth Thomas Rymer (1641–1713), arch-priest of neo-classicism. In *The Tragedies of the Last Age Considered* (1678) and *A Short View of Tragedy* (1692–93) he shows us this particular type of criticism carried to a *reductio ad absurdum*. Iago for Rymer is impossible. Why? Because it is a recognized fact that *all* soldiers are honest, and because it is also recognized that *all* human beings should show gratitude to those who are good to them. This is simply Horace's doctrine of types, suggested by the art of Greece, run to excess.

Dryden, as we have seen, broke away. His famous *Essay of Dramatick Poesie*, published in 1668, presents in dialogue form the struggle between those neo-classicists who looked to France for inspiration and those freer critics who could appreciate Shakespeare. The *Essay of Dramatick Poesie* is a work which, like Aristotle's *Poetics*, should be read by all who would study not only the development of literary criticism, but the essentials of the art of the drama. Dryden's critical remarks are, it is true, not confined to this work. One of his most penetrating statements, indeed, appears only as a manuscript note in a copy of Rymer's work. " It is not enough," he says there, " that Aristotle has said so, for Aristotle drew his models of tragedy from Sophocles and Euripides: and, if he had seen ours, might have changed his mind." [1] He was not alone in this verdict; he was not even the first to give utterance to it, for in 1628 François Ogier had come to a similar decision, declaring

that the Greeks wrote for Greece, and achieved success in the judgment of the cultured people of their time; and that we shall imitate them much better if we allow something to the genius of our country and to the taste of our language than if we force ourselves to follow step by step both their style of invention and their poetic forms, as some of our authors have done.[2]

[1] On these manuscript notes see the Scott-Saintsbury *Works of Dryden*, xxv, 379; and Saintsbury's *Loci Critici*, pp. 157–158.
[2] " Préface au Lecteur," prefixed to the *Tyr et Sidon* (1628) of Schelandre.

Yet, whatever predecessors he may have had, Dryden's words ring strong and true, testifying to the innate good sense and the profound realization of literary values which he brought to the enriching of criticism. The motto of his great *Essay of Dramatick Poesie* might well be found in that marginal annotation to Rymer.

THE ADUMBRATION OF NEW IDEAS. With the eighteenth century new styles in criticism and in drama began to make their appearance. The older neo-classic ideals still held their ground; in France Voltaire (1694–1778) robustly and obstinately upheld them, and in England Addison (1672–1719) gave cultured and ' safe ' judgments of an uninspired sort based on the same established system. Gradually, however, the fresh spirit is to be traced at work. This fresh spirit seems due to two main forces operative at that period. One was the appreciation of Shakespeare. In the London theatres the plays of the Elizabethan era were regularly played; hardly a week passed without the opportunity being given of witnessing some comedies or tragedies by Shakespeare, Jonson, Fletcher, or Massinger. Now, most of these had broken every one of the rules, and, in spite of that, critics found in them matter which they could not but praise. The usual method of escape was by an appeal to " nature." Shakespeare " warbled his native wood-notes wild "; he was " Nature's darling." As a result of this, whereas in seventeenth-century France nature was only theoretically superior to the supposed rules of the ancients, in England it became practically so. True, it hardly dawned upon anyone, except Dr Johnson—and in his case but dimly—that Shakespeare, precisely because he did break the rules, might be pointing out a newer and truer way for the theatre; yet there were the facts, facts which had to be faced and which inevitably induced men to a more liberal way of critical thought. This liberalism may have been the most potent influence in the development in London of fresh experiments in dramatic writing. Sentimental comedy and *bourgeois* tragedy, far off though these may be from Shakespeare's dramas, are the expression of a desire to attempt something other than time-worn forms and to escape from mere imitation. This sentimentalism is the second great force making for a change in critical idea. To France these plays soon passed, and there met with an enthusiastic reception from Diderot (1713–84) and his companions, who immediately attempted to find rational justification for their style. Diderot's discussion of serious comedy (1758), La Chaussée's prologue to *La Fausse Antipathie* (1733), and Beaumarchais's essay on the serious drama (1767) are documents which, however much they cling to the neo-classic conceptions for their terminology and arrangement of material, strike an unquestionably modern note. The combined influence of Shakespeare and of the sentimental dramatists is to be traced too in the famous *Hamburgische Dramaturgie* of Lessing (1729–81), where a determined attempt is made to reconcile the findings of Aristotle with the achievements of Shakespeare and the moderns.

ROMANTIC CRITICISM. Already in this time signs of a mighty change in literary orientation had become visible. The precursors of romanticism, in theory and in practice, had come into being. Gray was writing his *Odes*, Collins was indulging in reveries on the theme of Gaelic romance; Chatterton, Mrs Radcliffe, and a host of others, geniuses and charlatans, were tentatively feeling their way toward a new poetry and a new prose. Romantic criticism arose as a necessary complement to the activities in the sphere of creative art, Hurd, the Wartons, and others striving to display to men the beauties of the long-despised Middle Ages. Unfortunately, in England the drama lay somewhat apart. During the late eighteenth century the theatres were not in a flourishing condition. Sentimentalism had become mawkish and artificial, and the tragic drama was inert and powerless. With the coming of the new century melodrama sprang into being, and the theatres for long subsisted on show and stirring spectacle. Discovering the low standards of public taste, the poets of the time tended either to ignore the theatre of their own times entirely or else to pen 'closet' dramas, like Byron's *Werner*, never intended, or "in any shape adapted, for the stage." Renewed study of Shakespeare, however, and of Shakespeare's contemporaries, along with a fresh appreciation of the true glories of Greek literature, gave rise to a reconsideration of the great masterpieces of the past. Coleridge led the way, developing an entirely new type of critical analysis in his lectures and in his *Notes on Shakespeare*. Hazlitt at the same time strove to investigate the manifestations of the comic spirit as expressed by Shakespeare, the Restoration dramatists, and the novel-writers of the eighteenth century, while Lamb revealed and illuminatingly discoursed on the lovelinesses of the Elizabethans. The achievements of this new school were remarkable, but it possessed one or two characteristics in the early period of its development which prevented it from reaching final conclusions. In the first place, its methods were largely *subjective*, dependent on the tastes and upon the caprices of the several critics. Hardly ever can one trace here the larger unprejudiced and scientific acumen which gives to Aristotle's *Poetics* its supreme position in the history of criticism. Secondly, it ignored almost entirely the theatre as such. For Coleridge Shakespeare might have been a pure poet, and his works might never have been intended for the stage. Not one of these critics attempted to investigate the circumstances which surrounded the great works of dramatic art during the different periods of theatrical history. No word is said of the particular forms assumed by the Greek stage; of the Elizabethan playhouse conventions the writers are ignorant or make no mention. It was only in later times that these circumstances, often of prime importance for an understanding of particular dramas, were fully appreciated and utilized in the service of criticism.

On the Continent there was something of a more practical nature. Schiller (1759–1805) and Goethe (1749–1832) were men fully acquainted with the necessities of the stage, and their pronouncements therefore have the stamp of firmness, while such a scholar as Schlegel (1767–1845) could introduce a comparative treatment denied to others. Eagerly the Germans were devoting themselves to research in theatrical and dramatic history and were groping in the philosophic realms of abstract æsthetic; as a result their critical work has a value of real permanence and a strength based on their appreciation of actuality. France, too, saw the development of this newer style of criticism. The nineteenth century was an age of revolt, and because of the dominance of the neo-classic tradition in the French theatres that revolt seemed more violent and more impetuous than was the romanticism of England. After all, France had still to enjoy the thrill of discovering the real Shakespeare, while in England Shakespeare had never been forgotten. Hugo's defence of the grotesque came, therefore, as a real blow, and controversy raged over his daring innovations as it could never have done on the other side of the Channel.

MODERN CRITICISM. The turning-point in critical theory came about the eighties of the century. By that time the researches of the scholars had succeeded in opening up vast fields of knowledge concerning both the theatre and the drama of the past; the first fervour of romanticism had gone; and there was time for reflection and for comparative analysis. From all sides the old problems were approached and rediscussed. The study of psychology led some men to attempt an investigation into the sources of laughter and of tragic emotion. Others, like Sarcey, Brunetière, and Archer, turned to the essential principles of the dramatic art itself. Still others, after a study of playhouse conditions, endeavoured to recall the impression created by the greater masterpieces of drama when these were originally produced in theatres now no longer existent. The wealth of knowledge, the sure basis of actuality, the critical acumen, and the freedom from prejudice find no parallel save in that first glorious essay in this style, the *Poetics* of Aristotle.

That does not mean, of course, that all the problems are solved and all the questions finally settled. Criticism, after all, however ' scientific ' may be its method of approach, can never become one of the exact sciences, and even the most brilliant deductions and the most penetrating appreciations leave much unsaid. The art of dramatic criticism, in spite of these long centuries and in spite of the high attainments of the present age, might almost be counted in its infancy, for it has not yet quite reached an all-comprehensive view of the material on which it works. On the diverse manifestations of the theatre, from high tragedy and fine comedy on the one hand to the most pitiful of melodrama and farce on the other, even on that distant cousin of Thalia and Melpomene, the marionette and the puppet show, have been written volumes innumerable; brilliant studies have been made of Æschylus and Seneca, of

Shakespeare and Molière ; but only too often the difficulties inherent in this subject have prevented a true analysis of the qualities shared alike by Shakespeare and Æschylus, by Molière and Aristophanes. It seems that herein lies the greatest opportunity for the critics of the future, although the difficulties inherent in the subject and the enormity of the task may make us wait long for the work which shall do for the world's drama what Aristotle did for the drama of Athens. It is in this direction, however, that we should look, and for anyone launching himself on a survey of this critical thought the comparative method seems indeed an absolute necessity.

(ii) THE MEANING OF DRAMA

Obviously, in starting off on any survey of this kind, we must pause to ask ourselves what precisely we mean by the words ' drama ' and ' dramatic,' or, to put it in another way, what we regard as being the essence of the dramatic art when that is opposed to the arts of poetry, painting, or fiction. It is, plainly, an art, but in what terms are we to define those particular qualities which distinguish it from other arts ? At first sight it might appear that this would be a comparatively easy task; but deeper reflection reveals its difficulties, difficulties which perhaps may best be illustrated by a brief analysis of some attempts made in the past to find a suitable answer and a clear definition.

THE THEORY OF IMITATION. One of the first and one of the commonest theories is that which may be called the idea of imitation, although the word ' imitation,' admitting of both a broader and a narrower interpretation, requires very carefully to be considered. In its most succinct and crudest form this theory may be expressed in Cicero's phrase as quoted by Ælius Donatus; for him drama is " a copy of life, a mirror of custom, a reflection of truth." This definition, if so it may be called, has been quoted by succeeding critics hundreds of times, and has been taken as the basis of countless disquisitions, particularly in the period of the Renascence. Even in comparatively modern times it has found its supporters, for it fell in with the artistic aims of the realists of the nineteenth century.

Zola's object in writing *Thérèse Raquin* was fundamentally that suggested by Cicero. " I have introduced useless and supernumerary characters," he says,

> in order to place, side by side with the fearful agonies of my heroes, the banality of the life of every day; I have attempted continually to harmonize my setting with the ordinary occupations of my characters, so that they might not seem to ' play,' but rather to ' live,' before the spectators.[1]

The same conception, too, with slight modifications, is at the root of much theorizing concerning the sentimental comedy and the *bourgeois* tragedy. When Beaumarchais declares that " if the theatre is a faithful picture of what happens in the world, the interest aroused in us must of necessity have a close relationship to the way in which we look at reality," [2] we realize that " the mirror of truth " is still his ideal for the theatre.

Now, if this conception be taken in its strictest interpretation, then a drama is simply an excerpt from life. That is to say, the aim of the true dramatist ought to be the providing on the stage of as faithful a replica as may be of a scene which either has actually occurred or has been conceived in such terms as to make it lifelike; the dialogue of that drama will be the finest which introduces an almost exact phonographic reproduction of real conversation among living persons; and the greatest beauty of the play will be its faithfulness to reality. Cursorily considered, we might perhaps be tempted to believe that there is something to be said for these ideas, but a moment's reflection will indicate their falsity. Apart from the fact that one might deem the greatest playwright to be the recording gramophone, we soon come to realize that this ideal of drama is an impossibility, for a play can never be an excerpt from life. Even if we suppose that an author reproduces in a single scene the exact words which had been actually spoken by some persons whom he has taken for the models of his *dramatis personæ*, the very fact that this scene is cut off from others which follow or precede makes it artificial, or, to put it in another way, makes it a thing of art. The author has deliberately chosen this particular

---

[1] Preface to *Thérèse Raquin* (1873), p. 11.
[2] *Essai sur le genre dramatique sérieux* (1767)

section from life because it best serves his particular purpose in the writing of the play. Still further, unless the dramatist employs some mechanical instrument for recording the sounds, he can never hope accurately to reproduce in their minutest details the precise words spoken; and if, as is most usual, he is inventing both scene and characters it were but a fond dream to imagine that had that scene occurred in reality the characters, if living persons, would have spoken just in those terms. Exact realism, then, is a thing impossible and cast beyond the moon.

Nor do the greater dramatists even aim at this particular object; this is not the ideal toward which they guide their efforts. It may be that the power of observation and a good memory (or handy tablets such as Mr Bernard Shaw imagines Shakespeare to have used) are part of a dramatic author's necessary equipment, but clearly that which makes him an artist and gives him his final distinction is a power of selection and, along with that and even greater than it, what may be called an informing power, by means of which he is able to suggest infinite significance in his scenes and in the words of his characters. We may without fear, then, lay aside the narrower realistic views; were we to hold to these we should be bound to rule out as bad drama or as completely undramatic the work of Æschylus, Aristophanes, Shakespeare, and Molière.

There still remains, however, the broader interpretation of the theory of imitation, and here we may turn to the ideas of Aristotle and his commentators. The fundamental principle upon which Aristotle bases all his assumptions is that art in general consists of imitation. Unfortunately, the word he uses —μίμησις, 'imitation'—he nowhere attempts to define, and, so far as we can judge, he uses it in a variety of senses. It were needless here to enter into a lengthy discussion of this problem; sufficient be it to note that only rarely does Aristotle seem to think of imitation as a faithful reproduction of reality. When, for example, he says that tragedy "seeks to imitate better," but comedy "worse men than are," we realize that he is employing the word in a very wide sense; and this realization is strengthened when we find him declaring that "epic . . . and tragic poetry, and, moreover, comedy, and dithyrambic poetry, and the greatest part of the art pertaining to the flute and the lyre, are all entirely imitations." Indeed, we might almost say that Aristotle is here thinking either of the utilization of things in reality—such as sounds and words—as opposed to the reproduction of reality, or of the power which art has of creating emotions such as might have been aroused by scenes of real life. It would be nonsense to suggest that he imagined flute music or poetry to be an 'imitation,' in the sense of an exact replica, of things found in life, although for the drama, as we have seen, this misconception endured over centuries. Such a broad interpretation of the imitative quality in drama finds a reflection in some more modern theorizing concerning the functions of the playwright, and, as this is an important question, a few of these ideas may here be glanced at. " I imagine," says Hugo,

> that it has been said, " The drama is a mirror in which nature is reflected." But if this mirror be an ordinary mirror, a flat and polished surface, it will provide but a poor image of the objects, without relief—faithful, but colourless; it is well known that colour and light are lost in a simple reflection. The drama, therefore, must be a focusing mirror, which, instead of making weaker, collects and condenses the coloured rays, which will make of a gleam a light, of a light a flame. Then only is the drama worthy of being counted an art.[1]

This emphasis on the art is all-important, and may be taken along with Sarcey's realization that mere nature on the stage would appear uninteresting and even false. "I hold," he declares,

> that reality, if presented on the stage truthfully, would appear false to the monster with the thousand heads which we call the public. We have defined dramatic art as the sum total by the aid of which, in the theatre, we represent life and give to the twelve hundred people assembled the illusion of truth.[2]

Dimly, but only dimly, some critics had had a vague conception of this truth in earlier times. Hédelin saw it, and stated his opinion that " the stage does not present things as they have been, but as they ought to be." " The Poet," he believed, " must . . . reform everything that is not accommodated to

---

[1] Preface to *Cromwell* (1828), p. xl.
[2] *A Theory of the Theatre*, with an Introduction by Brander Matthews (Brander Matthews Dramatic Museum of Columbia University, New York, 1916), p. 31.

the Rules of his Art; as a Painter does when he works upon an imperfect Model." [1]   Goethe, too, gave the same advice:

> He who would work for the stage should . . . study the stage, the effects of scenography, of lights and rouge and other colouring matter, of glazed linen and spangles.   He should leave Nature in her proper place.[2]

The whole truth is finally summed up by Coleridge in one of his lectures.   For him the drama " is not a copy, but an imitation of nature," and the question could not be more succinctly settled.

In turning back upon these various ideas expressed by modern critics it seems that the most fruitful of all is that which speaks of drama as a kind of concentrating glass wherein the gleam is magnified and compressed into a light and the light into a flame.   In any consideration of the greater dramatic masterpieces we realize the truth of this analysis, for the master playwright, in taking a hint from nature, instead of being satisfied with mere episodes, at one and the same time orders what he has observed of, or has thought concerning, life and raises to a pitch of excitement and interest scenes which, had they occurred in reality, would have been but dull and uninspiring.   Here obviously is one of the great functions of the dramatist.

Yet this does not lead us very far on our way.   We started off in the endeavour to find a definition of the dramatic, and all we have succeeded in doing is to indicate that drama is an art.   After all, every art orders and concentrates in this manner, and it is in this sense, according to Aristotle, that all the arts are based on imitation.   So far we have found no characteristic which will enable us to make a clear distinction between this particular art of drama and the other kindred arts of poetry and fiction.

BRUNETIÈRE'S " LAW."   Peculiarly enough, the number of serious attempts to discuss this matter is comparatively few.   Perhaps it may be well to start here with that so-called " law " enunciated by Brunetière late in the nineteenth century and much discussed by critics during the last twenty years.   Put

[1] *The Whole Art of the Stage* (1684), p. 65.
[2] B. H. Clark, *European Theories of the Drama* (1929), p. 339.

in briefest terms, we may say that this "law" devised by Brunetière depends on the recognition of will as the prime characteristic of the drama. " In drama or farce, what we ask of the theatre, is the spectacle of a *will* striving towards a goal, and conscious of the means which it employs. . . . The novel is . . . the contrary of the drama," for in the novel the author endeavours " to give us a picture of the influence which is exercised upon us by all that is outside of ourselves." [1] To make clear these ideas of Brunetière two other quotations may be given. The first is the French critic's own summary:

> The general law of the theatre is defined by the action of a will conscious of itself; and the dramatic species are distinguished by the nature of the obstacles encountered by this will.[2]

The second quotation is William Archer's translation of a summary of his views:

> Drama is a representation of the will of man in conflict with the mysterious powers or natural forces which limit and belittle us; it is one of us thrown living upon the stage there to struggle against fatality, against social law, against one of his fellow mortals, against himself if need be, against the ambitions, the interests, the prejudices, the folly, the malevolence of those around him.[3]

This theory in turn has been analysed and criticized by Henry Arthur Jones, who for his part formulates a new " universal law of drama ":

> Drama arises when any person or persons in a play are consciously or unconsciously ' up against ' some antagonistic person, or circumstance, or fortune. It is often more intense when, as in *Œdipus*, the audience is aware of the obstacle, and the person himself, or persons, on the stage are unaware of it. Drama arises thus, and continues when or till the person or persons are aware of the obstacle; it is sustained so long as we watch the reaction, physical, mental, or spiritual, of the person or persons to the opposing person, or circumstance, or fortune. It relaxes as this reaction subsides, and ceases when the reaction is complete. This reaction of a person to an obstacle is most arresting and intense when the obstacle takes the form of another human will in almost balanced collision.[4]

[1] *The Law of the Drama* (Brander Matthews Dramatic Museum of Columbia University, New York, 1914), p. 73.
[2] *Id.*, pp. 79–80. [3] *Play-making* (1926), p. 23.
[4] Introduction to Brunetière's *Law of the Drama, ed. cit.*, pp. 36–37.

Now, all these disquisitions are mighty well, as Mrs Oakly
would say, and each separate judgment may be proved by
reference to a number of great dramas. We may immediately
agree that in drama of any kind, be it farce or comedy, tragedy
or melodrama, there is the spectacle of will consciously exerting
itself, there is generally a conflict, there is generally a great
crisis, there is generally the view of some protagonist ' up
against ' something or some one. Yet none of these things is
inevitable, and none seems to distinguish drama from other
forms of art. What are we to say of Aristophanes' *Frogs*?
Perhaps we may twist and turn and find there the spectacle of
will, the crisis, the conflict; but, however subtly we may
exercise our ingenuity, we realize that, good theatre though
the *Frogs* is, it does not wholly agree with these definitions.
What, too, do we make of Hardy's *Tess* or Richardson's
Pamela? Let us apply the theoretical ' laws ' of drama to
them and they become masterpieces of the theatre. In other
words, these judgments made by Brunetière and Jones may
indicate what interests us most in great dramas (as also in
narrative fiction), but they do not in any way serve to delimit the
dramatic *kind*, and, after all, what we are seeking is a definition
which shall indicate the peculiar features owned by the art of
drama and by none other of the arts.

SARCEY'S THEORY AND SHAW'S PRACTICE. Here, to a certain
extent, Sarcey comes to our aid. Instead of seeking for
abstract characteristics of the drama, he looks to the concrete
and the practical, insisting that the one thing which peculiarly
marks the art of the theatre is the presence of an audience.
" We cannot," he says, " conceive of a play without an audience.
Take one after another the accessories which serve in the
performance of a dramatic work—they can all be replaced
or suppressed except that one." His final judgment is
summed up in a few words: " A play without an audience is
inconceivable." [1]

A moment's reflection shows us that this observation carries
us considerably forward toward a theoretical and critical

[1] *A Theory of the Theatre, ed. cit.*, pp. 22, 24. It is interesting to notice
that Bacon in the seventeenth century had already observed this requirement and had touched upon the " crowd emotions " (*De augmentis*, English
translation, 1640, p. 107).

delimitation of the dramatic kind. According to this view, while painting is the art of expression through the medium of colour and line on a two-dimensional plane, literature the general art of expression through the medium of words, poetry the particular art of expression in emotional, usually rhythmic terms, and fiction the art of expression by means of a story told in prose, drama is the art of expression by means of a story told to an audience assembled together in one place. At once, however, we see another thing. This idea of Sarcey's helps us considerably, but we immediately recognize that, as providing a definition of drama, it is incomplete. A drama is never really a story *told* to an audience; it is a story interpreted before an audience by a body of actors. Thus, in addition to these spectators, the drama demands, or presupposes, the enunciation of the words, not by one man, but by several. This, of course, brings us fully into the realm of the theatre as distinct from, although including, the drama, and the problems so raised must for the moment be left aside for later consideration. One thing, however, must be emphasized continually, and that is that the drama may never be taken to exist as merely a written or a printed work of literature. If we are to appreciate it for what it is—that is to say, as a drama—we must first suppose that the author had both actors and audience in view when he was penning his lines, and, secondly, we must supply mentally for ourselves these two factors as we read any example of dramatic art. Sarcey's judgment, then, may be expanded so as to read: " A play without an audience and actors to interpret it is inconceivable."

These two factors themselves lead to something else, for both are delimiting and both raise the question of physical endurance and capability. Purely physical considerations never enter into the field of other literary forms. A novel may be as short or as long as we will; a poem may be a lyric of four lines or an epic in twenty books, each containing thousands of verses; but the playwright must ever be bound by the facts that his play is designed to be produced in a material theatre, interpreted by actors who are, after all, only human, and before an audience which is exceedingly human. A poet may write independent of everything save his stock of notepaper and his considerations

31

regarding a publisher's limit of adventurousness; the same precisely is true of the novelist. Both may be vaguely influenced
by the taste of the public, reacting thus to the fashion for epic
or for three-volume novels; but the restrictions imposed on
them are widely general and can never be regarded as hard and
fast 'laws' from which no author may diverge. The dramatist,
it is at once realized, stands in an entirely different position.
Normally the action of his work must be limited to a space of
time not too lengthy to tire and weary the body of spectators
gathered together for the purpose of listening to that work.
This space of time, through observation of dramatic tastes over
centuries, has been conventionally fixed at from two to three
hours. It is true that there are exceptions, such as Mr Bernard
Shaw's *Back to Methuselah*, but such exceptions are apparent
rather than real, and simply serve to prove the rule. *Back to
Methuselah* is not really one play, but a series of plays written
on kindred themes, and as such it has to be performed when
put on the stage. The complete *Hamlet* or the complete *Man
and Superman* may certainly be performed in one evening, but
such productions are in every way exceptional and definitely
stretch the powers of endurance to the uttermost limit. We
may, once in a while, go to the theatre at six and sit there, with
one break for dinner, until eleven, but when we do we regard
it as a feat and are not likely to repeat the experiment the
following night. Apart from this, there is the question of the
actor's powers of endurance. Nearly every play will include
one part at least which is lengthier and 'heavier' than the
others, and it stands to reason that no actor, unless heroically
endowed with almost superhuman energy, could continue night
after night to give interpretations of parts which necessitated
his presence on the stage at, say, six-fifteen and thereafter kept
him busy until nearly eleven. For various purely material
reasons, then, the dramatist has to submit to a general, but
unwritten, law that his play shall not presuppose a time of
action greater than about three hours.

Still further, because of the human material with which he
is working, he must normally take care that no one of his
characters remains on the stage the whole time. A drama
which presented, say, the person of Napoleon present before

us from the beginning of the first act to the close of the last would also be inconceivable, for we could hardly imagine an actor sufficiently gifted with strength and energy to enable him to carry out this interpretation night after night. The whole thing (which, as will be seen, involves more than has here been summarily discussed) is put trenchantly by Mr Bernard Shaw:

I am not governed by principles; I am inspired, how or why I cannot explain, because I do not know; but inspiration it must be; for it comes to me without any reference to my own ends or interest. . . .

This is not being ' guided by principles '; it is hallucination; and sane hallucination is what we call play or drama. I do not select my methods: they are imposed upon me by a hundred considerations: by the physical considerations of theatrical representation, by the laws devised by the municipality to guard against fires and other accidents to which theatres are liable, by the economics of theatrical commerce, by the nature and limits of the art of acting, by the capacity of the spectators for understanding what they see and hear, and by the accidental circumstances of the particular production in hand.

I have to think of my pocket, of the manager's pocket, of the actors' pockets, of the spectators' pockets, of how long people can be kept sitting in a theatre without relief or refreshments, of the range of the performer's voice, and of the hearing and vision of the boy at the back of the gallery, whose right to be put in full possession of the play is as sacred as that of the millionaire in the stalls or boxes.

I have to consider theatrical rents, the rate of interest needed to tempt capitalists to face the risks of financing theatres, the extent to which the magic of art can break through commercial prudence, the limits set by honour and humanity to the tasks I may set to my fellow-artist, the actor: in short, all the factors that must be allowed for before the representation of a play on the stage becomes practicable or justifiable: factors which some never comprehend and which others integrate almost as unconsciously as they breathe, or digest their food.

It is these factors that dictate the playwright's methods, leaving him so little room for selection that there is not a pennyworth of difference between the methods of Sophocles or Shakespeare and those of the maker of the most ephemeral farce.[1]

This puts the whole matter in a few well-chosen words. Some of the implications raised here must be considered in greater

[1] *New York Times*, June 2, 1912.

detail later on; here we note how these considerations, which every dramatist, be he great or be he weak, must take into account, serve to indicate, if not to define, the style of dramatic art as opposed to the arts of poetry and fiction. The dramatist works with words, but they are the words he puts into the mouths of characters designed to be interpreted by actors before an audience. The drama, we may say, is a mirror of life only in the sense that it provides a kind of physical semblance of human existence on the stage; otherwise, the actual scenes and characters conceived of by the playwright are so circumscribed and dominated by outside requirements (quite apart from the imaginative power of the playwright himself) that they can never be regarded as excerpts from life.

THE QUESTION OF ILLUSION. This leads us to the question of illusion, which has been raised already in connexion with the theory of imitation. The whole problem is expressed in one general query: Does the dramatic performance put before us delude us into believing that what we see is life? Among the earliest Renascence critics Castelvetro decided that " the show on the stage must reproduce the forms of the thing represented—nor more, nor less." Has this judgment any real significance?

As is obvious, such a query throws into relief, not the imaginative or creative faculty of the dramatic artist, but the emotions of the audience—the ' reactions ' felt by the whole body of spectators. There are some who would be inclined to answer this question in the affirmative, adducing various instances of *naïve* spectators who apparently took it to be so.[1] The story of the farmer who offered Richard a steed for much less when that monarch was grandiloquently offering his kingdom for a horse may serve as representative of one type of anecdote; the story of the good lady who loudly warned Hamlet of the poisoned rapier may serve as representative of another. It is, however, seriously to be questioned whether any one of these anecdotes is genuinely authenticated, and, even if one or several were proved to be true, the fact remains that

[1] Thornton S. Graves has an interesting essay on this subject—" The Literal Acceptance of Stage Illusion " (*South Atlantic Quarterly*, xxiii, 2, April 1924).

no member of an average audience is truly cheated into believing that what he sees on the stage is real; at least, no member of an average audience is capable of believing consciously that the stage-picture and the characters set before him are not mere images, maybe resembling the ' real,' but certainly not part of that. With the perspicacity which came from his study of philosophy, Coleridge seized on and analysed what for most is the experience of the theatre:

> The true stage-illusion in this and in all other things consists—not in the mind's judging it to be a forest, but in its remission of the judgment that it is not a forest. . . . For not only are we never absolutely deluded, or anything like it, but the attempt to cause the highest delusion possible to beings in their senses sitting in a theatre, is a gross fault, incident only to low minds, which, feeling that they cannot affect the heart or head permanently, endeavour to call forth the momentary affections.[1]

This insistence on a "willing suspension of disbelief," to borrow Coleridge's phrase employed in a different connexion, is all-important. It is true that we may, in witnessing realistic and problem dramas, *relate* the fictional events shown on the stage to the ' real ' life around us, but even then there is no question of taking the fictional for the real, while the fictional must ever be regarded as a symbol or concentration of the ' real,' not as a substitute for it.

THE BASIS OF THE DRAMATIC. After these preliminary considerations we may be, perhaps, in a position to suggest the main features by which drama, as an art-form, is distinguished, externally at least, from other arts. A rough definition might thus be framed: Drama is the art of expressing ideas about life in such a manner as to render that expression capable of interpretation by actors and likely to interest an audience assembled to hear the words and witness the actions. Such a definition certainly differentiates the particular form of dramatic art clearly from poetry and from the novel, but, as will be realized, it indicates merely the external form and circumstances of dramatic presentation. May there not be —this we have to ask ourselves—some inner characteristics too

[1] Lecture on "The Progress of Drama" (1818), printed in *Literary Remains* (1836–39).

by which the dramatic is distinguished from the poetic and the narrational? Here the common use of the words 'drama' and 'dramatic' may well be considered for a moment. The adjective 'fictional' is employed in a non-technical sense only for one thing, the untruth; 'poetic' similarly means simply 'fit for poetry'; but both 'drama' and 'dramatic' have at once a more extended use and a more specific connotation. We read in the papers of the "Dramatic Reunion of Two Brothers," and are told there of how two sons of one father have been separated for thirty years through some silly quarrel: as old men they find themselves unexpectedly in a small country hotel, speak to one another as strangers, discover each other's identity, and are reconciled at last. Every one is, of course, familiar with the frequent utilization of such headings in the daily journals, although seldom do we stay to consider the implication of the particular adjective or noun employed. If we do we shall find that, for the journalist, and so for the public to whom he addresses himself, the word 'dramatic' has a connotation signifying the unexpected, with, usually, the suggestion of a certain shock occasioned either by a strange coincidence or by the departure of the incidents narrated from the ordinary tenor of daily life. Now, the very fact that this word 'dramatic' can thus be freely and commonly used must indicate that in this strangeness, unexpectedness, and sense of shock the public recognizes something which it finds as a main element in works of dramatic art. For, be it noted, here is not a plain transference of meaning, but the direct use of a literary term for that which is found, even if but rarely, to resemble it in ordinary life. When we turn to individual dramas themselves we realize that the public is right. In ancient classic days Aristotle devoted a considerable section of his *Poetics* to a detailed discussion of 'recognitions' and 'discoveries,' just such things as are labelled 'dramatic' nowadays when they occur in real life, and things forming, as it were, the basic stock-in-trade of the Athenian playwright. By no means were these confined to the classic theatre. Such a play as *Hamlet* is full of 'dramatic' incidents of this kind. The return of the elder Hamlet as a ghost, the simulated madness of his son, the killing of Polonius in mistake for Claudius, the shuffling with the foils, the contrast between Hamlet and Fortinbras—all of these provide us with a series of shocks, greater or less in accordance with the emotional intensity of the particular scene. Nor is comedy in any wise different. Take as an example Wilde's *The Importance of being Earnest*. This presents us with a continuous array of such shocks, extending from the major one of Algernon's pretence that he is " Earnest's " brother to the brilliant verbal witticisms, unexpected and startling in their mirth-provoking qualities. Farce, melodrama, high comedy, and tragedy all betray the same characteristic, a characteristic frequently emphasized by the dramatist at important or strategic points of his play. A ' good curtain ' usually includes just such a shock, and the concluding acts of many dramas are based on an application of this feature. The curtain rings down on the end of Mr Galsworthy's *Strife* with the shock of discovering that, after all this bitter struggle we have been witnessing, matters are finally settled just as they had been at first; the close of Mr Lennox Robinson's *The Lost Leader* has what may be called the shock of uncertainty, when a chance blow kills the man who might have been the hero arisen from the grave. Instances might be multiplied endlessly; here, beyond those already given, it may be sufficient to cite the plays of Mr Bernard Shaw, who, better perhaps than any living author, has grasped the secret of theatrical success. Of his plays his first, *Widowers' Houses*, will serve as well as any. The discovery of the rejuvenated and altered Lickcheese, the constant turns and counter-turns in idea and plot, all provide a set of shocks of various intensity. In Mr Shaw's works the unexpected is thus constantly being exploited. The " But then Anne knew " in the first act of *Man and Superman*, the judgments of Confucius in *Back to Methuselah*, the decision of the wife in *Candida*, the neat excuse of Shakespeare to Elizabeth in *The Dark Lady of the Sonnets*—these examples, culled at random, show how regularly the Shavian drama is based on this idea, and, as has been shown, it is not only Mr Shaw who relies upon this source of effect.

To the purely external features of dramatic art indicated above, therefore, we may add this other—the constant utilization

of the unexpected leading toward emotional or mental shock
—indeed, the very basis of plays upon this quality in plot-
idea. Thus, in Mr Rudolf Besier's *The Barretts of Wimpole
Street* it is the shock of discovering the relationship between the
tyrannical father and his family, the shock of witnessing the
awakening of Elizabeth to strength and life, the shock of seeing
and believing in Robert's unconventional, because far-seeing,
faith and hope that give to the whole play its essentially
dramatic quality. Indeed, we may be almost prepared to say
(and in this again we shall be close to Aristotle) that the more
subtly and the more powerfully the major and the minor
shocks are planned in any play the more intensely dramatic
that play will be. A drama may be inconceivable without
audience and actors; it is also inconceivable without an
essential basis of carefully conceived situations designed (unlike
the situations necessary for narrative fiction) to arouse and
stimulate and startle by their strangeness, their peculiarity, or
their unconventionality.

(iii) THE DRAMATIC CONVENTIONS

Drama is an art, and so, like all arts, must have its conventions; a discussion of these may therefore well follow this
preliminary investigation into the general significance of the
dramatic form. Here, however, we must be doubly on our
guard, for dramatic conventions must inevitably depend on,
and be influenced by, the way in which we regard the art form
itself. Thus, both a dramatist who believes in the possibility
of securing illusion and the dramatist who denies that that is
feasible may agree that drama is an art, but the conventions
each will employ will differ markedly from one another.
Certain conventions, too, will be determined by the requirements and technical devices of particular types of staging, by
the arrangement of the auditorium, even by the circumstances
in which the audience come to witness the plays. Many of
these conventions, being related thus to a definite age and style
of playhouse, need not here be referred to, but there are at
least some which, vaguely adumbrated in ancient Greece and
carried on in diverse forms down almost to our own day,

must here be summarily discussed. Some attention, at any rate, has to be given to that which for centuries formed the focus of dramatic criticism—the three unities.

THE THREE UNITIES. The development of what may be called the unities idea is easy enough to follow. Aristotle had said that tragedy, in contradistinction to the epic, had a circumscribed fictional time; the epic might—indeed, generally did—deal in lengthy periods of time, whereas drama normally confined itself to a short period. In addition to this, he had emphasized the desirability of preserving some kind of unity in the action, pointing out that this unity must be organic and could not be secured by the mechanical device of making some one man the centre and cause of the plot—a mere series of incidents relating to one person not in themselves containing dramatic unity, although they might have the unity demanded, say, by the art of biography. Here it has to be borne in mind that a Greek drama habitually had a chorus as an integral, or even as a chief, element in its structure, and that in tragedy this chorus was in full view of the audience from beginning to end of the play. Because of this feature peculiar to it there was demanded a greater restriction in the fictional space given to the action than is necessitated in modern plays. After all, the chorus was an adventitious element, and we have to regard it as one of those topical and temporary features which here must be ruled out of account. Not all Greek tragedies were confined to what may be styled a period of verisimilitude, but obviously they had to be considerably restrained if any sort of impression of life was to be provided by the performances.

Without recognizing the topical and temporary requirements, the Renascence theorists took over and narrowed these judgments of Aristotle and this practice of the Greek playwrights. The course of their ideas may readily be traced, and readily, too, may be traced the introduction, alongside the unities of time and of action, the only two suggested by Aristotle, of a third unity, that of place. This last is clearly demanded as a corollary by the unity of time. If we believe, adopting the theory of stage illusion, that the fictional action should be restricted to a length of time roughly the same as that taken up by the performance of the play on the stage, then it follows that we should also restrict the place of the fictional action to one locality.

The development of these ideas starts with Robertelli's commentary upon Aristotle, which appeared in 1548, and in the *Discorsi sulle comedie e sulle tragedie* (1554) of Giraldi Cinthio. These both decided that there ought to be a limitation of the space of fictional action—the former stipulating a maximum of twelve hours. The year following that which witnessed the appearance of Robertelli's work saw the appearance of Segni's *Retorica et poetica d'Aristotele* (1549), wherein the length of time was extended to twenty-four hours; a closer restriction was advised by Maggi (1550),[1] who suggested a period of about three hours; while the young Minturno [2] was prepared to admit in exceptional cases as much as two days. Scaliger, in 1561, condemned both the swift passing " from Delphi to Thebes, or from Thebes to Athens, in a moment of time," and the attempts made to extend the time of action. Two years later Minturno, revising his earlier judgments, decided that the dramatic poet had to bow to an eternal law:

> The actual period of time supposed to transpire during the performance of a dramatic work is not within the determination of the poet. Even if we suppose that a hundred tragedies and a hundred comedies are presented in the theatre each will be found to demand the same definite period of time. . . . Whoso studies well the works of the most famous among the ancients will find that the action put upon the stage terminates in one day, or, at any rate, does not extend beyond two; just as the action of the longest epic poem does not exceed one year.[3]

For Castelvetro in 1570

> the time of the representation and that of the action represented must be exactly coincident, . . . and the scene of the action must be constant, being not merely restricted to one city or house, but indeed to that one place alone which could be visible to one person.[4]

This is the extremest form of enunciation, and is expressly based on the theory of stage illusion, but even Castelvetro was

---

[1] *In Aristotelis librum : De poetica communes explicationes* (1550). For this and a few other references I am indebted to a thesis by Dr F. E. Budd, *The Idea of Tragedy in the Renaissance* (1927).

[2] *De poeta libri sex* (1559). [3] *L'Arte poetica* (1563).

[4] H. B. Charlton, *Castelvetro's Theory of Poetry* (1913), p. 84. It was Castelvetro who really established finally the ' law ' of the unities.

forced to admit the possibility of an upward limit of time extending to twelve hours. From this time on, indeed, controversy raged regarding the true interpretation of this unity of time. Some logically said that it should mean simply " a time of fictional action equivalent to that of the representation "; others, observing the difficulties thus raised, would allow a dramatist a space of twelve hours; still others were prepared to accept a " natural day " of four-and-twenty hours. In France Jean de la Taille (1572) spoke vaguely of " one day " and " one place." [1] The same year Ronsard expressed his willingness to accept the convention, asserting that

> tragedy and comedy are circumscribed and limited to a short space of time, that is, to one whole day. The most excellent masters of this craft commence their works from one midnight to another, and not from sunrise to sunset, in order to have greater compass and length of time.[2]

In Spain Cervantes (1605) cast scorn on a comedy, " the first act of which is laid in Europe, the second in Asia, and the third in Africa." [3] Almost identical words are employed by Sir Philip Sidney (1595) in his *Apologie for Poetrie*, in which there is condemnation even of the classic *Gorboduc*, because " it is faulty both in place and time, the two necessary companions of all corporal actions." [4] Quite naturally, these ideas were passed on by the Renascence to the pseudo-classic seventeenth and eighteenth centuries. Chapelain (1595–1674) admitted a " single natural day " for time and demanded a " single place " for the action.[5] Corneille in 1660 decided similarly that " there is absolute necessity for the dramatic author to observe the unities of action, place and time." [6] In 1671 Milton declared that " the circumscription of time, wherein the whole drama begins and ends, is according to ancient rule, and best example, within the space of twenty-four hours." [7] More than half a century later Voltaire was defending the unities enthusiastically, and his example was

---

[1] " De l'Art de la tragédie," essay prefixed to *Saül le furieux* (Paris, 1572).
[2] J. E. Spingarn, *A History of Literary Criticism in the Renaissance* (1920), p. 207.
[3] *Don Quixote.*   [4] *Ed. cit.*, p. 63.
[5] B. H. Clark, *European Theories of the Drama* (1929), p. 127.
[6] *Discours de l'utilité et des parties du poëme dramatique* (1660).
[7] Preface to *Samson Agonistes.*

followed, even in the age of romance, by many another, among whom is to be ranked no less a revolutionary than Lord Byron.

This array of almost unanimous theorists does not mean, of course, that even in early times opponents of the unities were not to be discovered, but whatever objections they raised were continually overcome by the massed attacks of the classicists. A study of these objections, however, is not unentertaining, and at the same time serves to show the inherent weakness in the orthodox conceptions. When D'Aigaliers writes against them in 1598 he brings forward several arguments: (1) that the ancients themselves did not always observe the law of time; (2) that in any case we " are not bound by their manner of writing "; (3) that the observance of the unity merely leads to absurdity; (4) that, taking the commonly accepted classic analysis of an ideal tragedy, we cannot bring these mutations of fortune within the fictional period of one day; and (5) that plays in which the law is observed are demonstrably no better than those in which it is neglected.[1] For some years after his time the opposition was silent. Lope de Vega (1609) certainly was prepared to allow an extension of time to writers of historical dramas, but even he was swayed by faith in the orthodox critics; and it was not till the twenties of the seventeenth century that the voice of the rebels became clearly audible again. In 1623 Tirso de Molina pointed out the " inconvenience " of making " a discreet gallant . . . fall in love with a prudent lady, court her, make love to her, woo her—all within a single day, if you please, and after claiming her for the morrow, must needs marry her that very night." [2] This unnaturalness was stressed also by Ogier, four years later, and this critic added to the arguments for the attack a critical note on the *deus ex machina* and the messenger in ancient drama; his final judgment is that theatrical " poetry . . . is composed only for pleasure and amusement " and that the unities are likely to detract from these. It was Ogier, too, who was the first adequately to express the opinion that the religious surroundings and acting conditions in a Greek theatre

[1] J. E. Spingarn, *A History of Literary Criticism in the Renaissance* (1920), p. 209.
[2] Translated by B. H. Clark in *European Theories of the Drama* (1929), p. 94.

were so totally different from the circumstances in which a modern play was acted that there should be no possibility of servile imitation of the " ancients." Some half a century after this Dryden pointed out that the rule was not even a real rule of these ancients at all; Terence, he demonstrated, had " neglected " it, while some of the Greeks had fallen into grievous absurdities in an effort to follow the severer critics.[1] His true objection, however, is of another kind, being practically the same as that put forward by Ogier; speaking of the French, he thus expresses himself:

> By their servile observations of the unities of time and place, and integrity of scenes, they have brought on themselves the dearth of plot, and narrowness of imagination, which may be observed in all their plays. How many beautiful accidents might naturally happen in two or three days, which cannot arrive with any probability in the compass of twenty-four hours?[2]

With fine good sense and a keen appreciation of the various absurdities, Farquhar took up the attack in the first years of the following century; indeed, he carried it on more than one stage farther, for, adopting a point of view adumbrated by Sir Robert Howard in the period of the Restoration, he insisted on the logical errors of the critics. " The less rigid Criticks," he says,

> allow to a Comedy the space of an artificial Day, or Twenty Four Hours; but those of the thorough Reformation, will confine it to the natural or Solar Day, which is but half the time. Now admitting this for a Decorum absolutely requisite: This Play begins when it is exactly Six by your Watch, and ends precisely at Nine, which is the usual time of the Representation. Now is it feazible in *rerum Natura*, that the same Space or Extent of Time can be three Hours, by your Watch, and twelve Hours upon the Stage, admitting the same Number of Minutes, or the same Measure of Sand to both? I'm afraid, Sir, you must allow this for an Impossibility too; and you may with as much Reason allow the Play the Extent of a whole Year; and if you grant me a Year, you may give me Seven, and so to a Thousand. For that a Thousand Years shou'd come within the Compass of three Hours is no more an Impossibility, than that two Minutes shou'd be contain'd in one; *Nullum minus continet in se majus*, is equally applicable to both.[3]

---

[1] *An Essay of Dramatick Poesie* (1668).   [2] *Ibid.*
[3] *A Discourse upon Comedy* (1701).

Clearly the same logic may be applied with equal force to the unity of place.

> Here is a New Play, the House is throng'd, the Prologue's spoken and the Curtain drawn represents you the Scene of *Grand Cairo*. Whereabouts are you now, Sir? Were not you the very Minute before in the Pit in the English Play-house talking to a Wench, and now, *Presto pass*, you are spirited away to the Banks of the River *Nile*. Surely, Sir, this is a most intolerable Improbability; yet this you must allow me, or else you destroy the very Constitution of Representation: Then in the second Act, with a Flourish of the Fiddles, I change the Scene to *Astrachan*. *O, this is intolerable!* Look'ee, Sir, 'tis not a Jot more intolerable than the other; for you'll find that 'tis much about the same distance between *Egypt* and *Astrachan*, as it is between *Drury-Lane* and *Grand Cairo*; and if you please to let your Fancy take Post, it will perform the Journey in the same moment of Time, without any Disturbance in the World to your Person.[1]

Naturally, the whole trend of critical opinion swept, toward the close of the eighteenth century, onward to romantic standards, although some writers here, such as Byron, and various critics in France still would have wished to apply the old rules. Goethe pronounced against the unities firmly in 1825,[2] and two years later Hugo launched an energetic offensive, declaring that, in spite of the rules, the Greek theatre was much freer than the modern, because

> the one obeys naught save the laws that are suited to it, while the other applies to itself basic conditions absolutely foreign to its spirit. One is artistic, the other is artificial.[3]

From an examination of these various views it is obvious that the whole theory of the unities in the modern theatre depends on the assumption, which already we have dismissed, that the individual spectator is deluded into believing the fictional representation to be reality. Admitting this, there would be justification for those who would limit the fictional action to the actual time of performance, but the others are logically absurd who were prepared to allow a fictional time of twelve or twenty-four hours; for them nothing is to be

---

[1] *A Discourse upon Comedy* (1701).
[2] *Conversations of Goethe with Eckermann and Soret,* translated from the German by John Oxenford (1850), i, 206.
[3] Preface to *Cromwell* (1828), p. xxix.

said at all. The one group falls into a ridiculous folly, and the other bases its critical theory upon a false premise.

This being so, it would appear that no more need be done than decently to inter the unities in the grave dug deeply by the romanticists, but once more a certain amount of care is necessary. It may be absurd to suggest a limitation of three, twelve, or twenty-four hours, but one may well ask whether, more liberally and generously interpreted, and regarded not as ' rules,' but as critical observations, the unities may not still preserve something of value. In discussing these unities Lessing had to admit that, while these were but logical requirements demanded by the presence of the chorus in the Greek theatre, they did bring something of worth to the playwrights. The Greeks, he noted,

> submitted willingly to this restriction; but with an adroitness, with a sense of understanding, such that in seven cases out of nine they gained more than they lost. For they allowed this restriction to be the motive for so simplifying the action, carefully eliminating from it everything superfluous, that, reduced to its absolute essentials, it became simply an ideal of the action which was developed most felicitously in that form which demanded the least amplification from circumstances of time and place.[1]

Herein Lessing seems to be aiming at a great truth, a truth which applies not only to the drama of the Greeks, but to the greater dramas of all time, for, looking at the majority of these greater dramas, especially the tragedies, are we not often struck by the fact that the dramatists have deliberately imposed restrictions on themselves when these restrictions were not imposed upon them from without? Even where the fictional time is, on analysis, demonstrably lengthy, the playwrights have frequently employed diverse devices calculated consciously to give an impression of swift-moving events in the theatre. Shakespeare certainly seems to have endeavoured in his finest tragedies to cheat us into believing that the action is rapid and the space of time occupied is short, or, to put it more precisely, to conceal from the audience that, for the sake of verisimilitude, he has had theoretically to allow somewhat lengthy intervals between some of his scenes. A few examples

[1] *Hamburgische Dramaturgie,* No. 46.

may here suffice. In *Hamlet*, after the events of the two days
embraced in Act I, Scenes I to v, there is actually an interval
of a couple of months, as, again, there is a space of a week
between Act IV, Scene IV, and Act IV, Scene v; but no
spectator or reader feels this extension of time. *Hamlet* seems
to move rapidly on from the first visitation of the ghost to
the final catastrophe. If the intervals are realized they merely
make the play appear like a tale told in a prologue (Act I), a
set of three acts (II–IV), and an epilogue (Act V). *Othello* has
a structure similar to that of *Hamlet*. Act I is confined to a
day. Then comes the voyage. Acts II and III take up a
couple of days, and then, after the interval of a week, there
are Acts IV and V. Here again, however, in spite of the
division into prologue, two acts, and epilogue, there is a swift-
ness suggested which makes us forget the actual time analysis.
Macbeth and *Lear* are more extended, and in them, precisely
because of this, we find a certain weakness not apparent in the
other two tragedies. In *Macbeth* the interest is sustained at
white heat up to the murder of Duncan, is carried on in a way
till after the death of Banquo, and then rapidly declines,
although Shakespeare by his poetry makes strenuous efforts
to revive our flagging attention. The murder of Duncan
occurs in Act II, Scene II; Act II, Scene III, is the scene of
the discovery. Banquo is murdered in Act III, Scene III, and
his ghost appears in Act III, Scene IV. On studying such
indications as Shakespeare has left to us of the time duration
of this play, we find that a long interval occurs just after the
death of Duncan and that thereafter there is a continual series
of intervals throughout Acts IV and V. These intervals
cannot be concealed by Shakespeare as he concealed those of
Hamlet and *Othello*, and our waning interest must in part be
attributed to them. The structure of *Lear*, as is obvious,
is inclined to be epic, and, as such, although when read it may
have an added grandeur, yet when seen in the theatre it has
not the effect of the other three. It is certainly interesting to
notice that only when we come to the romantic tragi-comedies,
where the interest is palpably less and the emotional intensity
is weakened, do we get the really violent breaking of this unity
of time. The long sixteen years' leap between the acts of

The Winter's Tale would have been virtually impossible in a high tragedy; it would have completely dispelled that closely concentrated emotion which it is the business of tragedy to present to us.

This judgment finds confirmation in Mr F. L. Lucas' book on *Tragedy* (1927), where he notes that

> the modern dramatist seldom takes these Elizabethan liberties with time and place. The fascination of form has grown stronger; by spreading the action over years we feel that the tension of a piece is weakened and that the magic cauldron goes off the boil. . . . In tragedy a terrible inevitability is gained by beginning, not at the very beginning but just before the catastrophe, when the tragic mistakes have been made and are beyond God Himself to undo.[1]

If, then, we find that, not only does Shakespeare, the romantic libertine, introduce a ' double clock ' system into his plays, but that modern playwrights have, as it were, returned to the ancient Greek conventions, we must believe that in those conventions lies somewhat of permanent and essential value for the art of tragedy.

The same is true of the unity of place. It may be confessed that on Shakespeare's stage there was little or no scenery, so that both theoretically and practically he might shift his locality as often as his heart desired; yet this we find, that the more closely he has held to a single locality, the more powerful and intense is the effect he has produced. *Othello* has virtually two settings only—Venice and Cyprus; *Hamlet* for the most part moves within the precincts of the castle at Elsinore. The latter part of *Macbeth*, on the other hand, is distracting because of the succession of short scenes cast now in Scotland, now in England. And is this not the real source of weakness in *Antony and Cleopatra* ? If we compare Dryden's *All for Love* with Shakespeare's Roman tragedy we realize that the effect of the former drama, weaker though it be in poetic expression, in true tragic power, and in subtlety of characterization, springs from that concentration of effort which accompanies the limitation of scene.

It is remarkable, in this connexion, that many of our modern

[1] P. 79.

dramatists, no doubt quite unconsciously, preserve the unities of time and place, or veer but little away from them. Mr Bernard Shaw's *Getting Married* would have pleased the most rigid of the classicists, as would any one of the component plays making up the cycle called *Back to Methuselah*. The action of *Candida* falls almost within the twenty-four hours' limit, and that of *Heartbreak House* extends from the evening of one day to the evening of the next. Nor is this characteristic confined to Mr Shaw's work; it is marked both in other English and in Continental drama, the playwrights evidently feeling a certain necessity in the restrictions they thus voluntarily impose on themselves. It is perfectly true that for certain plays the unities can never be applied; it is also perfectly true that the modern expressionistic movement seems to favour short, heavily stylized scenes; but in the main we may be prepared to say that, just as drama itself presents a kind of concentration of life, a certain amount of restriction in so far as place and time are concerned may aid the dramatist considerably in his task.

THE UNITY OF ACTION. The unity of action, although in origin it is closely allied to the other two, must be kept distinct from them, for it raises problems of an entirely different kind. In general, it may be said that this unity of action presupposes that (1) no sub-plot of importance should be made to appear in any serious play, and (2) no admixture of tragedy and comedy is permissible. Both of these assumptions raised much controversy in the early period of modern criticism, and once more it may be useful to consider briefly some of the views put forward. In 1609 we find Lope de Vega determined that we must not " mingle tragic style with the humbleness of mean comedy," [1] and Sidney, a few years previously, had spoken of " these grosse absurdities, . . . neither right Tragedies, nor right Comedies: mingling Kings and Clownes, not because the matter so carrieth it: but thrust in Clownes by head and shoulders, to play a part in majesticall matters, with neither decencie, nor discretion." [2] This tragi-comedy, Addison thought,

---

[1] *The New Art of Writing Plays,* translated by W. T. Brewster (1914), p. 30.
[2] *An Apologie for Poetrie,* ed. cit., p. 65.

is one of the most monstrous inventions that ever entered into a poet's thoughts. An author might as well think of weaving the adventures of Æneas and Hudibras into one poem, as of writing such a motley piece of mirth and sorrow.[1]

These ideas are based evidently on the classical doctrine of 'kinds,' which teaches that there are certain unchangeable literary forms and types, each distinct from the other, which may never be confused or mixed with one another artistically. In England, however, the dramatists of the Elizabethan age had succeeded in producing some very amusing and some very moving plays of just this mixed sort, and, as these were universally acknowledged to be good theatrical pieces, English critics for the most part had to find for them some adequate excuse. This they did by appealing from the 'ancients' to 'nature.' Dryden thus, in the person of Neander, put in a plea for such plays on the ground that there is diversity in nature and that a similar diversity is pleasing in works of dramatic art: [2]

A continued Gravity keeps the Spirit too much bent; we must refresh it sometimes, as we bait in a Journey, that we may go on with greater ease. A Scene of Mirth mix'd with Tragedy, has the same effect upon us which our Musick has betwixt the Acts, which we find a Relief to us from the best Plots and Language of the Stage, if the Discourses have been long. I must therefore have stronger Arguments ere I am convinc'd, that Compassion and Mirth in the same Subject destroy each other, and in the mean time, cannot but conclude, to the Honour of our Nation, that we have invented, increas'd, and perfected a more pleasant way of writing for the Stage, than was ever known to the Ancients or Moderns of any Nation, which is Tragi-Comedy.

And this leads me to wonder why *Lisideius* and many others should cry up the Barrenness of the *French* Plots, above the Variety and Copiousness of the *English*. Their Plots are single, they carry on one Design which is push'd forward by all the Actors, every Scene in the Play contributing and moving towards it: Our Plays, besides the main Design, have Under-Plots, or By-Concernments, of less considerable Persons, and Intrigues, which are carried on with the Motion of the main Plot: As they say the Orb of the fix'd Stars, and those of the Planets, though they have Motions of their own, are whirl'd about by the Motion of the *primum mobile*, in which they are contain'd: That

[1] *The Spectator*, No. 40, April 16, 1711.
[2] *An Essay of Dramatick Poesie.*

Similitude expresses much of the *English* Stage: For if contrary Motions may be found in Nature to agree; if a Planet can go *East* and *West* at the same time; one way by Virtue of his own Motion, the other by the force of the first Mover; it will not be difficult to imagine how the Under-Plot, which is only different, not contrary to the great Design, may naturally be conducted along with it.

Dryden, however, does not stand alone. If he was the "first Mover" of the neo-classic school Dr Johnson was, a century later, the very high priest and dictator of the Augustans, yet with a retained naturalness and a lack of mental servitude which is seen nowhere more clearly than in his famous pronouncement on this precise theme.

I know not whether he that professes to regard no other laws than those of nature, will not be inclined to receive tragi-comedy to his protection, whom, however generally condemned, her own laurels have hitherto shaded from the fulminations of criticism. For what is there in the mingled drama which impartial reason can condemn? The connexion of important with trivial incidents, since it is not only common but perpetual in the world, may surely be allowed upon the stage, which pretends only to be the mirror of life. The impropriety of suppressing passions before we have raised them to the intended agitation, and of diverting the expectation from an event which we keep suspended only to raise it, may be speciously urged. But will not experience show this objection to be rather subtle than just? Is it not certain that the tragick and comick affections have been moved alternately with equal force, and that no plays have oftener filled the eye with tears, and the breast with palpitation, than those which are variegated with interludes of mirth?[1]

The plea was, of course, taken up later by the romanticists, notably by Hugo, who declared that

Christianity draws poetry to truth. Like Christianity, the modern muse sees things in a fashion higher and broader. It recognizes that not everything in creation is humanely *beautiful*, that the ugly is there alongside the beautiful, the deformed near the graceful, the grotesque on the reverse of the sublime, evil with good, shadow with light.[2]

It will be observed here that all these judgments, although we might call them romantic in contradistinction to the classical, are based on the assumption that drama is a mere

[1] *The Rambler*, No. 156.   [2] Preface to *Cromwell* (1828), p. xi.

' mirror ' of nature and that what is to be found in nature may with propriety be introduced into plays. This error was seized upon by Sarcey with a sure touch :

> Most of those who rebel against the sustained seriousness of tragedy, who advocate the mixing of the tragic and the comic in the same play, have set out with the idea that it is thus things happen in reality and that the art of the dramatist consists in transporting reality to the stage. It is this very simple view that Victor Hugo sets forth in his admirable preface to *Cromwell* in that highly imaginative style which is so characteristic of him. . . . That is superb eloquence. But the great poets are not always very exact thinkers. The question is badly put. We are not at all concerned to know whether in real life the ludicrous is mingled with the terrible; in other words, whether the course of human events furnishes by turns to those who are either spectators or participants food for laughter and for tears. That is the one truth which no one questions and which has never been questioned. But the point at issue is altogether different. Twelve hundred persons are gathered together in the same room and form an audience. Are these twelve hundred persons likely to pass easily from tears to laughter and from laughter to tears ? [1]

Sarcey's answer to this rhetorical question is, of course, in the negative, but, in pointing out Hugo's error, he seems to have run into one of his own. Whatever we may wish to think on the standards of abstract theory, the fact remains that, when witnessing, let us say, the plays of Shakespeare, we can pass easily from the sublime to the ridiculous, from the tragic to the comic. Perhaps Tirso de Molina was right when he noted a

> difference between Nature and Art: that what the former began, cannot be changed; thus the pear-tree will bear pears to eternity and the oak the uncouth acorn, and notwithstanding the difference of soil and the varying influences of the atmosphere and climate to which they are subject, she produces them over and over again. Amid other changes, species is constant. Does it matter how much the Drama may modify the laws of its ancestors, ingeniously mixing tragedy with comedy and producing a pleasant type of play of the two—and partaking of the character of each—introducing serious characters from the one, and waggish and absurd characters from the other ? [2]

[1] *A Theory of the Theatre, ed. cit.*, pp. 34–37.
[2] Translated by W. A. Hope in B. H. Clark's *European Theories of the Drama* (1929), p. 95.

This whole question we shall have to return to later; but here it must be noted that, so far as we may judge from concrete examples, tragedy and comedy are not truly dissimilar, and are not so fundamentally opposed to one another that they can be treated only in isolation. There is, in point of fact, more in common between high tragedy and fine comedy than there is between certain types of tragedy or between certain types of comedy. In Greece and in England alike tragedy and comedy both took their rise not only at approximately the same time, but out of the same forms. In Greece the choral song chanted round the altar of the god developed along the twin lines of tragic and of comic or satirical expression. The services of the Church, out of which sprang the collective mysteries of the Middle Ages, gave rise both to the tragic themes of Abraham and Isaac and to the comic interludes of Mak and the shepherds. Plato, treating the subject in a more or less abstract manner, discerned in his *Philebus* both pleasurable and painful elements in all laughter; it was he, too, who made Socrates in *The Banquet* force his companions to admit that it was the business of the same genius to excel both in comedy and in tragedy; while modern investigators have shown clearly how closely allied are the two moods, or *Les Passions de l'âme*, to employ the title of that book of Descartes wherein the relations between sadness and laughter are subtly discussed. In the flourishing period of Greek tragedy comedy was allowed to enter in perhaps not so freely as in Shakespeare, but at any rate consciously and of set purpose.[1] Many are the individual writers who have excelled in the two great branches of drama. In England Shakespeare wrote his *As You Like It* as well as *Hamlet*, Jonson his *Every Man in his Humour* as well as *Sejanus* and *Catiline*. Synge succeeded both in *The Playboy of the Western World* and in *Riders to the Sea*. Again, the same nations have produced both species contemporaneously. In France Racine framed his brilliant neo-classic tragedies while Molière was penning and acting his sparkling comedies. In

---

[1] Thus, Æschylus permitted the Herald to enter into his *Supplices* and the Nurse into his *Choephoræ*, while the *Antigone* of Sophocles has its Watchman and the *Orestes* of Euripides its Phrygian Slave.

Italy Goldoni flourished, if not contemporaneously with, at least in the same age as the finest tragic dramatist of that land, Vittorio Alfieri.

The fact is that tears and laughter lie in close proximity. It is but a step from the one to the other. " The motor centres engaged," remarks Sully, " when in the full swing of one mode of action, may readily pass to the other and partially similar action." [1] We feel nothing incongruous in practice in laughing at the jests of Mercutio and at the same time witnessing the tragic story of " Juliet and her Romeo," just as we feel nothing incongruous when in a novel of Dickens we pass from hilarious laughter to the most tearful forms of the pathetic. In all essentially creative ages the two have been freely used together in every kind of literary art. The Greek dramatists, as we have seen, did not confine them to watertight compartments: the Elizabethans freely mingled them. The doctrine that the two are fundamentally opposed is largely the development of later criticism—not so much of ' free ' criticism, as exemplified in Aristotle and in the romantics, as of ' derivative ' and ' artificial ' criticism, as exemplified in Horace and the neo-classic writers of France and of eighteenth-century England. It is noticeable that wherever a critic of the neo-classic school breaks away into a more independent or natural position there vanishes from him the necessity for any strict division between the two moods or species.

This being so, the final test, in so far as a work of dramatic art is concerned, will not be one based on ' nature,' but on the artistic effect of the whole. If the comic and the tragic elements be fused harmoniously one with the other, then the result will be justified by the general impression so obtained. It will be found that between certain forms of comedy and certain forms of serious drama there can be no such communion, and that, on the other hand, there are certain types of tragedy which undoubtedly betray an emotional affinity to corresponding types of comedy. A realization of this is expressed by Shelley in his *Defence of Poetry*. " The modern practice," he says, contrasting the ancient stage with the

[1] J. Sully, *An Essay on Laughter* (1902), p. 70.

Elizabethan, " of blending comedy with tragedy, though liable
to great abuse in point of practice, is undoubtedly an extension
of the dramatic circle; but the comedy should be as in
King Lear, universal, ideal, and sublime." If we imagine
King Lear with the Fool cut away and his place taken by a
set of characters such as appear in *The Taming of the Shrew*
we shall, I think, realize the peculiar affinity that exists between
the tragic spirit of Lear and the comic spirit of the jester.
On the other hand, we could not imagine a satisfactory union
of the peculiar comedy of Lear's fool and, let us say, the heroic
drama of the Restoration. That heroic drama, strangely
enough, finds its comic affinity in the sphere of manners.
Dryden has written plays, such as *Secret Love, or The Maiden
Queen*, where something of the heroic note is struck in some
scenes, something of the manners note in others; and the
two seem well to harmonize. Etherege, the real founder of
the true manners style, presented in his first play, *The Comical
Revenge, or Love in a Tub*, a tragi-comedy where rimed heroic
scenes alternated with pure Restoration comedy. The reason
of the harmony may be discovered probably in the fact that
both are artificial. The heroism of the Drawcansir serious
dramas is as far removed from the physical realities of life as
is the airy dallying of the comic muse of Congreve. It is
the artificiality which forms the link between the two.[1]

Passing still farther, we may find a bond of union between
the comic parts of the sentimental drama of the eighteenth
century and the domestic drama of the same age. The
domestic drama depends upon reality. How true a picture
it may be of actual life will, of course, rest with the particular
genius of the dramatist, but it will never seek to enter either
the realms of the Shakespearian tragedy or the dominion of
the artificial heroic species. The romantic comedy of
Shakespeare, therefore, unless considerably altered, would
hardly harmonize with its spirit, and still further the comedy
of manners would be wholly alien to its outlook and aim.
The comedy that is associated with the sentimental *genre*,

[1] This artificiality, of course, depends largely upon intellectual qualities.
The wit of the comedy of manners and the rhetoric of the heroic tragedy
are thus bound together by the common tie of rational as opposed to
emotional creation.

however, also makes an appeal to reality. It may be often a spurious form of comedy, but that is not of importance here. What is of importance is that it is able to go along with the domestic tragedy without producing that clash of two spirits which is noticeable in some transition plays—the plays that come between the Elizabethan and the Caroline periods, and those between the eras of Restoration wit and of eighteenth-century sentimentalism.

This, then, is a point we are bound to note in all attempts to relate in any way the spirits of tragedy and of comedy—the correspondence of certain types of tragic and of comic expression. There is, besides, a species of converse truth which is no less observable. Not only are certain types of comedy unsuited for certain types of tragedy, but, as will be perfectly apparent, tragedy and comedy can both develop along separate lines so as to become, in an extreme form, fundamentally opposed. Thus, for example, a violently cynical spirit will effectually extinguish even the possibility of a certain type of tragic expression. Let us take *Othello* as an example. If *Othello* is to be appreciated aright an atmosphere, a mood, must be created in the mind fitted for the reception of the tragic spirit of the play. Let but one thought of cynicism as regards the development of the plot enter in, and the whole effect will be lost. Rymer thus found it impossible to appreciate this tragedy, partly no doubt because of neo-classic prejudice, but mainly because he was not prepared to accept certain axioms which Shakespeare had laid down. Cynicism, on the other hand, is not inimical to the heroic tragedy, precisely because that heroic tragedy is far beyond the reach of cynicism. Men of the Restoration age might laugh at humour, cynically jeer at love, but they could appreciate in their own way the Love and Honour dramas. Farce, for a different reason, is alien to almost all forms of tragedy. There could be no purely farcical under-plot in either a Shakespearian or a Restoration tragedy. Dryden could take *Troilus and Cressida*, heroicize the characters of the lover and his mistress, creating thereby a truly tragic conclusion, and at the same time make cynical the figure of Pandarus; but he could not have introduced in

55

the midst of his serious scenes the slightest element of farce without irretrievably ruining his drama. In working along the two lines of heroics and of cynicism he realized their affinity; farce he kept for his purely comic inventions.

THE UNITY OF IMPRESSION. The whole thing might, in one way, be summed up by saying that in drama the one essential unity is unity of impression. This unity of impression is, of course, closely linked to the ancient unity of action, but places essential stress, not on the creative process involved in the construction of the play, but on the effect which the whole drama will have on an average audience. It has found its most fervent exponent in Sarcey, and, although we have seen fit to combat some of his views regarding tears and laughter, some passages in which he enunciates his theories must be quoted here in full :

> To be strong and durable an impression must be single. All dramatists have felt this instinctively; and it is for this reason that the distinction between the comic and the tragic is as old as art itself.
> It would seem that when drama came into being the writers of ancient times would have been led to mingle laughter with tears, since drama represents life, and in life joy goes hand in hand with grief, the grotesque always accompanying the sublime. And yet the line of demarcation has been drawn from the beginning. It seems that, without realizing the philosophic reasons we have just set forth, the dramatic poets have felt that in order to sound the depths of the soul of the audience they must strike always at the same spot; that the impression would be stronger and more enduring in proportion as it was unified. . . .
> Try to recall your past theatrical experience; you will find that in all the melodramas, in all the tragedies, whether classic or romantic, into which the grotesque has crept, it has always been obliged to take an humble place, to play an episodic part; otherwise it would have destroyed the unity of impression which the author always strives to produce.[1]

In these words is contained a great truth—a truth which has a greater reference to drama than to other literary forms. Drama, as we have seen, must be excessively concentrated, and this very concentration demands the securing of a unity

[1] *A Theory of the Theatre, ed. cit.*, pp. 41–42, 45.

of impression. On the other hand, by unity of impression is not necessarily implied mere monotony and sameness of emotion, for the unified impression as such may be gained by means of the utilization of a variety of emotions. This, however, may be said: that every great drama shows a subordination of the particular elements of which it is composed to some central spirit by which it is inspired, and that any drama which admits emotion not so in subordination to the main spirit of the play will thereby be blemished. Freytag has expressed this conception by saying that in every great drama there is an "idea," and that "through this unity of action and significance of the characters, and, finally, the whole structure of the drama are produced."[1] This observation is not true of the novel or of narrative poetry, where much that is subsidiary and even apparently extraneous may be introduced without ruining the main plan of the work.

It is rather interesting to note that, in their insistence on impression, these modern critics were anticipated by the ancient writers on Sanscrit drama.[2] According to them there were eight principal *rasas*, or impressions, which might be aroused by a dramatic poem—*Srīngára*, which we might call the emotion of love ; *Víra*, the emotion of heroism; *Karuna*, the emotion of pathos or tender grief; *Randra*, the emotion of anger; *Hásya*, the emotion of laughter; *Bhayánaka*, the emotion of fear or terror; *Bibhatsa*, the emotion of disgust; and *Adbhuta*, the emotion of wonder or admiration. Each of these may have many subdivisions, and in any one work various *rasas* may be employed, although the types of drama are determined by reference to that *rasa* which is most important and although it is recognized that every *rasa* is in agreement with some and 'hostile to' others. As will be observed, this system of critical approach is in essential agreement with that of those who emphasize as all-important the 'idea' or 'impression' received from witnessing a dramatic work of art.

THE QUESTION OF DRAMATIC RULES. It must be emphasized that such judgments as have been referred to above

[1] *Die Technik des Dramas* (1863), p. 7.
[2] See S. M. Tagore, *The Eight Principal Rasas of the Hindus* (1879).

are not 'rules' in the old sense of the word, for a clear distinction has to be made between observations founded on a study of concrete examples of dramatic art and a set of 'laws' based either on the real and supposed model of the 'ancients' or on merely mechanical, abstract theorizings. Thus, Hédelin endeavours to substantiate " the Rules of the Stage " by declaring that they " are not founded upon Authority, but upon Reason; they are not so much settled by Example, as by the natural judgment of Mankind," [1] meaning by that simply abstract philosophizings and mechanically conceived generalities. With sound common sense Dr Johnson seized on the flaws in such arguments as those of Hédelin:

> That many rules have been advanced without consulting nature or reason, we cannot but suspect, when we find it peremptorily decreed by the ancient masters, that *only three speaking personages should appear at once upon the stage*; a law, which, as the variety and intricacy of modern plays has made it impossible to be observed, we now violate without scruple, and, as experience proves, without inconvenience.
> The original of this precept was merely accidental. . . .
> By what accident the number of acts was limited to five, I know not that any author has informed us; but certainly it is not determined by any necessity arising either from the nature of action, or propriety of exhibition. . . .
> It ought to be the first endeavour of a writer to distinguish nature from custom; or that which is established because it is right, from that which is right only because it is established; that he may neither violate essential principles by a desire of novelty, nor debar himself from the attainment of beauties within his view, by a needless fear of breaking rules which no literary dictator had authority to enact. [2]

Such a liberal outlook is fundamentally the same as that of Lessing, who declares that " the one thing a tragic poet must not do is to leave us cold; so long as his work creates interest in us he may treat the trivial little formal rules as he pleases." [3] There is no need now to trouble ourselves with the old controversy; but this we must realize, that within what may

[1] *The Whole Art of the Stage* (1684), p. 22.
[2] *The Rambler*, No. 156, September 14, 1751.
[3] *Hamburgische Dramaturgie*, No. 16.

be called the idea of the rules there yet lurks some truth. Perhaps we might phrase it better if we said that in drama as an art-form there are certain conventions which have been observed by all the greater writers and that, so far as we may judge, there is some kind of essential necessity in the observance of these conventions. The neo-classical critics may have gone far astray in the application, but perhaps they were right in the principle, when they insisted on the careful consideration of certain dramatic truths. The drama as a whole may seem as wide a sphere as is poetry or the novel; yet, because of the peculiar conditions in which it is presented to the public, it is more restricted, and its exponents have to work with more careful and more conscious artistry if their creations are to have a universal appeal.

It is, indeed, only a few of the rules, based entirely on a misunderstanding of historical conditions, which can be wholly rejected. Such a one is the Roman and neo-classic plea for decorum. Horace's " Let not Medea murder her sons in public. . . . [Do not] introduce on the stage things which are fit only to be acted behind the scenes," [1] is repeated in Minturno's emphasis on " things which cannot be done in tragedy " and in de la Taille's recommendation that " care must always be taken to put nothing on the stage which cannot be performed easily and with decorum," [2] and all alike are based on what may be called a misreading of Athenian drama. On the Greek stage the heavy costumes of the actors as well as the religious circumstances surrounding the performance of a play forbad anything in the nature of violent action and particularly prohibited any representation of murder. The later ' rule,' therefore, was based on no valid theory or observation, but was due merely to the false attempt at worship of the ancients. Similarly may be dismissed the rule regarding the limitation of speaking parts, as well as the rule which demands nor less nor more than five acts—these too are founded on naught but foolish admiration of whatsoever was done in Athens. Rules of this kind obviously may be disregarded, but in general we shall find that most of these neo-classic laws,

[1] *Epistle to the Pisos.*
[2] " De l'Art de la tragédie," in *Saül le furieux* (1572).

although mistaken, have within them more than a fragment of essential verity.

When we turn from such rules to consider drama as an art-form we realize at once that there are many conventions which must be kept if it would not lose its essential spirit. " It will be necessary," remarks Sarcey,[1] " to resort to conventions in order to give the impression that a long time has elapsed when we have only six hours at our disposal," and he might have gone on to say that conventions might be used, too, for precisely the opposite effect—creating the impression of concentrated or compressed time. This is only one series of conventions, and there are many besides. Again, Sarcey may be called upon for his simile of the scene-painter. " Suppose," he says,[2]

> a scene-painter should give to his canvas backgrounds the tones he has observed in nature, his picture, lighted by the glare of the footlights, would appear grotesque. So do facts and sentiments drawn from reality and transported just as they are to the stage.

In the theatre conventions always rule, and it is the duty of the dramatic critic to understand their scope and necessity that he may the better appreciate the artistry of the playwright-creator.

(iv) THE JUDGMENT OF DRAMA

Here there arises the whole question of the broader appeal of drama and of the methods and principles which must be adopted in the criticism of the theatre. Already we have seen that, in order to judge the worth of a particular piece of dramatic art, the theatre, if not physically present, must be visualized, and that all endeavours have to be made in the reading of the play to imagine its production in a playhouse, with scenery and histrionic interpretation of the parts. This imaginative process is not nearly so easy as at first sight it may seem, for difficulties both of an historical and of a psychological kind immediately confront us. Before we proceed farther, therefore, a discussion of some of these difficulties seems necessary.

---

[1] *A Theory of the Theatre, ed. cit.*, p. 27.   [2] *Ibid.*, p. 32.

THE THEORY OF DRAMA

THE DIFFICULTIES OF DRAMATIC THEORY. In the first place, there are comparatively few readers who possess naturally, or have trained themselves to possess, the power of so visualizing theatre, scenery, and actors. It is true that certain modern dramatists, such as Mr Bernard Shaw, provide lengthy stage-directions calculated to appeal more to the reader than to the producer, but even these aids do not always have the effect desired, for the mind refuses to give concrete embodiment to the description, however elaborate, of the setting and of the characters in the play. The majority of readers are so dominated by purely literary conceptions that they fail to grasp imaginatively the effect of a particular scene in the theatre. There are some dramatists who ' read ' better than they ' play '; others, such as Ben Jonson, who ' play ' better than they ' read.' Clearly, the first duty of one who essays dramatic criticism is to distinguish these two and to build up in himself the power of assessing, so far as may be, the theatrical worth of a play a production of which it is impossible for him to witness.

The second difficulty lies in the facts that the theatre has continually changed in shape and in equipment, and that many great dramatists have written deliberately either for a single actor or for a particular troupe. In studying *Hamlet* we must place ourselves in imagination in the Globe playhouse and create for ourselves an image of the Elizabethan actor Burbage. In studying *Venice Preserv'd* we must enter Wren's Theatre Royal in Drury Lane and witness there the actress for whom Otway undoubtedly created his chief female part, the incomparable Mrs Barry. A true basis of judgment, therefore, must be formed by an adequate knowledge, not only of dramatic history, but of theatrical history as well. The critic need not be a scholar, but he must be capable of making use of all that which the scholar has been able to unearth concerning the playhouses of the past.

Even farther than that must he go, for, since the drama is distinguished by the fact that it is an art-form presented to an audience gathered together in one place, the critic must be able to assess rightly the influence which such an audience has had on any individual playwright. That playwright, if he is to be successful, may never forget the spectators before whom his work is to be performed. A poet like Blake may, in seclusion, produce his prophetic rhapsodies independently of his public; he may write more for the readers yet unborn than for the readers of his time; but the dramatist must always bear in mind the audience before whom he is to present his work. This dependence of the dramatist on the public necessarily leads toward the confusion of diverse forces. The temporary and the topical will mingle in his work with the permanent and the eternal. Hamlet will give his advice to the players and rail at the child-actors at the very time that he is engaged in a soul-struggle which proves his kinship with the tragic heroes of past ages and of the future. The dependence of the dramatist on the theatre, on the actors, and on the audience, we may place as one of the chief difficulties in any endeavour to analyse the qualities common to all the great dramatists of the world.

The theatre also is partly responsible for still another great difficulty—the sharp line of demarcation between the classic and the romantic dramas. These are two main divisions of tragic effort dealt with by Professor Vaughan in his admirable work on *Types of Tragic Drama*; and undoubtedly the plays of ancient Greece, with their descendants, the plays of Racine, Voltaire, and Alfieri, present to our view qualities alien to the characteristics of the Elizabethan, Spanish, and German dramas. Sometimes, it must be felt, there is nothing in common between Shakespeare and Sophocles, so startlingly different are the technique and the expression of those two dramatists. The very conception of the tragic spirit differs so entirely in these two men that almost nothing might appear to unite them save the mere fact that both wrote in dialogue works to be presented before an audience. This difficulty, one of paramount importance, we shall consider in greater detail later.

Not only, however, is there this line of demarcation between the typical drama of Greece, France, and Italy and the drama of England, Spain, and Germany; there is also a striking variety of types, both of tragedy and of comedy, within the bounds of the dramatic productivity of any one nation. England may be taken as an example. What, we may well ask ourselves, is there truly in common between *Arden of Feversham* or Moore's

Gamester and the romantic tragi-comedies of Beaumont and Fletcher? How can Shakespeare's dramas share in any way the spirit of Dryden's *Conquest of Granada*? What relation is there between Steele's *Conscious Lovers* and *A Midsummer Night's Dream*? Or between Jonson's *Volpone* and Congreve's *Way of the World*? It would almost appear as if the only method of treating these types would be to consider them either purely from the historical point of view or else purely from the point of view of each apparently independent species. It is this difficulty of discerning the qualities common to the various types that has led to so many " Chronologies " of English drama and to the numerous specialized works on the separate divisions of tragedy and of comedy.

Other difficulties, obviously, there are in any consideration of an art-type such as this; but they are difficulties surmountable. We shall not, however, be able to proceed far if we do not always bear in mind at least these chief problems that lie in our path. There must be no attempt to slur them over. A result will be attained not by overlooking the difficulties, but by appreciating to the full their importance and by passing beyond their boundaries. It is not by ignoring the presence of the audience in Greece, in Elizabethan England, or in the England of the Restoration that we shall be able in some way or another to connect the *Œdipus Tyrannus* of Sophocles, the *Hamlet* of Shakespeare, and the *Aureng-Zebe* of Dryden, but by an appreciation of the fundamentally differing characteristics of those three audiences, and by a consequent discounting of the purely local and temporary elements called forth in the respective dramas by those three separate bodies of spectators.

THE THEATRE AND DRAMA. Of all the problems which face the dramatic critic by far the greatest is that which concerns the relationship between the play as such and the theatre. We are agreed that drama is distinguished from other forms of literary endeavour in that it is written designedly for performance in a theatre, and it follows logically that the full effect of such a play can come only from a theatrical representation. Owing to the facts that hundreds of thousands of plays have been written and that even in such a metropolis as London only a few hundred productions can be given in the course of a year, it is necessary for us to have the printed texts for reference, but that which alone gives full consummation to any drama is the stage presentation. So much may be agreed to at once, but concerning the implications arising therefrom there is considerable controversy and doubt. Here, perhaps, we may start with Schlegel's statement of the case:

> It is evident that the form of dramatic poetry, that is, the representation of an action by dialogue without the aid of narrative, demands the theatre as its necessary complement. . . . Visible representation is essential to the dramatic form, . . . [therefore] a dramatic work must always be regarded from a double point of view—how far it is *poetical* and how far it is *theatrical.*[1]

It is precisely here that the main difficulties arise, and these must be fully considered ere we go farther. In the first place, it is a matter of common knowledge that there are many dramas 'poetically' weak which are 'theatrically' strong. *Charley's Aunt* cannot be styled a great piece of literature, but it is excellent theatre of its kind. A melodrama of the early nineteenth century may be lacking entirely all the graces of style and even of adequate characterization, but when it was originally played, and even now when it is revived, it may possess these theatrical qualities which Schlegel defined as meant " to produce an impression on an assembled multitude, to rivet their attention, and to excite their interest and sympathy." [2] On the other hand, a play may be lamentably lacking in almost every theatrical requirement and yet possess the most glorious poetry in the world. Marlowe's *Tamburlaine* is thus not good theatre, for it contains nothing but a series of episodes from the life of one ambitious man, but in sheer lyricism of writing it passes far beyond the plays of its own time. The first question is, therefore, that raised by the problem of knowing how to balance these often opposing qualities.

The difficulties, however, do not cease here. Not only may an individual play be theatrically strong and poetically weak, but certain productions may bring forth qualities which in

[1] *A Course of Lectures on Dramatic Art and Literature,* translated by John Black (1840), pp. 24, 31.
[2] *Ibid.,* p. 33.

others we should have missed. Examples, obviously, are not far to seek. Let us take for one Shakespeare's *Taming of the Shrew*. An ordinary stock-company production of this in ordinary Elizabethan clothes with ordinary settings can be a most dull and uninspired affair; the thing seems antiquated and the joints creak abominably. The jests fall flat, and the whole spirit of the play is monotonous. Contrast this with such a production as Sir Barry Jackson gave at the Court Theatre in 1928, with Mr Scott Sunderland excellently cast as Petruchio. It was not merely the modern dress that made it come alive. The antique flavour completely vanished; the jests took on new meaning; and Petruchio and Kate, instead of being merely actors dully mouthing out certain lines they did not believe in, became interesting and dominating personalities. The same, of course, is true of all plays. *Hamlet* as performed in our own times by Mr Henry Ainley, by Mr John Gielgud, and by Herr Moissi is an entirely different thing, quite apart from any diverse cutting of the play; each brings something new, something of his own, to the performance, so that the impression created on the public at each production differs subtly yet materially in emotional quality. If, then, productions of a single play thus differ from one another, wherein is to lie the basis of our dramatic criticism? Are we to say that *The Taming of the Shrew* is a rather dull play, or an excellent piece of comedy? Are we to see in *Hamlet* something majestic in force, or something directly and poignantly appealing as a tragic happening that might have been of to-day, or something fraught with pathos and with tears?

Before attempting to decide this question it may be well to consider for a moment what has been said on the matter, so that conflicting views may be, as it were, opposed to one another. Molière, being a practising dramatist and actor, has every right to come first. It is he, certainly, who speaks through the mouth of Dorante in *La Critique de l'École des femmes*:

> Speaking generally, I would place considerable reliance on the applause of the pit, because, amongst those who go there, many are capable of judging the piece according to rule, whilst others judge it as they ought, allowing themselves to be guided by

circumstances, having neither a blind prejudice, nor an affected complaisance, nor a ridiculous refinement.[1]

The same view is shared by Farquhar, who found that " the Rules of English Comedy don't lie in the Compass of *Aristotle*, or his Followers, but in the Pit, Box, and Galleries," [2] and by Castelvetro, who placed his faith in the *moltitudine rozza*. Here, then, theatrical applause is to be taken as the standard of success. The other side may be given as expressed by Alexandre Dumas *fils* in his criticism of Scribe:

> M. Scribe did not attempt to write comedies; he sought merely to write *for the theatre*; he had no wish to instruct, to moralize, or to correct people; he wanted simply to give them amusement. He did not ask for that glory which immortalizes the dead; he was contented with the success which brings popularity to the living and with the fecundity which brings riches. He was a first-class prestidigitator—a wonderful juggler. He brought before you a situation as if it were a *muscade* [' juggler's ball '] and tossed it about, now in tears, now in laughter, now in terror, during two, three, or five acts, and there it was still in the *dénouement*. It was always the same; he had nothing to say.[3]

This amounts to declaring: Scribe won applause in the theatre, but his plays are not good ones. How can we reconcile the two opposing ideas?

Difficult indeed is the finding of an adequate answer to this problem, but the following may be suggested as a profitable line of approach. Since the play is a play because it is intended for performance, clearly the purely theatrical quality is that which has first right to claim our attention. It is the fact that *Hamlet* and *Othello* are good theatre that makes them, in the first place, fine drama; that is to say, in the development of plot and in the characterization there is to be discovered a certain skill which renders them peculiarly suitable for histrionic representation. Indeed, these two plays, however badly they may be performed, will always make an appeal of some kind in the theatre, not necessarily because of the beauty of the dialogue, for that may be utterly lost, but because of the very structure, the treatment of the theme itself. On the

---

[1] Scene VI, translated by H. van Laun: *The Dramatic Works of J. B. Poquelin-Molière* (Edinburgh, 1878), ii, 256.
[2] *A Discourse upon Comedy* (1701).
[3] Preface to *Un Père prodigue* (1859).

other hand, there are but few people who would elect to go to a bad performance of *Hamlet* rather than to a good performance of some wretchedly written, unliterary play by some unknown Mr Smith.   In the first case, the whole production will strike an unsatisfactory note; in the other, the skill of the players, being itself artistic, will provide a unity independent of the actual drama that is being performed.   In a *commedia dell' arte* performance, to judge from the extant scenarii, the actual piece put upon the stage must often have been ridiculous enough, but contemporaries seem agreed that the productions of some of these troupes reached the highest levels of artistry. This reference to the *commedia dell' arte* serves to indicate another thing.   A typical Italian company of the sixteenth century did not have any authors: the dialogue was all, or mostly, improvised; and thus we have a theatre in which no playwright appears, in which dramatic criticism as such has naught on which to exercise its ingenuity.   The fact that the *commedia dell' arte* remained for years the most popular form of theatrical artistry seems to prove that it is the stage representation which is, after all, of prime account.

Over against this, we find that, whereas many plays popular in their own time have irretrievably perished, whereas the *commedia dell' arte* show is nothing now but a shadow and a dream, there are plays, such as *Œdipus Rex*, *Hamlet*, and *Othello*, which remain permanent masterpieces, inspiring the theatre to ever new efforts as decade follows decade.   Unquestionably the greater part of their strength lies in their poetry— to use that word in a general sense so as to apply to all writing of creative order; it is this which has preserved them as living things over the long stretch of years from the time they were written up till to-day.   It would be wrong, however, to speak merely of their poetical power, for the ' poetry ' of a *Hamlet* or an *Othello* is not as the poetry of a *Paradise Lost* or a *Divina Commedia*.   It is poetry applied to, and ever kept subservient to, dramatic necessity.   We might put it in some such way as this.   The author Shakespeare finds or devises an excellent theatrical plot—that of a prince of Denmark who seeks revenge for the murder of his father.   Out of this plot he frames an equally excellent scenario, planning the situations so that they shall be thrilling and effective, arranging the exits and entrances with a sure knowledge of stagecraft. Had this scenario been one taken over by a *commedia dell' arte* troupe, the performer assuming the *rôle* of Hamlet would have improvised the actual words in his part, and the good performer would obviously have found more fitting, more memorable, and more characteristic words than one less gifted in this special form of histrionic artistry. What Shakespeare has done is to put himself, as it were, in the place of the finest, most gifted, and most inspired actor of this kind and to write down for him the most delicate and subtle dialogue he could possibly have imagined. This, we may say, is what is meant by perfect dramatic poetry; it is simply inspired improvisation captured by the artist as it is extemporized and made permanent. When an actor speaks of a ' good ' part he does not always mean merely a ' fat ' part; more often he means a part with such dialogue that every line, every word, rings true. Similarly ' good dialogue ' does not by any means invariably signify poetic dialogue; it is dramatic language subordinated to character and eminently suitable for histrionic enunciation. The perfect dramatist is he who is able to put himself in the place, not of a series of living characters, but of a company of actors each of whom is taking a certain part in his play, and who at the same time has the ability to prevent his own personality from intruding into what should be the dialogue of another's. There may be as much poetry, as much sheer lyricism, as you like in a drama; only, that poetry must not seem the poetic speech of one man, and it must be subordinate to the essential requirements of the stage performance.

In some such way as this must we look at plays; in some such way must we judge their virtues or defects. Shakespeare and Molière are consummate artists in the realm of drama because of their power in this direction. In our own times Mr Bernard Shaw has a similar power of thus improvising dialogue essentially linked to the ' part ' played by the actor. These are masters, and by comparison with them we may discern the weaknesses in many of the others.

THE QUESTION OF MORAL. Even if we come to some agreement on these matters, however, other problems remain,

and of these perhaps the most perplexing is that of the ' moral.'
When we witness a performance of *Charley's Aunt* we laugh
heartily and come away pleased with a good evening's entertainment. When we go to see a production of *Hamlet* or
The Trojan Women or *Ghosts*, even when we see a production
of a comedy such as *Volpone* or *Le Misanthrope*, something
remains with us; our view of life is deepened; the dramatist
and the actors have given us more than mere entertainment.
The question that we must ask ourselves here is: do we expect
from a fine theatrical performance this something more or
should entertainment be the sole end and aim of the playhouse?

There are some who would answer this question by saying
that what may for convenience be styled ' morality ' is utterly
unnecessary in drama. Ogier was of this school, declaring
that dramatic poetry " is made for pleasure and amusement
alone," [1] and so apparently was Molière. In the person of
Dorante the latter asks " whether the great rule of all rules is
not to please; and whether a play which attains this has not
followed a good method." [2] On the other hand, for centuries
critics had followed critics in echoing the judgment that
" delight and instruction " were the twin aims of the dramatist.
A certain practical purpose is implied in Aristotle's famous
" purgation " theory. Ælius Donatus affirmed that " comedy
is a story which deals with various habits and customs of public
and private affairs, from which may be learned, on the one
hand, what is useful in life, and, on the other, what is to be
avoided." [3] Sir Philip Sidney thought that in comedy we
see the petty vices laid bare and in tragedy the royal evils
which " teacheth, the uncertainty of this world, and upon how
weake foundations guilden roofes are builded." [4] Pierre
Corneille, after declaring that " the aim of the drama is simply
to give pleasure to the spectators," finds that some sort of
moral is included in the pleasure thus conveyed.[5] " A school
for the prevention of abuse " was Goldoni's ideal for the
theatre,[6] while Lessing adopts without criticism the current
view:

[1] *Op. cit.*   [2] Scene VII ; *ed. cit.*, ii, 267.
[3] *Excerpta de comœdia.*   [4] *An Apologie for Poetrie, ed. cit.*, p. 45.
[5] *Discours de l'utilité et des parties du poëme dramatique* (1660).
[6] *Mémoires* (1787).

Comedy will correct through laughter; but not through mockery; not just those vices which cause laughter, not even simply those persons in whom those laughable vices are exposed. Its real general importance lies in the laughter itself, in the exercise of our capability of appreciating the laughable, of appreciating it readily and quickly under all cloaks of emotion and fashion, in all admixtures with bad or good qualities, even in the wrinkles of solemn gravity.[1]

It is not in the moral maxims that the moral lies:

I will not say that it is a fault when the dramatic poet so arranges his plot that it may serve for the affirmation or confirmation of a great moral truth. But I must say that this arrangement of the plot is certainly not necessary; that there may be most instructive and perfect plays that have not a single maxim in view; that we make a mistake in looking on the final moral sentiment to be found at the close of various tragedies of the ancients, as though that stood for the entirety of the piece.[2]

To " delight and teach " is Ben Jonson's aim for drama;[3] " to instruct delightfully is the general end of all poetry," thinks Dryden;[4] Farquhar believes that " Comedy is no more . . . than a *well-fram'd Tale handsomly told as an agreeable Vehicle for Counsel or Reproof.*"[5]

It may at once be admitted here that Lessing's declaration regarding moral maxims is essentially and permanently true. A play such as *Ghosts* may deliberately preach a certain thesis; but assuredly most of the greater masterpieces of dramatic art have no such definite aim in view. It may also be admitted that in comedy the object of the average playwright is to arouse laughter and not to point any moral. When Congreve wrote *The Way of the World* or Wycherley *The Gentleman Dancing Master*, neither of these authors proposed to do more than find a ridiculous plot which might be amusing in the theatre. Wycherley had, we may believe, no thought of ' reforming ' gallants who, after the Grand Tour, came back unable to speak their own language or testy fathers who adopted the " Spanish way " in the training of their daughters. The actual idea, then, of an instructive purpose we do not normally look for in a drama, although an individual writer may produce an effec-

[1] *Hamburgische Dramaturgie*, No. 12.   [2] *Ibid.*
[3] *Timber, or Discoveries* (1641).   [4] *Essay of Dramatick Poesie* (1668).
[5] *A Discourse upon Comedy* (1701).

tive drama written around some special view of life or some special thesis. That does not mean, however, that the ' moral ' is absolutely extraneous to drama. Goethe has said that " if a poet has as high a soul as Sophocles, his influence will always be moral, let him do what he will," [1] and herein perhaps lurks the real truth.

THE TECHNIQUE OF DRAMA. In endeavouring to secure a basis for the adequate appreciation of particular works of dramatic art it is obviously necessary to consider what may be styled the technique of drama, which will include all the means open to the playwright for the expression of his ideas. This subject is one so vast that it can only be touched upon here, but at least a few suggestions may be offered for further consideration. The dramatist, we may say, is given the task of providing the actors with such dialogue as will enable them adequately to interpret their parts, and at the same time such as will form, when taken together, a complete harmony. When, therefore, any dramatist sets to work he will have, at the outset, three things to determine—the theme which is to be dealt with, the characters by means of which that theme is to be displayed, and the medium (the actual dialogue) through which both are to be given expression. This order agrees with that which Aristotle set forth in his *Poetics*; for him the elements going to the make-up of a play consisted of the Fable, the Characters, the Diction, the Thought, the Decoration, and the Music, and he declared categorically that

> of all these parts the most important is the combination of incidents, . . . for tragedy is an imitation, not of men, but of action —of life; and life consists in action, and its end is action of a certain kind, not quality. Now men's character constitutes their quality; but it is by their actions that they are happy, or the contrary. Tragedy, therefore, does not imitate action for the sake of imitating character, but in the imitation of action that of character is of course involved; so that the action and the plot are the end of tragedy; and the end is of principal importance.[2]

[1] *Conversations of Goethe with Eckermann and Soret*, ed. cit., i, 372, 373.
[2] *Poetics*, Chapter VI. The reading of the first sentence of this quotation is in the simplified form, now, I believe, usually preferred. Butcher makes a plea for a wider sense of πρᾶξις than ' action,' but it is difficult to discover a more fitting word in English.

Logically, this judgment contains absolute truth. Since drama is the art of telling a story in dialogue, then no drama can exist without some kind of a plot, however slight. Even an apparently motionless play, such as Maeterlinck's *Les Aveugles*, has a plot, a story—flimsy perhaps, but nevertheless the background against which the characters are outlined. Here, however, there at once confronts us a difficulty in appreciation. The plot may be the mainspring controlling, as it were, all the intricate machinery of the play, but in itself it has but little worth. The Greek tragic writers utilized mere threadbare tales of legend; Shakespeare, with a divine hand, drew his stories from scattered volumes of Italian *novelle* or from dramas which had been written by his predecessors. In analysis the plots of these major dramatists are seen to be merely the framework on which is embroidered the gorgeous tapestry of the poets' invention. The chief interest of *Hamlet* is derived from the figure, the character, the words of the hero; in *A Midsummer Night's Dream* it is the atmosphere of the play which makes that comedy memorable, the delicate aroma of spring-flowering poetry, the fairy-world and all its charm. The difficulty here, of course, is one peculiar to the dramatic art itself, and therefore some decision must immediately be made before we can hope for a sure basis for our critical appreciation. Drama is a thing written for the theatre, and the theatre is a place where men come to see as well as to hear. The physical action, accordingly, is absolutely demanded on the stage, and it will be found that those plays which most frankly embrace physical action are likely to be the most popular. Melodrama and farce are attractive precisely because they make free and unashamed use of the purely material. In high tragedy and fine comedy, perhaps, the over-insistence on " drums and battle " or on rough-and-tumble horse-play will distract our attention from richer qualities, yet the greater dramatists, those born to their profession, have ever shown a willingness to bow to the will of the theatre in this regard. It has been said that the basis of Shakespeare's tragedy is melodrama, and the judgment is a just one; nor does his comedy lack the element of farce— the ass-head given to Bottom, the floundering Falstaff in the buck-basket, the cross-gartered Malvolio, all of these incidents depend for their amusement on the resources of farce. The same is true of the works of Mr Bernard Shaw. In almost every one of his plays there is evident the deliberate employment of devices calculated to appeal, not to the mind, but directly to the eye; the farcical, the physical, here too joins hands with the truly comic, the inward or spiritual. In other words, the great dramatist is he who, accepting the conditions of the theatre, realizing that the theatre demands as a first requisite a fable and all that a fable implies, proceeds from that to present a richer, a deeper, a profounder, or a more poignant impression than the mere action itself could have conveyed. This is a subject to which return must be made; for the moment we must keep strictly to the mere technique, the aspect which we started to consider at the beginning of this section.

This fable, the prime necessity of drama, must be expressed, of course, by means of characters, who will derive their interest largely from their subordination to the main theme, the fable itself. In criticizing any drama, therefore, the characters must not be considered as separate entities, but only as parts of a larger whole. It was the error of much romantic criticism thus to extract individual persons from Shakespeare's plays and regard them as living beings independent of their surroundings. Much of value may emerge from such disquisitions, but these are not truly dramatic criticism, which has ever to concern itself with the whole play considered as a basis for the performance in a theatre. The characters, then, are subordinate to the action in the sense that through the characters the playwright endeavours to elucidate, explain, and illuminate a certain action. Most clearly can the dramatist's methods be seen when we turn to historical subjects. Shakespeare reads, in Holinshed, the facts regarding the reign of Henry IV, and, taking these facts as given to him (thus forming the fable), he proceeds to explain them and to make them dramatic by the thoughts and speeches he gives to his characters and by the selection he makes both of persons and of incidents. He divines that the theme is capable of dramatic treatment, seeing in it the opportunity of introducing those turns of surprise and the unexpected which we have seen to be necessary for a stage performance; to the facts as given he adds others with the same end in view, presenting to us the unlooked-for contrast of tavern and Court, of Falstaff and Hotspur; and then he throws light on all the action by the personality he gives to each of his figures. When Mr Drinkwater seizes on the story of Mary Queen of Scots he starts by introducing the unexpected in his contrast of modern and ancient, and then proceeds to interpret the facts by an analysis of the Queen's dual nature. The story of Robert Browning and Elizabeth Barrett is similarly chosen by Mr Besier. In dealing with this story he brings in the unexpected, as we have already seen, and, having done that, gives his explanation of the known facts by his interpretation of the father's character. Clearly, too, is the interpretative or explanatory purpose shown in Mr Shaw's treatment of *St Joan*.

The same process is inevitably adopted when the dramatic author either invents his story or takes over a story invented by another. The tale of the Moor of Venice in Cinthio is a good *novella*, but it is told by the Italian in ordinary narrative and without that peculiar effect to which, even when we meet it outside of the theatre, we give the name 'dramatic.' Shakespeare adopts this theme, and, selecting such incidents as will serve his purpose and adding others, he endeavours to explain the whole action by interpreting the characters of Othello, Desdemona, and Iago in a certain way. This method of procedure might, at first sight, seem not to require over-much emphasis here, but only too often, in so-called dramatic criticism, do we meet with writers who have overlooked this particular part of the creative process in the forming of a play. Moreover, we discover here a certain slight distinction between ordinary narrative and dramatic exposition. A novel or a tale may be inherently 'dramatic,' but there is no real need for it to be so. The novelist does not have imposed upon him the constant demand for surprise and shock. He may carry us leisurely and even unemotionally forward through a series of events, without startling us in any one chapter, without introducing anything which, because it has come to us as strange, gives us the shock of surprise. Clearly, then, the criticism which we devote to a novel must be founded on principles far different from those on which are founded the methods of true dramatic criticism.

This leads us to another consideration. In the novel, as we have seen, the author has a canvas as large as he may will it. His actual work may be expressed in thousands of pages, and he may introduce within that large canvas, and under no apprehension of spoiling its proportions, a whole series of digressions, whether in the form of description or in that of subsidiary events. For the dramatist there is no such freedom. He remembers that his play must be confined to an acting-space of not more than three hours, that multiplicity of characters will not only confuse upon his small canvas, but will injure the possibility of getting his work presented in the theatre, and that all subsidiary incidents are debarred him, who has barely time to develop his main theme fully. The novelist may expand; the dramatist has always the inexorable necessity of condensing.

Nor is this true only as regards the number of characters and the choice of situations; it applies also to the treatment of such characters as are finally decided to be absolutely essential for the adequate interpretation of the plot. It is obvious that a novelist may elaborate as fully as he likes both antecedent events and the situations with which he is dealing in particular. Thus, in presenting before us, say, a man of thirty at some critical period of his existence, he is at perfect liberty to spend half a hundred pages in telling us where this man was born, how he was educated, what were his earlier beliefs, his aims, his love affairs, his business ventures, his hopes, and his despairs. He may tell us what books he has read, or with whom, at various periods of his career, he has come into contact. Or, again, he is at perfect liberty to narrate to us in minute detail, as Mr James Joyce does in *Ulysses*, the most trivial events occurring within a deliberately circumscribed period of time; nothing is too small to be told, for such a writer has no outer conventions limiting his work such as the theatre imposes upon drama. The playwright, then, is fettered in the presentation of his characters. He is forced to show us his figures only for a few minutes of their lives, and what has gone before he can rarely do more than hint at vaguely. It is a commonplace of dramatic criticism that a successful exposition is the most difficult thing of all to achieve, and the reason of the difficulty lies precisely in the fact that in the exposition the audience has to be provided artistically with such information regarding the characters as is necessary for an understanding of the play. An audience gets bored when information of this kind is provided for it by direct enunciation; unconsciously the spectators feel that here a departure is being made from the sphere of drama, which is action, to the sphere of ordinary narrative. The true aim is expressed lucidly enough by Pierre Corneille:

> I desire the first act to contain the basis of all the episodes and shut the door to everything else that might otherwise have been introduced. Frequently this first act does not provide all the necessary information for the entire understanding of the subject, and all the characters do not appear in it, but it is sufficient that they are mentioned, or that those on the stage are made to go in search of them. . . . An actor . . . must . . . give information to the listener . . . through the passion which moves him, and not by means of a simple narration.[1]

The author, then, has the difficult task of providing information to the intellect of his spectators while often appealing directly to their emotions.

A poor exposition, such as that in *The Tempest*, is tedious simply because it is a departure from the technique or artistic methods proper to the dramatic form. In a good exposition the information is provided by allusion and, as it were, from within the action itself. We may take the first scene of *Hamlet* as an illustration. The sudden challenge of the sentry, Bernardo, and the ensuing crisp conversation strike at once the proper dramatic note. Within a few lines and without effort we know that these are the battlements of a royal residence, that it is midnight and bitter cold, and that some gloom overshadows those on guard. Barely ten lines have been spoken since the opening of the play when Horatio and Marcellus enter, giving still more physical action, and by the

---

[1] *Discours de l'utilité et des parties du poëme dramatique* (1660).

time the challenges are finished the spectators know that this royal residence is in Denmark and that the gloom overshadowing these men is caused by a ghostly visitant. Not for one moment is our interest permitted to flag, for immediately the ghost appears, and in the confusion that follows we are informed, again naturally and dramatically, that Horatio is the chief of these watchers, that he is a scholar, and that even he, who has been sceptical concerning this story of a ghost, recognizes in the supernatural form before him the image of a king revered and recently deceased. Here, it is true, the brilliance of the exposition is somewhat marred by Horatio's lengthy speech regarding historical events, but, having had this excitement, this dramatic series of shocks, we are prepared for a moment to listen to his quieter and less dramatic narrative. Much more could a novelist have given us—not only concerning the events, but concerning the persons involved; Shakespeare the dramatist has perforce to limit himself to those few details which are absolutely essential.

In assessing, then, the craftsmanship of any play we must take this question of technique into consideration, and ask ourselves with what skill the particular dramatist has provided the necessary background and how far that background in itself is adequate and skilfully blended with the action revealed before us. At the same time our knowledge of theatrical conditions must be brought into play, for theatrical conditions, changing as they do from age to age, confront the dramatist with differing problems and requirements. In a theatre innocent of scenery, such as was the Elizabethan, a certain elaborate description of the setting was clearly a necessity; description of this kind, on the other hand, is out of place in a modern theatre, where the scenographer can supply ample indication of the scene of action, and thus the plays of the romantic poets in which descriptions of landscape are introduced in imitation of Shakespeare are marred as much by what is extraneous, because unnecessary, as would be an Elizabethan drama in which, because of omission, we were left doubtful as to the place of action. Fundamentally, however, the problems facing a playwright of to-day are the same as those which faced his predecessor in 1600. For the reading public Mr Shaw may write lengthy stage directions telling, if he desires, what his hero read the week before last or describing the joke in *Punch* which he chuckled over on Friday or reproducing the menu of his yesterday's dinner; but so far as the drama is concerned these stage-directions are as though they had never been written. It is through the dialogue, and through the dialogue alone as interpreted by the actors, that he can convey his story to the assembled audience.

Difficult as may be the providing of information regarding antecedent events, perhaps even more difficult is the suggesting of intermediate events as the action of the play is unfolded. Normally, a drama is divided into several parts, to which we give the name of acts or scenes, each act being part of the larger whole but distinct and independent in so far as it has its own beginning, after an interval, and its own end. Now, not only has the dramatist to introduce an artistic unity, with beginning, middle, and end, in each act, while keeping that act subordinate and subservient to the general theme of his play; he must provide suggestions in his dialogue which will connect immediately any one act with that which went before. Again a particular concrete instance and a comparison with ordinary narrative treatment may be useful. This time *Macbeth* may serve. In the first scene we have the witches, and there the coming of Macbeth to the desert heath is anticipated. The second scene gives explanation of Macbeth's position: he and Banquo have just won a battle and are returning to greet Duncan; the King's words anticipate the following scene when he bids Ross go to greet Macbeth with the new title of Thane of Cawdor. The witches reappear in the third scene, and to them enter Macbeth and Banquo. On hearing their prophecies Macbeth is "rapt," and we wonder whether perhaps the prophecies were indeed true novelties to his mind. Ross (anticipated in the second scene) arrives to confirm the second prophecy, and at once our wonder is increased on seeing how easily Macbeth already thinks of murdering Duncan. In Scene IV Macbeth greets Duncan, and we hear that the King intends to visit the victorious general in his castle. This is immediately followed

78

by a scene in which Lady Macbeth is discovered reading one
of her husband's letters, and at once her comments reveal
the fact that she and he have discussed this matter of Duncan's
murder before, and, when Macbeth himself enters, her
reference to his " letters " indicates that this, part of which
has been read to us, is only one of several. Now, a novelist
writing on this theme could have indulged, first of all, in an
account of the relationship in which the various characters
stood to one another, in a description of the battle, in a
detailing of the letters sent by Macbeth to his wife, and,
secondly, in a series of comments on the thoughts passing
in the minds of his characters. Some little in this way the
dramatist may do by means of soliloquy, but, compared with
the opportunities afforded to the other, his means are meagre
in the extreme. That which is most important, however, is
the fact that, whereas the novelist may provide absolute
continuity, tracing thus Macbeth's march from the field of
battle over the heath to Duncan's camp and thence to his
own castle, the dramatist has to work in a series of leaps, as
it were, merely suggesting in the dialogue of his various scenes
that which otherwise he has to keep silent.[1] He must concentrate, and he must suggest far more than his words actually
tell. In *Macbeth* the whole spirit of the play depends upon
our appreciation of the significance underlying certain phrases
which, at first sight, might appear to be of little import. Here,
too, the dramatist is bound to remember the fact that his
work is to be addressed, not to a reading public, but to
spectators in the theatre, and that that which might be easily
grasped by the one will not be so easily grasped by the other.
This might be put in another way. Whereas the reader
normally seems to work intellectually, in the sense that his
appreciation of allusions is conscious, rational, and based on
an actual comparison of passage with passage, the spectator,
moved emotionally and rapt in the spirit of the play,
appreciates allusions subconsciously or unconsciously, for he
has no time to compare or reason; and again, whereas the
reader may appreciate more rapidly the purely verbal allusion,

---

[1] On this question of Shakespeare's silences see the introductory lecture
in *Studies in Shakespeare* (1927).

the spectator is more likely to be impressed by the allusion or suggestion accompanied by physical action. Once more some concrete instances may serve to make this clear. The rimed reference to Macbeth in Scene I and the account of the battle by the bleeding soldier in Scene II are both calculated to impress themselves on the minds of spectators. A reader might readily miss the connexion between (1) Duncan's bidding Ross to greet Macbeth as Thane of Cawdor, (2) the second prophecy of the witches, and (3) the actual greeting of Macbeth by Ross: but in the theatre each of these is closely accompanied by action. Ross is a material entity, and we see him going out on a mission; the witches are material, too, and rise,

> each at once her choppy finger laying
> Upon her skinny lips;

and when Ross re-enters we recall at once, without conscious effort, the mission on which he had gone. This, then, is a truth on which we should do well to lay deepest stress: the subtlety in suggestion of which the dramatist makes use is entirely different from the subtlety in suggestion employed by the novelist. One further example will provide a clear illustration. In *Hamlet* Horatio comes on in the first scene as a man to whom the others bow in authority; he is a rational man, a scholar, and a sceptic until his own eyes have seen the ghost. In the second scene he is shown to be Hamlet's friend, and he accompanies Hamlet to the battlement in Scene IV. There he seems to be afraid of the effect which the ghost has had on Hamlet's mind, and he opposes to his " wild and whirling words " a cautious rationalism. Thereafter he vanishes until the second scene of Act III, when Hamlet, calling " What ho! Horatio! " is immediately answered by " Here, sweet lord, at your service." Now, in reading we do not miss this Horatio, unless we have succeeded perfectly in visualizing imaginatively the whole of the scenes and the whole of the characters; but in the theatre Horatio is a physical form, and his reappearance thus opportunely makes us realize, unconsciously, that he has been in constant attendance on his prince all the time, and the fact that he has actually not made his entry on the stage since the first act leads us, again unconsciously, to be prepared for any suggestive allusions to conversations which we know would, in real life, have taken place between them. As a matter of fact, Hamlet's words to Horatio indicate that the latter has been suggesting that this ghost was, after all, either a figment of the fancy or else an evil spirit and that the prince is endeavouring to find proof for his belief in it.   This, however, is a theme I have worked out elsewhere,[1] and here it need not be entered into fully.   The Horatio-Hamlet relations I have taken in this instance only as an example of the way in which the dramatist is forced to work and of the special methods of approach which we must adopt in endeavouring to appreciate the greater tragedies and comedies.

THE STYLE.   Lastly there is the medium which the dramatist employs.   All of the action and all the characters can be revealed only by language, and it is obviously pertinent to inquire how far the particular medium employed by the particular playwright harmonizes with, or is fitted to give expression to, the spirit and theme of his work.   One thing must be remarked at the very beginning, and that is that the language of drama is assuredly not the language of ordinary life, although, on the other hand, it fails if it be artificial.   Everyday conversation, put in a play, would be intolerably tedious, and no great drama, however ' realistic ' it may seem, employs such speech.   Going back to the idea of the concentrating mirror, we may say that fine dramatic dialogue is the compression, the abstract, of what would have been most characteristic in a scene that had been enacted in real life.   The dramatist has only a few moments at his command, and therefore he must be sparing and economic in his utilization of words.   On the other hand, while it must never be forgotten that dramatic dialogue has ever to be artistic (in the sense that it is the deliberate invention of the artist's imagination), a single false note of artificiality will ruin a scene.   In writing his play the dramatist chooses characters for whom he selects a certain conventional utterance, and to this convention he must remain true.   Thus, if he be writing ' realistically,' endeavouring to give an abstract of ordinary life, a sentence which simply could not have been uttered in ordinary conversation will strike this wrong note.

[1] *Studies in Shakespeare* (1927).

His scene may be one of a humble cottage and the time of action the early hours of the morning. Let us suppose that three peasants are conversing and that the playwright has given to his scene this abstract of what might have been heard in a real cottage; let us then suppose that one of the trio asks the time and another answers:

> Look, the morn, in russet mantle clad,
> Walks o'er the dew of yon high eastward hill—

and immediately any audience would burst into roars of laughter. Yet the same audience would never dream of laughing at these very same words as spoken by Horatio, because of the fact that Shakespeare has chosen a certain conventional utterance for the characters in *Hamlet* with which the two lines are in complete harmony. The language, then, need not be ' realistic ' in order to make us see in the scenes an abstract of real life, for Horatio and Hamlet live no less powerfully than the characters of naturalistic drama. The language of *Hamlet* is not artificial, it is elevated; and between the semblance of ordinary prose conversation (the ' realistic ') and the rimed verse dialogue such as appears in *Romeo and Juliet* (the ' poetic ') there are many gradations, of which blank verse, that which comes between rimed verse and prose, is the most important. For convenience, indeed, we may say that a playwright has, as his choice of medium, these three modes of utterance. This does not, however, imply that throughout the course of any one play he requires to adhere strictly to the one form. From early times it has been recognized that comedy tends to find fitting medium of expression, if not actually in prose, at any rate in a kind of verse which is akin to prose in its eschewing of rich imagery and in its commonplace use of words, whereas tragedy, no doubt because of the appeal therein made to the emotions, tends toward higher poetic expression and richer flights of rhythmic language. This is a truth against which there can be no argument, but even Horace divined that

> sometimes comedy . . . may exalt her voice, and Chremes when in a passion may rail in tumid strain: and so a tragic writer may often express grief in a prosaic style.[1]

[1] *Epistle to the Pisos.*

Probably from Horace Daniello took this idea:

> The tragic poet certainly has the liberty to lower his style, when he wishes, so as to approach humble speech, so as to weep and lament. . . . Similarly the comic author has the liberty to employ, occasionally, some of the grandiloquence of the tragic poet.[1]

These remarks emphasize the fact that, while there may be one medium chosen for the foundation of any particular play, contrast may well be provided by the judicious employment of another form. Such variation may work in two ways. There may, on the one hand, be the employment of " prosaic style " at a moment of tense passion, as at the close of *King Lear*, where words in themselves, however rich and however pregnant with significance, fail before the tremendous cataclysm of emotions into which we are hurled. It will generally be found that the most poignant and the most terrible scenes of tragedy are dealt with by the greatest dramatists with this awful restraint; it is only the lesser writers who think to increase the tension by the outpouring of useless verbiage. More commonly, on the other hand, the variation in the use of the various media corresponds to the types of characters introduced or to their moods. Thus, in *The Merry Wives of Windsor* the basis of the play is prose, being comic, but the lovers are made, for the sake of contrast, to express themselves in verse. Similarly, the basis of *Hamlet* is verse, being tragic, and contrast is provided by the use of prose for various purposes—for Hamlet's madness and intimate conversations in Act II, Scene II, and in Act III, Scenes I and II, and for the two Clowns in the churchyard. Shakespeare's employment of these media seems to have been deliberate and exact, planned not according to any abstract rules, but according to the requirements of the particular scene and for the sake of contrast. In modern drama the ' poetic ' blank verse has almost disappeared in favour of a prose which is regarded as more ' realistic,' but it is to be questioned whether the playwrights have not lost a means of expression which provided their forerunners with an exquisite opportunity for subtle balancing of characters and of scenes. Verse drama perished because it became imitative

---

[1] *La Poetica* (1536).

and literary, instead of carrying on the Elizabethan traditions of creativeness and dramatic purpose; it has perished justly, yet maybe a new age will arise to revitalize the form and give back to the theatre this powerful medium of expression.

The study of the language, or diction, of drama may, of course, be carried far beyond the bare suggestions hinted at here. It may be employed historically to the general development of dramatic types, or it may be carried farther in an analysis of dialect speech used for purposes of contrast. Dialect, indeed, on examination will be found to be one of the chief tools ready to the hand of the comic dramatist. Dialect in itself is not amusing, and a tragedy, such as Mr Masefield's *Tragedy of Nan*, may be expressed entirely in non-standard speech, but the contrast afforded by the juxtaposition of a dialect or of several dialects and the standard form will almost always grant to the playwright a means of raising laughter in the playhouse. This subject, clearly, is one too vast to be dealt with here, but we cannot hope to be able to appreciate aright or to criticize drama adequately unless we add to a study of action and character a detailed study of the employment of various types of diction.

(v) THE FORMS OF DRAMA

In surveying the manifold species included within the one general class of the dramatic art it is evident that there is one primal and essential distinction between plays that are serious, profoundly dark, and sad, and plays that are gay, bright, and animated; to these, from earliest times, have been given the names of ' tragedy ' and ' comedy.' Beyond this major division there are various admixtures of the two chief kinds, to which the term ' tragi-comedy ' has vaguely been applied, all of these species depending upon the tone of the piece or the specific impression which it is obvious the dramatist wished to evoke. All serious plays, however, are not tragedies, and all blithe plays are not comedies; we realize that there is not only a distinction across, but a distinction downward. To the form tragedy, the aristocratic representative of the serious drama, corresponds melodrama, its plebeian relative, and to comedy, likewise the aristocratic representative of the gay drama, corresponds farce. Leaving aside the variant forms of tragi-comedy, therefore, we find four main kinds of drama, associated in pairs—tragedy, melodrama; comedy, farce. Any attempts to define these accurately are rendered exceedingly difficult by the multiplicity of particular examples of each, but some sort of investigation is necessary here before we proceed farther, and a start may be made with the time-honoured forms of tragedy and comedy.

TRAGEDY AND COMEDY. From earliest times two main points of distinction were discovered to differentiate these two species: the one, it was said, dealt with adversity and unhappiness, employing for that purpose exalted characters, the other dealt with joyousness and mirth, making use of humbler figures. These ideas may be traced down from the time of Aristotle's *Poetics* to the eighteenth century. In the fourteenth century Dante was calling his epic a " divine comedy " (*La Divina Commedia*) simply because comedy " begins adversely and terribly, but closes on a note of happiness, delight, and charm," being expressed in a style " mild and humble." [1]

According to Daniello (1536), the materials ready to the hand of the comic writer were " familiar and domestic occurrences, not to say base and even vicious, while the tragic poets treat of the deaths of high kings and the ruins of great empires." [2] Minturno (1559) thought that tragedy should deal with " serious and grave happenings " and that it concerned " those of high rank," while comedy recognized " the middle sections of society—common people of the city or the country." [3] The same conceptions are re-echoed by Scaliger about the same period: " Comedy introduces characters from rustic, or low city life. . . . Tragedy, on the contrary, introduces kings and princes. . . . A tragedy begins more tranquilly than a comedy, but the ending is full of horror." [4] So, too, Castelvetro, for whom " the common action of a private citizen is the subject of comedy, while the actions of kings are the subject of tragedy." [5] A century later Chapelain is found

---

[1] *Epistle to Can Grande.* [2] *La Poetica.* [3] *De Poeta.*
[4] *Poetices libri septem* (1561). [5] *Poetica d'Aristotele* (1576).

declaring that " in Tragedy, which is the noblest form of drama, the poet imitates the actions of the great; in Comedy, those of people in middle or low condition. The ending of Comedy is happy." [1] According to this distinction, it will be observed, especially when the qualification was made, as often, that tragedy need not necessarily have an ending of disaster and death, any play which introduced princes was tragic, any play that introduced clowns or common folk was comic. By the seventeenth century there had already risen critics who divined the fallaciousness of this reasoning. Thus, Pierre Corneille in 1660 declared his opinion that

> when one puts on the stage a simple love intrigue between persons of royal birth, and when these run no risk either of their lives or of their states, I do not think that, even though the characters are illustrious, the action is of such a sort as to raise the play to tragic levels.[2]

Johnson, a century later, saw the errors into which this theory could lead the writers. " They seem to have thought," he opines,

> that as the meanest of personages constituted comedy, their greatness was sufficient to form a tragedy; and that nothing was necessary but that they should crowd the scene with monarchs, and generals, and guards; and to make them talk, at certain intervals, of the downfall of kingdoms, and the rout of armies.[3]

It was in this period that the ' domestic ' tragedy was coming into prominence, and that domestic tragedy inevitably led to the expression of the idea that true tragic sympathy could be evoked for the humble as well as for the great. Thus, Beaumarchais in 1767 wrote that

> the genuine heart-interest, the true relationship, is always between man and man, and not between man and king. And thus, instead of the exalted rank of the tragic characters adding to my interest, on the contrary it diminishes it.[4]

Now, an examination of these various critical passages at

---

[1] Translated by B. H. Clark in *European Theories of the Drama*, p. 127. Dryden also accepts this view in 1679 (Preface to *Troilus and Cressida*).
[2] *Discours de l'utilité et des parties du poëme dramatique* (1660).
[3] *The Rambler*, No. 125, May 28, 1751.
[4] *Essai sur le genre dramatique sérieux* (1767).

once shows us that fundamentally the classicists were wrong. It is absolutely impossible to make any real distinction between tragedy and comedy on the grounds alone of the characters represented, although, as we shall see, there may have been some historical justification for the introduction of exalted figures in the early tragic drama. Moreover, it is seen that even the classicists themselves recognized that no valid distinction could be made on the lines of the ending of the play. While a comedy had to close happily, a tragedy did not necessarily require to ring down the curtain on death. What, then, is the distinction between the two? Clearly it lies, as Johnson knew, in the effects which each type has upon the mind, or, to put it in another way, tragedy and comedy are to be defined according to the impression which the dramatist wishes each to have on the assembled audience in the theatre. In vague terms we may say that in tragedy the impression is dark, in comedy light; that in tragedy we are deeply moved and our sympathies profoundly stirred, in comedy the impression, because lighter, is less penetrating and our sympathies are not so freely called into play. For the moment this must suffice, for a fuller discussion must be reserved to the sections devoted particularly to these two forms. It is important that we have recognized at any rate the principle by which each shall be defined.

MELODRAMA AND FARCE. And what now of melodrama and farce? These too are to be defined partly according to the impressions they are intended to convey, but a comparison of melodrama and tragedy, or of farce and comedy, indicates something more—the qualities which are required to make tragedy so profound a form of expression and comedy so animated an expression of the human spirit. Concrete instances will make the position clear. We call Brandon Thomas' *Charley's Aunt* a farce: we call Kyd's *Spanish Tragedy* a melodrama. What are our reasons for thus labelling those two? In the first place, there is to be noted the use of the words farce and melodrama, so that we may not be misled by ancient or popular associations. Farce, according to the etymologists, is a word derived ultimately from the Latin *farcio*, 'I stuff,' so that farce means the type of drama " stuffed with low humour and extravagant wit." [1] The word came into frequent use in England only toward the end of the seventeenth century, and was then and thereafter employed not always in a strict and circumscribed sense. There was a certain degenerating movement in comedy which started from about the year 1675, and the tastes of the audience ever more and more drew the dramatists to introduce weaker and frailer types of humorous drama. A fashion sprang up for three-act plays. These three-act plays were generally not so witty or so brilliant as the fuller five-act dramas of the more regular authors; but the word farce was applied to them solely in contradistinction to the richer and more extended comedies of the time. Farce, then, came to mean simply a short humorous play. As, however, in a short play there is usually no time or opportunity for the broader display of character and of plot, farces came rapidly to deal only with exaggerated, and hence often impossible, comic incidents with frequent resort to mere horseplay. With this signification the word has endured to modern times. Melodrama has a somewhat similar development of meaning. Derived from the Greek μέλος, ' a song,' it originally signified only a serious drama wherein a number of lyrics were introduced, becoming in some respects equivalent to opera. In this way both a tragedy of Æschylus and a piece by Metastasio might be included under the one term. With the operatic tendencies of the eighteenth century, however, melodrama, as distinguished from tragedy, tended to become increasingly more sensational, neglecting the characterization and the true tragic spirit for the sake of mere effect. Song, show, and incident became the prevailing characteristics in it, as buffoonery and extravagant development of plot did in farce.

In both farce and melodrama, therefore, there is an undue insistence upon incident. As, however, we found that farce was opposed to fine comedy and that melodrama was one of the chief antitheses to high tragedy, we may expect to find that all great drama, whether it be tragedy, comedy, or a species in which both are mingled, will be distinguished above all things

---

[1] The development of meaning in this word, from the world of physical things to the realm of theology and thence to the theatre, may be fully studied in the *New English Dictionary*.

by a penetrating and illuminating power of characterization, or at least by an insistence upon something deeper and more profound than mere outward events. Farce and melodrama will be found to be distinguished from fine comedy and from high tragedy in that they have nothing, or practically nothing, that makes an inward appeal, although, on the other hand, even a high tragedy, such as *Hamlet*, may have decidedly melodramatic or sensational elements in the plot, and a fine comedy, such as *A Midsummer Night's Dream*, may utilize for stage purposes elements which, if not precisely farcical, depend in some way or another on mere external merriment.

It is, then, some inner quality—the stressing of the spiritual as opposed to the merely physical—that makes tragedy out of melodrama and comedy out of farce. At the same time note may be made of the fact that this inner quality is not static, but moves progressively toward an ideal. If we contrast the theatre of the Greeks with the theatre of the Elizabethans we shall note how much deeper and more profound the modern tragedy has become. Supreme poetry may be found in both; but there is an atmosphere in *Hamlet* and in *Lear*, even in lesser plays such as Webster's *Duchess of Malfi* and Otway's *Orphan*, which is lacking in Sophocles' *Œdipus Coloneus* and *Philoctetes*. This inwardness, to use Professor Vaughan's phrase,[1] is the marked characteristic of modern as opposed to ancient drama, and it is arrived at partly from a deeper power and sense of psychological analysis—the presentation of *états de l'âme* rather than of mere situation—partly by that greater freedom of the romantic drama which permits of development of character, and partly also by a new atmosphere connected with these two things, yet in some ways independent of both. The very fact that we can watch Lear changing from a headstrong, imperious monarch to a chastened human being, the very fact that we can watch the development of character in a figure such as Monimia,[2] shows to us the power that lies in the romantic drama discovered only in the Middle Ages and

[1] The ultimate form of his decision is that " the unvarying tendency of tragedy—and even the work of Ibsen is no exception—has been from the less to the more ideal, from the less to the more inward " (*Types of Tragic Drama*, p. 271).
[2] In Otway's *Orphan*.

unknown to the rigidity of the Greek stage. That this inwardness has increased rather than degenerated in the still more
recent period is a fact that requires little proof. Modern inves-
tigations into the realms of psychology have opened up new
ways for the playwrights, and in a dramatist of the genius of
Ibsen we discover that character and atmosphere have been
stressed far more deeply than in preceding drama. If we
come still later into the present century and glance at the plays
of Maeterlinck we find there has been yet a farther advance
from the inwardness of Elizabethan drama, for Maeterlinck's
peculiar genius, reinforced by his philosophical beliefs, is able
to carry us into a strange world where only the subconscious
self, the soul, is heard.

> The mysterious chant of the Infinite, the ominous silence of
> the soul and of God, the murmur of Eternity on the horizon, the
> destiny or fatality that we are conscious of within us, though by
> what tokens none can tell—do not all these underlie King Lear,
> Macbeth, Hamlet? And would it not be possible, by some inter-
> changing of the *rôles*, to bring them nearer to us, and send the
> actors farther off? Is it beyond the mark to say that the true
> tragic element, normal, deep-rooted, and universal, that the true
> tragic element of life only begins at the moment when so-called
> adventures, sorrows, and dangers have disappeared? Is the arm
> of happiness not longer than that of sorrow, and do not certain of
> its attributes draw nearer to the soul? Must we indeed roar like
> the Atrides, before the Eternal God will reveal Himself in our
> life? and is He never by our side at times when the air is calm,
> and the lamp burns on, unflickering? . . .
> Indeed, when I go to a theatre, I feel as though I were spending
> a few hours with my ancestors, who conceived life as something
> that was primitive, arid, and brutal; but this conception of theirs
> scarcely even lingers in my memory, and surely it is not one that
> I can share. I am shown a deceived husband killing his wife, a
> woman poisoning her lover, a son avenging his father, a father
> slaughtering his children, children putting their father to death,
> murdered kings, ravished virgins, imprisoned citizens—in a word,
> all the sublimity of tradition, but alas, how superficial and material!
> Blood, surface-tears, and death! What can I learn from creatures
> who have but one fixed idea, and who have no time to live, for
> that there is a rival, or a mistress, whom it behoves them to put
> to death? [1]

[1] " The Tragical in Daily Life," in *The Treasure of the Humble* (George
Allen and Unwin, 1897), translated by Alfred Sutro.

This, probably, is the most important piece of creative criticism on the drama that has appeared for the last century. We see it expressed in the theatre itself, not only in *Pelléas et Mélisande*, but in many of the domestic dramas of Ibsen. There is an attempt in both to pass from the Shakespearian conception of tragedy to another conception more fitting to the modern age. There is an endeavour to move from the tragedy of blood and of apparent greatness to the tragedy where death is not a tragic fact and where apparent greatness is dimmed by an inner greatness. Shakespeare found the world of character, of inner tragedy; the modern age has found the world of the subconscious, adapting it, as every age has adapted the desires and the moods of its time, to the requirements of the theatre. It is for this reason that we may regard this and similar pronouncements of Maeterlinck as among the greatest contributions to the development of the drama since the end of the sixteenth century. It is a proof that the creative instinct in the theatre is still vital and pulsating.

In comedy the same or a similar movement may be traced. If we contrast a play of Terence with a play of Shakespeare or a play of Congreve we discover that, whereas in the Roman piece most of the stress of the comic spirit was laid upon incident with occasional characterization, the comedy of Shakespeare depends largely on character, with the introduction of that peculiarly modern branch of the comic to which we give the name of humour, and that the comedy of Congreve depends largely upon an inner wit, independent often of incident and of plot. It may still be true that the spectators in any theatre will always demand action as such, and that the most successful plays, particularly comedies, will be those which introduce most freely the purely material. Shakespeare's comedies are thus good acting pieces because he has been careful to elaborate artistically an interesting story, paying attention both to the inner comedy and to the outer. The plays by the masters of the school of manners introduce these two elements in a similar way. *Love for Love*, *The Old Bachelor*, *A Trip to the Jubilee*—in all of these Congreve and Farquhar have been careful to make an appeal to the outward sources of laughter. Yet, in spite of that, in spite, too, of the perennial attractions of pure farce, the same movement may be traced in the realm of comedy as was evident in the realm of tragedy. Here, also, the unvarying tendency is " from the less to the more inward."

THE CONFLICT. The facts just mentioned become still more apparent when we come to consider that cardinal part of drama, the conflict. All drama ultimately arises out of conflict. In tragedy there is ever a clash between forces physical or mental or both; in comedy there is ever a conflict between personalities, between the sexes, or between an individual and society. In tragedy the " pity and terror," [1] to use Aristotle's famous phrase, issues out of this conflict; in comedy the essence of the laughable is derived from the same source.

It is obvious that in tragedy there may be manifold varieties of the principle of conflict manifested not only in different dramas but even in one single play. The purely outward conflict is the first type to catch our attention. Here a struggle between two physical forces (which may be characters), or between two minds, or between a person and a force beyond that person, is to be found most fully expressed in the drama of ancient Greece. Because of the restrictions of the Athenian stage, inducing as they did a theatrical productivity of statuesque proportions and atmosphere, the tragedy of Æschylus, of Sophocles, and of Euripides presents the paradox of depending upon action, in the sense that the tragic conflict is an outward conflict, and yet of ruling out action, in the sense of movement, from the development of the plot. It might be more correct to say, as Professor Vaughan has pointed out, that the Greek drama is a drama of situation, a particular species of dramatic effort handed on to the neo-classic playwrights of France and Italy. This situation is nearly always one of outward struggle; struggle of a man with some force outside himself, as with Orestes and the Furies, or struggle of man with man, as with Agamemnon and Clytemnestra, Ulysses and Andromache.[2] This outer conflict is obviously the most primitive of all types of tragic struggle. It requires genius to raise it to the height of impassioned art. A minor dramatist working on a romantic

---

[1] On the validity of the phrase, however, see *infrā*, pp. 120–121.
[2] In Seneca's *Troades*.

theme in a romantic manner may in some place reach a height that is truly arresting; but only a Racine and an Alfieri can make of the drama of situation a thing of pulsating truth and interest. The outer conflict, on the other hand, is not, of course, confined to the classic or to the neo-classic schools. The founder of the English romantic drama, Christopher Marlowe, except in one scene of *Dr Faustus* and in the historical play of *Edward II*, presents nothing to us but the clash of external figures and forces. Tamburlaine the Great in the play of that title stands in opposition to the force of life; Barabas in *The Jew of Malta* is a tragic figure because of his similar position. The interest of both plays depends first on the clash between one dominating personality and a world of lesser figures, and secondly on the clash between that dominating personality and a power beyond and above it.

Opposed to this is the inward conflict, impossible of realization in its purest form. Inwardness, as we have seen, is a characteristic of the modern as contrasted with the ancient drama, and this inwardness is nowhere better seen than in the field of tragic struggle. In spite of the ridicule cast by academicians on the old formula of ' Seneca + morality = Shakespearian drama,' one cannot avoid believing that the old struggle in the moralities, with the stock figures of Humanum Genus or Everyman beset by temptations and befriended by good angels, must have been the inspiring force in the development, so marked in Elizabethan times, of a conflict going on within the mind of the hero, a conflict no longer of force with force, or even of mind with mind, but of emotion with emotion, of thought with thought. In the Elizabethan drama appears for the first time the conception of an inner struggle moving alongside of an outer conflict, the one mingling with the other, both contributing to the essence of the tragedy, but the former assuming greater and more dominating importance. Thus, in *Othello* we have the outward conflict between Othello and Iago, which takes up the attention of the eye; but beyond that there is Othello's own mind, and it is the battle that rages there which has made *Othello* into a masterpiece of the world's art. In *Hamlet*, similarly, there is the outward conflict between Hamlet and the Ghost, between Hamlet and Claudius, but the real essence of the tragedy lies within the mind of Hamlet himself. The outward struggle is more apparent in *Lear*; but it vanishes again in *Macbeth*, wherein the value of the play lies in the struggle so clearly marked within the mind and the heart of the murderous king.

As the romantic drama is not all of this type, so we find that the neo-classic dramas, based though they may be on the older Greek conception, and misled though they may have been by classical enthusiasm for the ' fable,' have nevertheless, many of them, combined the inward and the outward struggle in a primitive but arresting manner. The Love and Honour plays of our own Restoration period are but an extreme example of a tendency visible in Racine and in Alfieri. We may laugh at Dryden's conception of Almanzor or of Montezuma, but, after all, these characters are but simplified and exaggerated examples of the inner conflict. It is not in species that they differ from Othello and Hamlet; we might even say that the first at least of these two Shakespearian figures also displays a battle between love and honour. It is in the manner of the presentation that they differ, first in that they are not complex studies, and secondly in that the conflict is not presented naturally, but through the medium of self-conscious declamation and oratory. Declamation and oratory, more finely managed and made more probable, mar too the cognate dramas of Racine, although here the inner struggle often assumes enthralling forms. If we take *Andromaque*, a play typical of a whole school of French tragedy-writing, we find a conflict in the mind of Andromaque, arising out of her love for her child and faith to her dead husband, a conflict in the mind of Hermione, arising out of her jealousy toward Andromaque and love for Pyrrhus, a conflict in the mind of Pyrrhus, arising out of his love for his gods and love for Andromaque, and a conflict in the mind of Oreste, arising out of his love for Hermione and his hate of Pyrrhus.

The classical or the neo-classic play, however, must, by reason of its self-imposed limitations, present this inward struggle only in a highly circumscribed form. The romantic type, because of the ease with which it can introduce development of character, offers larger opportunities, particularly for the display of a conflict derived from the performance of some action. As was noted above, a still further development of the inwardness and of the inner conflict is visible in a number of romantic plays of modern times. In the works of Maeterlinck and his school there is an inward and an outward conflict; but the inward conflict is not the conflict of Shakespeare's heroes. There is a struggle here, not between love and honour, not between two thoughts or two emotions, but between the conscious and the subconscious mind, between human ties and the ties of the soul. In *Pelléas et Mélisande* we have the outward struggle between Pelléas and Golaud; but that is of small importance when placed alongside of the deeper struggle in the soul of Pelléas and in the soul of the husband. The force of this new orientation on the part of some dramatists of modern days is well seen if we compare this play of *Pelléas et Mélisande* with a play of similar theme, but derived from the direct Shakespearian tradition, Stephen Phillips' *Paolo and Francesca*. In the latter tragedy the inwardness is of the most ' human ' kind. The struggle in the heart of Paolo is one of simple love and honour; in that of Malatesta, of love for his wife and love for his brother. The conflict of Maeterlinck is removed one stage onward, and it is probable, as we have seen, that here, as in other ways, the theatre is adapting itself to the requirements of the time, and is showing itself ready for expansion to echo aright the demands of the newer age.

This principle of conflict in tragedy is, as was pointed out, no less marked a feature of comedy. Here also the outward and the inward struggle is to be seen, although it takes other forms and has different ends.

One of the commonest and most obvious sources of the comic in the world of the theatre is the opposition of an individual or of a profession to society as a whole. M. Bergson, in his entertaining book *Le Rire*, has declared that all laughter is social in character and that it is fundamentally the reproof of a particular society to any eccentricity on the part of a single person or of a special class. Whether the view be accepted or not, it is plain that here lies one of the great and most commonly utilized media for the comic playwright. Satire may frequently enter in, for it is difficult to exclude satire from comedy, but the essence of the comic lies in the implied or directly stated contrast and conflict. The old father of Terence, the hypocritical Tartuffe of Molière, the longwinded Polonius of Shakespeare, the Restoration fop of Congreve, the eighteenth-century beau of Cibber, the notorious Mrs Malaprop of Sheridan—all these are set over against a world of normal society figures. A world of Poloniuses would not be laughable, nor would a world of Malaprops. Nor would these figures be laughable if we imagined them detached and abstracted from their environment. The whole of our mirth arises from the fact that they are set in juxtaposition with other 'ordinary' types. So Polonius becomes amusing when we see him set against Hamlet and Horatio, Mrs Malaprop when contrasted with Faulkland and the rest, the Restoration fop when compared with the fine, cultured gentleman of the age.

This conflict of the individual and of society is, naturally, often indistinguishable from a conflict between two individuals; but a distinction may be made. We find often that in comedy the laughable element is increased by the direct opposition of two eccentric individuals one to another, and by the indirect opposition of both to society as a whole. Thus Dogberry and Verges are foils to one another, although neither is comic until we think of both as opposed to a world of normal intelligences. Benedick and Beatrice are similarly amusing, although in a different manner, but both take their humorous complexion, so to speak, from the presence beside them of Claudio on the one hand and of Hero on the other.

Comedy, however, does not always depend upon eccentricities or abnormalities, and it would appear as if a conflict between an individual or a group with society is not always present in the mind of the dramatist or of the audience, either directly or indirectly. One of the chief *motifs* of artistic comedy has no direct bearing on this—namely, the comedy that arises out of a conflict of the sexes. According to Meredith, true comedy demands a certain state of society where men and women meet on equal terms, the laughter arising out of the clash of the male and female temperaments. Now we may have whole series of tragedies which depend almost entirely on heroes alone. Marlowe's are thus purely masculine, and

even *Hamlet* is more masculine than feminine. On the other
hand, most comedy is certainly bisexual. We might search in
vain among thousands of our comedies to discover one single
play wherein there was not at least one principal woman
figure.[1] The humour of *Twelfth Night*, the gaiety and the
brilliance of *The Way of the World*, the sparkle of *The School
for Scandal*, are all heightened by, or else take their very
inspiration from, the conflict between the minds of men and of
women. This laughter of the sexes, as we may style it, is
apparently one of the most primitive emotions, and its source,
as is perfectly obvious, arises directly out of an implied or stated
antagonism. The man who is gaily outwitted by the woman,
as in Fletcher's *Tamer Tam'd*, the chiding woman mastered
by her husband, as in *The Taming of the Shrew*, the primitive
mate-hunt refined into cultured forms, of the woman for the
man, as in Fletcher's *Wild-goose Chase*, or of the man for the
woman, as in the same author's *Scornful Lady*, will always
remain stock situations in our theatre.

All of these are outward conflicts, struggles between an
individual and society, between two individuals, or between
the sexes. There is no hint here of a comic inner struggle.
This is not so easily developed as a sense of inner tragic conflict, and is but rarely to be discovered. Comedy more frequently deals with simple than with complex characters, and
accordingly has not the means whereby to suggest a struggle
between two emotions in the heart of the one man or of the
one woman. Where complexity enters into comedy there is
usually a hint either of the pathetic or of the tragic. There is
something laughable in Shylock's " My daughter! O my
ducats! O my daughter!" partly because of the incongruity
between the two objects, but partly because of the inner
struggle they reveal. Yet Shylock's words are not wholly comic;
they approach very near to the borders of the tragic. In the
same way there is occasional laughter that arises from the words
of Lear's Fool, because these words reveal in the mind of the
Fool a conflict between profound intelligence and disordered

[1] As Meredith has pointed out in his essay *On the Idea of Comedy and
the Uses of the Comic Spirit*, the women often overshadow the men. The
typical example is Millamant in *The Way of the World*.

wits. Here again, however, the figure of the Fool is not comic but pathetic, a fitting foil to Lear's agony. The inner conflict of this type, then, although it is the glory of all post-Elizabethan tragedy, will be found not fitted for pure comic expression.

There is, however, one type of inner conflict which marks out the works of the finest comic dramatists, a conflict not between two thoughts or two emotions, but between two fancies, leading toward what is usually known as *esprit* or wit. Wit is a word that has often been explained. Locke, as is well known, has defined it as being that quality of our mind that brings together ideas with quickness and variety. Addison adopted Locke's definition, but added that wit often deals not only with the congruity of ideas but also with their opposition. Whatever definition we adopt, we shall find that wit is opposed to humour and to the absurd in that it is intellectual, conscious, artificial, and refined. It is conscious and intellectual in that the creator of wit, although he may be laughed with, is never laughed at; he is deliberately saying laughable things. It is artificial in that it arises not out of natural buffoonery or unconscious eccentricity. It is refined in that it appears nowhere in primitive nations, having been developed by long centuries of intellectual pursuits and of cultured conversation. Fundamentally, wit arises out of the conflict of two ideas or of an idea and an object. The *bon mot* is the expression of a clash between two several fancies or ideas, combined for one moment together. In its most obvious form it issues forth as a pun; in its highest it appears as a merely implied confusion of two conceptions. It marks an intellectual acumen, the swift juxtaposition of two ideas fundamentally inharmonious.

It is this conflict of fancies that appears as the marked characteristic of modern comedy. It occurs in Shakespeare's plays as a kind of effervescence over the prevalent atmosphere of humour; it assumes chief place in the comedies of Congreve and his companions of the manners school. On this depends the charm of *The Way of the World*, *The School for Scandal*, and *The Importance of being Earnest*.

UNIVERSALITY. So far, if we may pause for a moment to summarize our results, we have found that conflict is a prime force in all drama; that an outward conflict is what appeals

most in the theatre; and that an inward conflict is what gives
majesty and distinction to comedy and tragedy. A play will
be great only when it leaves the borders of farce on the one
hand and of melodrama on the other; it will be a great
stage and literary success only when it combines the two
characteristics.

We may have, however, a tragedy or a comedy wherein
character is deeply stressed and the inward is consciously or
unconsciously marked, and which yet may not be a great
literary triumph. It may be laid down as an axiom that
beyond the characterization and the inwardness there must
go some general atmosphere or spirit which, as it were, enwraps
the whole development of the ' fable ' and tinges the characters
with a peculiar and dominating hue. This spirit or atmosphere
I shall call universality.

Let us again turn from abstract theories to concrete examples.
Let us take the anonymous Elizabethan tragedy of *Arden of
Feversham*. This is a well-conceived and a well-penned
drama: the very fact that it has been attributed to Shakespeare
proves that. Not only is the dialogue excellent, but the construction is balanced and harmonious, and the characters are
delineated in a manner reached by but few of the Elizabethan
playwrights. We cannot deny that the play is a good one;
and yet, when we place it alongside of *Hamlet* or *Lear* or
Macbeth, we feel not only that it is not as great as these, but
that it does not stand in the same class of dramatic productivity.
Hamlet and *Lear* and *Macbeth*, we say, are high tragedies:
Arden of Feversham is merely a serious drama. There is
evidently something lacking in the play, but it is nothing
directly concerned with plot, diction, or character. What
precisely is it that constitutes its failure? Or, conversely,
what is it, lacking in *Arden of Feversham*, which makes Shakespeare's plays great? *Arden of Feversham* is a domestic
tragedy: it is merely a dramatized ballad telling of a husband
murdered by his wife and her lover. It is a domestic play,
but domestic plays are not necessarily to be ruled out of the
realms of high tragedy; most of Ibsen's dramas rise to a height
approaching the masterpieces of Shakespeare; so do Otway's
Orphan and Heywood's *A Woman Killed with Kindness*. When

we come to look deeper we see that the real cause of failure does not lie in the subject but in the treatment of the subject. *Arden of Feversham* deals with an independent and isolated event, and we call it sordid, as we should call a similar newspaper account of some recent murder sordid. The emotion implied by this adjective cannot perhaps be very well defined accurately, but it signifies at any rate that the reader of the play or of the newspaper paragraph has not been thrilled by what has been put before him. The account seems bald and bare, uninformed by any broader and higher significance. There is, to use the word with which we started, no universality in the treatment of the theme. There is universality in *Hamlet* ; there is universality in *Othello*, which deals, we may note, with a theme somewhat similar to that of *Arden of Feversham*; there is universality in *Venice Preserv'd* and in *A Doll's House* and in *Rosmersholm*.[1] It is a spirit of universality that marks out every great drama, no matter when or where that drama was produced. In what this universality consists and how it is attained may be fittingly left to our more precise investigation of the nature of tragedy itself.

It will thus be perfectly obvious that the merely terrible event in life is not in any respect ' tragic.' This was noted in the sixteenth century by Jean de la Taille when he wrote that tragedy

> does not deal with such things as ordinarily occur every day and for a plain reason—such as a person dying a natural death, or a person killed by his enemy, or a person condemned to death by the law as a result of his crimes; for all such occurrences do not easily move us, would hardly bring a tear to my eye. Now the true and only end of a tragedy is to move and richly arouse the passions of each one of us; and for this purpose the subject must be so pitiful and poignant in itself . . . as immediately to arouse in us some emotion.[2]

The same observation was repeated in the nineteenth century by Sarcey, when he noted the high art required in the selection or the invention of the tragic theme. To this it all comes

---

[1] I do not intend here to institute any comparison between Otway, Heywood, or Ibsen and Shakespeare ; I am merely endeavouring to demonstrate that their finest plays belong to the same *class* of dramatic productivity.

[2] " De l'Art de la tragédie," in *Saül le furieux* (1572).

back—that in tragedy the impression created upon the minds of the audience can be secured only by taking a subject which, by its universality, suggested often symbolically and by implication, raises the single set of occurrences on to a plane the vastness of which is one of the chief elements in the arousing of the tragic impression itself.

Universality of a kind will also be found to mark out fine comedy. There is a sense in all great comedy, as there is in all great tragedy, that the events and the characters are not isolated. They are related in some way or another to the world of ordinary life. In the Tartuffes and the Bobadils and the Dogberrys of fine comedy we see, as it were, abstracts of mankind; there is nothing particular or isolated about them. If, however, we find in a comedy a person such as Dryden's Bibber, in *The Wild Gallant*, we have a feeling that that person is independent, that he is not connected with other figures, that he is a unique specimen of a particular madness. Extraordinary eccentricity is not truly laughable in a comedy; that which is risible is the fashions, the manners, the professions, the classes of mankind. Universality is demanded here as it is demanded in tragedy.

In a consideration of this universality in both comedy and tragedy Aristotle's remarks on certain characteristics of drama ought not to be neglected. In his *Poetics* he pleads that high tragedy has a certain idealizing power, and that there is a generalizing element in all fine comedy. " The poet and the historian," he declares,

> differ not by writing in verse or in prose. The work of Herodotus might be put into verse, and it would still be a species of history, with metre no less than without it. The true difference is that one relates what has happened, the other what may happen. Poetry, therefore, is a more philosophical and a higher thing than history [διὸ καὶ φιλοσοφώτερον καὶ σπουδαιότερον ποίησις ἱστορίας ἐστίν]: for poetry tends to express the universal [τὰ καθόλου], history the particular.[1]

It is evident that these words of Aristotle have more than a little in common with the plea for universality in drama put

[1] On the universality of Greek literature and on the exact signification of Aristotle's words Butcher's *Aristotle's Theory of Poetry and Fine Art* (1895) should be consulted.

forward in the preceding pages and discussed at greater length in those following. At the same time, Aristotle's τὰ καθόλου does not go far beyond the general spirit of a piece of art: it does not seem to take into account the many and diverse means by which the dramatists and the poets have secured their ' philosophic ' effect.

II

TRAGEDY

(i) UNIVERSALITY IN TRAGEDY

IN passing from the more general consideration of the main characteristics of the higher types of drama to a more detailed analysis of tragedy and of comedy in particular, it will be necessary, even at the risk of some repetition, to cover some of the ground already traversed, in an endeavour to investigate the methods and the styles of the various dramatists. As the question of universality is, as has been shown, one of paramount importance in any study of tragedy, it may form the groundwork of this analysis.

THE IMPORTANCE OF THE HERO. We have already seen that universality is an absolutely necessary element in every great tragedy. The question now arises as to how and by what particular methods it has been achieved by dramatists ancient, Elizabethan, and modern. Is it arrived at externally, is it instinct in the conception of character, or is it attained both from within and from without?

Here there is space only for a few considerations and suggestions.

We may well start our investigation by quoting a few words of Aristotle. The tragic hero, he states, " should be some one of high fame and flourishing prosperity." High fame and flourishing prosperity are phrases not exactly synonymous with kingship, but sufficiently close to it to make Aristotle responsible for all the later neo-classic dicta concerning the illustrious nature of the hero of tragedy. Where this subject of illustriousness is not dealt with by any later classical critic, we may assume that it was so much taken for granted that nothing needed to be said of it. For the Greeks domestic tragedy would have been impossible; for the Augustans it was anathema.

Not only classical precept, however, demanded a monarch or an illustrious person for a tragic hero. In medieval days, as has been seen, it was tacitly assumed that all tragedy dealt with kings and with princes, an assumption arrived at perhaps from dim memories of Aristotle and his followers. Chaucer's Monk says:

> Tragedie is to seyn a certeyn storie,
> As olde bokes maken us memorie,
> Of him that stood in greet prosperitee,
> And is y-fallen out of heigh degree
> Into miserie, and endeth wrecchedly.[1]

And the stories that he tells deal almost entirely with earthly potentates, save for a few Biblical and mythological personages.

The conception of tragedy as the falling from prosperity into misery and wretchedness we shall consider in greater detail hereafter; for the moment let us concern ourselves solely with this view of the tragic hero, a view shared by the classical and by the medieval tradition alike. When we consider this view in the light of the spirit of universality it is evident that here we have one of the crudest, although at the same time one of the commonest, methods of securing some atmosphere that goes beyond the mere figures presented on the stage. The presence of a person of prominence as a hero gives the sense that more is involved than is apparent on the surface. In the times when kingship meant more than it does to-day (at least for the majority of Western nations) men saw in the monarch-hero not merely an individual in the pangs of misery and despair, but a symbol of the whole fate of a kingdom. In later days, of course, this method of securing universality lost some of its initial force. When kings ceased to be all-powerful overlords there was necessarily abandoned the idea that a king's fortunes were bound up with the fortunes of his subjects; but for the age of classical Greece and for the medieval world it was a thoroughly legitimate method of gaining this end. In Elizabethan days its power and its value were already fading. The appearance of *Arden of Feversham* and of *A Woman Killed*

---

[1] It should be noted here that as drama was largely non-existent in the medieval world, except in the shape of the mysteries, ' tragedy ' means for Chaucer merely tragic tales such as his Monk puts forward, just as ' comedy ' means only a poem for Dante.

with Kindness in the late sixteenth and early seventeenth centuries may be regarded as the attempts of unconscious revolutionaries to overthrow the old conventions, to express something more in keeping with a newer age. Those plays are to be associated with the gradual rise of Parliamentary control and the emergence of the middle classes, just as Lillo's *London Merchant*, which was actually as revolutionary as the Jacobins, is to be looked at from the point of view of that rapidly changing English society of the mid-eighteenth century.

Perhaps, however, the conditions of our modern world are veering back to those which produced the monarch-play of the past. Since the seventeenth century the idea of democracy was continually in the air, and the power of the people was a potent thing. Within the last few years, strangely enough, this power of the people has tended, in many European countries, to bow to the will of the uncrowned king who establishes his control by voicing the will of a party—maybe even of a party created by himself. Where the dictator would have been impossible in Western Europe twenty years ago, he is now an established fact, and the power of a Lenin or a Mussolini differs perhaps only in theory from the power of an ancient prince. In other words, we again have in our midst rulers whose lives are intimately bound up with the fortunes of their people, so that the conception of the monarch-hero or of the ruler-hero is perhaps not so strange to us of to-day as it would have been to the preceding generation. In 1911 the drama seemed to be moving along the lines of militant democracy, where the individual was subordinated to the class or to the idea; in 1931 there are indications that we may have a recrudescence of the serious drama which deals mainly with those few extraordinary personalities of the dictator kind. Perhaps our interest in biographic drama is merely one aspect of this preoccupation with the extraordinary and dominating in character. However that may be, we realize that the conditions of the modern world make more understandable and therefore more arresting this most ancient device for the securing of a universal spirit in a dramatic theme.

Where, for one reason or another, the monarch or dictator

element is abandoned, we must remember that if we reject such themes of " fitting magnitude " then something must be introduced which may take the place of that emotion which the fall of a king or of a prince may arouse. There is the warning of *Arden of Feversham* ever before us. The theme of this play is ' lowered ' from the seventeenth-century point of view, and nothing is given in compensation. Herein, we shall find, lies one of the many difficulties of the domestic drama.

INTRODUCTION OF THE SUPERNATURAL. It must not be supposed, of course, that the introduction of a royal hero was the sole method employed by the ancient dramatists to secure universality. There are many others, not mentioned by Aristotle, but figuring in plays Greek as well as English. Of these probably the most potent is the direct presentation of some force that is extra-human, a force that at once serves as a fairly powerful means of obtaining an atmosphere broader than the mere individual events enacted upon the stage, and of providing some emotion of awe which, it will be found, is one of the prime essentials of tragedy. If we take the famous trilogy of Æschylus—*Agamemnon*, *Choephorœ*, and *Eumenides* —we discover that part at least of the spirit of these plays comes from the sense of the supernatural, presented not only visibly but by intellectual suggestion. The Furies enter upon the stage in person; the ghost of Clytemnestra rises and addresses the audience; and, over and above these, there is a vast, indefinite background of fate. A whole house is doomed. Disaster, misery, crime follow on the footsteps of its every scion. No one can escape; the curse lies beyond the power and control of the particular actors. Immediately, by this means, an otherwise ' sordid ' story of murder and revenge has been carried to higher levels, and assumes at once a peculiar significance of its own.

There appear, naturally, many divergent means of introducing this supernatural in tragedy, stretching from the crude presentation of a ghostly figure to the merest suggestion of an indefinable atmosphere where nothing is dogmatically stated, but where vague hints, half-visionary floating wisps of thought and feeling, are cast before the spectators. The introduction of a god into a play is the most simple of all, but this, as is perfectly obvious, was possible only in the dramas of Greece and in the primitive mysteries of medieval Europe. In Elizabethan plays, as in the modern theatre, the presence of a heavenly visitant is almost always impossible. The failure of Fletcher's *Cupid's Revenge* is due entirely to the insertion of the God of Love in human shape persecuting the mortal figures around him. There is at once something crude and incongruous in his presence. We have lost the religion that might have made possible for us his interference in the development of the plot, and we have lost the medieval *naïveté* that might have acquiesced in his appearance. More delicate use of heavenly agents may perhaps be found in the angels of Massinger and Dekker's *Virgin Martyr* or in the disguised spirits of Mr Yeats' *Countess Cathleen*; but for the most part the introduction of heavenly or diabolic forces in modern drama must be abnormal and unsuited to the tastes and beliefs of the age.[1] Ghosts, on the contrary, dominated the Elizabethan as they dominated the Greek stage. They were accepted by the spectators with a kind of awed wonder. They were dramatically true in those days; and even in this twentieth century there are some among us who have not abandoned faith in their reality and their power. In Æschylus, as we have seen, they made their early appearance. They were taken over by Euripides, and especially developed by him as spirits, symbols, and even instruments of revenge. Seneca seized upon them, and thence they passed over to Kyd and to the Elizabethan theatre generally. The ghost of Hamlet's father is therefore the direct descendant, with a clearly traceable genealogy, of the ghost of Clytemnestra in the *Eumenides*.

It will at once be observed that the dramatic force of the ghost, just as that of the monarch-hero, will depend largely upon the faith of the audience. If a ghost be put forward as an integral part of a serious play, *in propria persona*, a touch of cynicism or of active disbelief will kill at once the particular

---

[1] Although in such plays as those of Sir J. M. Barrie, or in Mr Yeats' *Countess Cathleen* and Mr Sean O'Casey's *Silver Tassie*, attempts seem to be made in the direction of discovering a fitting atmosphere for the introduction of supernatural powers.

mood which it is the business of tragedy to call forth in us. This truth apparently was realized, probably unconsciously, by Shakespeare, and his example is so important that perhaps a moment may be spent here in considering his special treatment of this theme. The Greek ghosts were for the most part ordinary supernatural visitants, which, though connected with the lives and the actions of the *dramatis personæ*, were fundamentally separated from them. With Shakespeare the supernatural is always related to the thoughts and the ideas of at least one living tragic character. *Hamlet* will serve as an example. In this play the prince is made to have his suspicions of the murder of his father before ever he sees the spirit. " I doubt some foul play," are his words at the close of Act I, Scene II. " O my prophetic soul !" he cries on hearing the truth from the immaterial lips of his sire (Act I, Scene v). The ghost in *Hamlet* is one of the crudest of all Shakespeare's ghosts, and yet how wonderfully it is suggested, and how far Shakespeare has escaped the difficulties presented by dogmatic introduction of the supernatural in an age of doubt and of speculation, may well be seen when we compare the ghost of *Hamlet* with the ghost of Andrea in *The Spanish Tragedy*. In the latter there is no preparation made for the spirit's appearance. It is thrust forward on to the stage at the start, and its very crudeness must startle and disappoint not only those who, in Jonson's words, are " somewhat costive of belief," but those who firmly believe in these visitants from another world.

It may be noted further that Shakespeare not only thus suggests, in the words of the hero, this connexion between the personality of Hamlet and the ghost itself, but in other ways tends to mitigate the crude appearance of the supernatural. The ghost in *Hamlet* is not wholly visible. Bernardo and Marcellus, certainly, see it; but to Hamlet's mother it is but as air, a mere hallucination in the mind of her son. It speaks, but it speaks only to him. It is materialized, and yet there is always the faint hint that, after all, it is connected with Hamlet's personality. The eternal elusiveness of Shakespeare is operating here. His suggestiveness is the suggestiveness of genius.

Not any of Shakespeare's ghosts in the other great tragedies are so corporeal as this of the " royal Dane." Banquo's spirit is more immaterial. It rises on the stage, but it is Macbeth alone who sees it. It is, if not wholly, at least partially, a creation of his own mind: or, rather, we cannot tell whether Shakespeare really intended it to be an independent creation or not. As with the ghost of Hamlet's father, so with the witches in this play of *Macbeth*, figures only partly connected with forces outside of physical nature, we have a sense of kinship between the supernatural and the emotions of the hero. Their thoughts and their words attune themselves to, and harmonize with, the thoughts of Macbeth. " Fair is foul, and foul is fair," is their cry in the first scene of the play; and Macbeth's " So foul and fair a day I have not seen " on his first entry is an echo symbolically conceived.

> Good sir, why do you start, and seem to fear
> Things that do sound so fair?

inquires Banquo after the triple prophecy, revealing in his surprise the state of Macbeth's soul, which had but responded to the utterance of his unspoken dreams. The thane is " rapt withal," rapt in the thoughts that rise within him, thoughts of kingship and of murder. The letter that he sends to his wife displays clearly enough the fact that the sinning pair had discussed the matter in days long before the witches had appeared to him on the heath. These witches, therefore, are in part corporeal, in part supernatural, in part the personified temptations of Macbeth himself. There is the sense that we are in touch with infinite, indefinable, and intangible forces of the universe; and yet there remains a doubt. The subtlety of Shakespeare disarms our preconception, whether that preconception be of belief or of disbelief.

THE SENSE OF FATE. The ghost, however, even when treated with the genius of a Shakespeare, will always remain a somewhat crude method of introducing the supernatural. Much more effective probably and more refined is the general sense of fate which is presented in a number of tragedies both ancient and modern. In a drama such as *Œdipus Tyrannus* we feel that there is something which constantly baffles human effort. [Fate appears above the stage like a fourth actor, playing a principal part, cheating, deceiving, betraying, watching with a grim smile the blundering actions of the miserable king.] With Shakespeare again this sense of fate in tragedy reappears, although once more in a modified form. The only drama of his in which it is deeply to be felt is *Romeo and Juliet*, and this play is separated in many respects from the other great tragedies.

There are two points which might here be noted. First, Shakespeare presents to us in this and in his other dramas both chance, or luck, and fate. With chance there is barely a sense of an outer-world power governing our actions, although that sense may be hinted at, vaguely and in hesitating accents; with fate, however, there is a direct assumption that a conscious or unconscious supernatural agent is guiding and shaping our actions. In *Romeo and Juliet*, as we have seen, the latter idea of fate is expressed. The lovers are " ill-starred " from the very beginning. Juliet has her premonitory vision of ill-fortune. Romeo's words of hope at the opening of Act V are shattered and transformed as if some leering immaterial being had heard them and was jesting with his miserable puppet below. In the other tragedies Shakespeare appears usually to have preferred to imply simply chance. It was chance that led to Hamlet's boarding the pirate sloop; it was chance that made Duncan come to Macbeth; it was chance that brought Bianca in with the handkerchief when Othello was eavesdropping. Fate, direct fate, occurs only in the one early play.[1]

On the other hand, it is very noticeable, particularly as according with his usual habit of suggestion and with his own elusive attitude toward matters of doubt, that Shakespeare has frequently intensified the fatal as opposed to the chance sense of his tragedies by the introduction of some conversation between his characters on supernatural themes and on the influence of the heavenly bodies upon human action. This conversation on starry influence, however, is inconclusive in the sense that it makes no definite assertions. " This is

---

[1] On Shakespeare's use of fortune Dr Smart's essay on *Tragedy* (English Association *Studies,* vol. viii) should be consulted.

the excellent foppery of the world," sneers Edmund, " that, when we are sick in fortune, often the surfeit of our own behaviour, we make guilty of our disasters the sun, the moon, and the stars." In the same play Kent, uninformed of Edmund's words, says,

> It is the stars,
> The stars above us, govern our conditions.

In other tragedies characters such as Iago, with his " It is in ourselves that we are thus and thus," echo the words of Edmund, while others repeat in different forms the beliefs of Kent. It has been already noted by Professor Bradley that Shakespeare puts all his anti-fate speeches into the mouths of his bad characters, Edmund and Iago in particular; but the converse to that has hardly been observed. It is true that these speeches are put into the mouths of evil persons, but those evil persons are clever and mentally alert; whereas the belief in fate and in starry influence is all in the mouths of good, honest people, who are, however, like Kent, usually stupid and unintellectual. Shakespeare again takes up an attitude neither approving nor disapproving. He utilizes the sense of fate, but never employs any direct intervention in human affairs on the part of the gods, nor deliberately enunciates a belief in supernatural influence. Even his use of chance is incidental. Except in *Romeo and Juliet* it never operates on the main plot of a play so as to bring about the catastrophe. That Hamlet was brought back to Denmark was a piece of chance, but the death-covered stage at the close of the play arose out of no chance; it was the direct result of the queen's indecision and weakness, of the king's duplicity, of Laertes' hate, and of Hamlet's loss of all care and interest in life.

TRAGIC IRONY. Besides these methods of securing a sense of supernatural forces above and beyond the drama enacted upon the stage, there are many others, probably less tangible and less immediately apparent, yet none the less effective. The simple use of tragic irony really presupposes, or at any rate hints vaguely at, a force outside human ken. With the Greeks tragic irony was truly the warping by the gods of a speech or a promise of one of the *dramatis personæ* in a drama. This

III

device is used but sparingly by Shakespeare, for it demands the assumption of a conscious fatal power in the universe—an assumption which, as we have seen, Shakespeare was not prepared to admit. The dramatic irony which arises out of theatrical circumstances is common in his works, but the deeper, more pagan, irony is largely absent. Minor supernatural effects, however, almost always introduced by narration, he employs constantly. We hear of the dead gibbering in the streets of Rome after Cæsar's fall; we are told of horses going mad in *Macbeth*. Yet here again the sense of the supernatural is only partial.

> The night has been unruly ; where we lay,
> Our chimneys were blown down, and, as they say,
> Lamentings heard i' the air, strange screams of death,
> And prophesying with accents terrible
> Of dire combustion and confused events
> New hatch'd to the woful time : the obscure bird
> Clamour'd the livelong night : some say, the earth
> Was feverous and did shake. . . .[1]

So we are told; but we cannot be sure that Lennox is not mistaken. The supernatural events are given in hearsay, not in reality. It is noticeable in this speech that not only are the strange events not introduced upon the stage, but those which are most peculiar, the lamentings in the air and the shaking of the earth, are prefaced by Lennox himself with the qualifying phrase " as they say." All he avers he has seen or heard is the fall of chimneys and the hooting of the owl. Somewhat of the same nature is Casca's account of the prodigies witnessed before the death of Cæsar.[2] He himself has certainly seen " a tempest dropping fire," a slave whose hand was burning, a lion which " went surly by," but the " men all in fire " that walked " up and down the streets " were viewed, not by him, but only by a group of terror-stricken women.

PATHETIC FALLACY. These last quotations from *Julius Cæsar* and from *Macbeth* also illustrate one other minor method of inducing a supernatural or semi-supernatural effect, a method employed most largely by Shakespeare. In his tragedies, and even in his comedies, there is utilized what may be styled a kind of pathetic fallacy, or rather, perhaps, a species of natural

[1] *Macbeth*, Act II, Scene III.   [2] *Julius Cæsar*, Act I, Scene III.

symbolism. It is apparent in a slight way in Portia's " It is almost morning," in the last act of *The Merchant of Venice*. More clearly is it to be found in the words of Pedro in the last act of *Much Ado about Nothing*:

> Good morrow, masters ; put your torches out :
> The wolves have prey'd ; and look, the gentle day,
> Before the wheels of Phœbus, round about
> Dapples the drowsy east with spots of grey.

It is evident in the darkness and the gloom of the castle in which Duncan is murdered, and in the storm scenes of *Lear*, where the lashing hail and the driving wind seem to sympathize with the aged king, the tempest outside symbolizing in a way the tempest of madness in his own brain. This natural symbolism has, of course, been used by other dramatic poets, ancient and modern, but not to the extent in which it appears in Shakespeare's dramas. The most marked example from the Greek stage is in the background of Sophocles' almost romantic tragedy of *Philoctetes*.

THE SUB-PLOT. The presence of the monarch-hero and the use of the supernatural in one of its many forms are, as we have seen, two of the most frequent means of securing a feeling of universality employed by the Greek and by the Elizabethan playwrights. We may pass now to consider a fairly common romantic expedient, denied, because of the restrictions of their stage, to the ancients. This is the use of the sub-plot. To counter the sense of individuality and of detached tragic spirit which is raised by the presence in all great dramas of an outstanding personality for the hero, the Elizabethans, and Shakespeare in particular, frequently made the sub-plot a duplication or an explanation of the main theme of the play. Thus Lear's circumstances and fate are not solitary and detached. He is driven out by the daughters who professed to love him, and is cared for by the daughter his own folly had driven away. In exactly similar manner Gloucester is cheated and betrayed by his loved son Edmund, while Edgar, whom he has injured, joins him in his misery and relieves his cares. This parallel so apparent in the sub-plot, and evidently introduced for a conscious purpose, gives the sense that the ill-treatment of Lear is no isolated thing: it is reflected elsewhere in the position of Gloucester, and, seeing this, we are led unconsciously to believe that it may have a much broader and wider significance. So, too, in *Macbeth* Banquo is assailed by temptations similar to those which had drawn the King to murder and to a life of crime. " Hush! no more," he says at the beginning of Act III, his evil thoughts dwelling upon ideas of kingship. Macbeth is thus not entirely alone; his position is not unrelated to the positions of others. Perhaps, also, we may see something of a similar phenomenon in *Othello* and in *Hamlet*. In both of these plays the sub-plot works rather by contrast than by parallel. The tragedy of *Othello* depends upon the apparent infidelity of a wife; and this theme of infidelity is caught up again in the relations between Iago and Emilia.[1] So in *Hamlet* the theme is revenge for a father's murder, and this is repeated in an altered form in the passion of Laertes at the death of Polonius. Here, as in *Othello*, however, the contrast is emphasized. Just as Iago is opposed to Othello, and Emilia's vulgarity to Desdemona's innocence, so Hamlet is opposed to the tempestuous and resolute Laertes, and Polonius, garrulous and weak, to the imaged figure of the " royal Dane."

Once more, as Shakespeare shows us, actual enunciation is not required in tragedy; suggestion, mere hints, facts mentioned in passing as purest trifles, suddenly and often unconsciously assume in the theatre tremendous and dominating importance.

SYMBOLISM IN THE HERO. The employment of a sub-plot related to the main theme of the play is not one much utilized in our modern drama. There has been a certain reaction to the sometimes formless romanticism of the earlier stage, and this, coupled with the new requirements of the twentieth-century theatre, has tended to reduce both tragedy and comedy to something approaching classical proportions. Hardly one of these methods we have already considered, therefore, may be freely and naturally employed at the present day. There are, however, other ways open to modern dramatists, and of these the chief perhaps is the identification, not necessarily expressed in so many words, of the hero with an ideal, with a faith, or

[1] Possibly also in those of Cassio and Bianca.

with a class—a method utilized to a minor extent by the Greeks, hardly at all by Shakespeare, and most largely by the dramatists of the last two centuries. If we refer once more to *Arden of Feversham* we shall find that Arden represents absolutely nothing outside himself. Had he been, as it were, the symbol of a type of men, had he embraced in himself the expression of a high ideal, had he passed beyond the limits of mere individual existence, then the play of which he was the hero might have risen almost to the level of Shakespearian greatness. Although lacking all other means of obtaining the feeling of universality, by royalty or suggestions of the supernatural or sub-plot, it would yet have taken on a new complexion; it would have gripped our attention and thrilled us as now it cannot do.

It has been pointed out by Professor Vaughan, who has thus followed the line laid down by Hegel, that the *Antigone* of Sophocles employs this device.[1] Creon there is the representative of a justice that is based on earthly laws; Antigone is representative of a justice that transcends law as we know it and touches the deepest instincts of our higher natures. In a way, too, Heywood's *English Traveller* rises thus above the limits of individuality, for Young Geraldine is more than an isolated figure. He is representative of a class of those honest and high-souled gentlemen who, after years of foreign travel, returned to their native homes, not *inglesi italianati, diavoli incarnati*, but with all their previous nobility strengthened, the dross of their beings purified by refinement and culture. It is this that makes Heywood's drama stand apart from the anonymous *Arden of Feversham*; it is the sense there is in it of something beyond the petty and the trivial and the temporary, something that has a value profound and universal.

Ibsen's plays abound in this identification. Dr Stockmann, in *An Enemy of the People*, is not merely an ordinary man: he embraces in himself a complete ideal of human life. He is representative at once of a class and of a faith; and the fact that he is so representative carries the action of the play to

[1] Although Professor Vaughan has not related the device to the securing of universality. For a criticism of Hegel's views in regard to this play see Dr Smart's *Tragedy*.

wider realms than those of a small Norwegian town and gives to the drama a universal appeal. Goethe's *Faust* presents a similar phenomenon; for *Faust* is in a way the interpretation of the spiritual beliefs and ideals of an entire age.

This, probably, will be one of the main resources of the dramatist of the future. Our age is one of wide ideals, of individual-absorbing faiths, of broad classes; even the dictators of to-day are identified with one of these. Mazzini's main objection to Shakespeare was that he had no definite outlook upon life, no political passion, no soul-dominating faith, and that as a consequence his stage figures too lacked these things —" l'avvenire è muto nelle sue pagine, l'entusiasmo pei grandi principii ignorato "—but the Elizabethan age was like that. The passion for a faith apart from religion grew largely in later years. It was present in the Civil War of 1642; it was present in the Rebellion of 1688; but it did not reach its intensity until the French Revolution had founded a new world on the ashes of the old. The tendency of literature, as of life, since 1789 has been toward the expression of socialization, toward a grouping of personalities under broader standards, although those broader standards may find symbolic expression in the shape of one outstanding intelligence; sometimes toward the very negation of personality, sometimes, as in anarchist thought expressed in literature by William Morris, toward the realization of personality only through grouping or collectivism. Future drama, expressing these tendencies, will probably therefore veer toward the presentation of vaster forces, of classes, of beliefs, either in abstract form, or, symbolically, through the concrete presence of a representative personality. Such plays as Galsworthy's *Strife* and *Justice* are not mere problem dramas; they are tragedies in which the forces and classes and beliefs of present-day existence meet and clash. In *Strife* the conflicting characters are not individuals, as they would have been in Elizabethan days; they are but figureheads, symbols of elements too vast to be presented within the limits of an ordinary theatre. Everywhere in modern art we can witness a passion for this idealization, for the embodying of abstract or collective forces in concrete form. It reaches its fullest expression in a universal drama such as Hardy's *Dynasts*. We might even expect to see in the future an enlargement and alteration of the theatre, corresponding to the fuller realization of this passion.

EXTERNAL SYMBOLISM. Closely connected with this identification of the hero of a drama with a class or a faith goes that other use of what may be called external symbolism, a device employed by playwrights of all ages, but probably with most effect in our own days. There is a typical instance of this in the wild duck which is introduced into Ibsen's play of that name. The horses in *Rosmersholm* are examples of the same tendency. Synge's *Riders to the Sea* has a similar atmosphere. There is in all of these an endeavour to fix on some one object outside the characters themselves and to treat that object as a force, or symbolic of a force, operating from without on the action of the drama, or else to treat it as symbolic of a vaster sphere of action, connecting the *dramatis personæ* with the universe at large. It serves the double purpose of fusing together in one atmosphere the varying figures of the play, connecting them with the audience and with the world beyond the audience, and of providing some suggestion of forces apart from the events given on the stage. The roaring waters referred to so often in Mr Masefield's *Tragedy of Nan* act somewhat in this way. The ring and the well in Maeterlinck's *Pelléas et Mélisande* are symbolic and permanent, things immutable as the characters are not. The background of Przybyszewski's *Snow* has the same force. Here the wide expanse of snow, visible to the audience through the windows of the cosily warmed room, provides a general atmosphere for the tragedy. The snow is not only a symbol of Bronka's mind; it is a symbol of something outside her, of something greater and eternal. Something of the same effect is provided by the game of cards in Heywood's *A Woman Killed with Kindness*, where the cards dealt and the progress of the game seem strangely to harmonize with both the events of the drama and the emotions of the characters. Occasionally, this external symbolism is expressed in the form of a person, and in this manner links itself with the use of the supernatural. The nurse in this last-mentioned play of Przybyszewski's is symbolic, half-connected with another world. The old madman in *The Tragedy of Nan* has a similar power. The witches give unity of tone and universality to *Macbeth*, as does the Ghost to *Hamlet*.

HEREDITY. The introduction, however, of such a symbolic person is usually eschewed in modern tragedy for reasons that will at once be apparent. The old sense of fate has gone, and the direct suggestion of a supernatural force is somehow incongruous. Science and explanation of facts by natural means have taken the place of superstition and the belief in a direct superhuman influence. This change of attitude is seen nowhere more clearly than in the disappearance of the ancient Greek theme of a doomed house and in the substitution therefor of the use of heredity. Heredity is the fate of our present-day existence, just as terrible and just as awe-inspiring to the modern atheist or scientist as ever the Three Sisters were to an ancient Greek. The most famous example of its utilization appears in Ibsen's *Ghosts*, but there are many other hardly less marked occurrences of it in modern drama. In *Ghosts* the real tragic spirit arises not from the pain and the suffering of the individuals alone, but from the realization in the minds of readers and audience that this is a curse that passes beyond the borders of the life and death of an individual, and that heredity has sway over all. In its purer form, of course, this theme could not often be treated without becoming tedious and monotonous; but it can be adapted in countless ways so as to appear in a disguised but not necessarily less potent shape. The two dramas mentioned immediately above, *The Tragedy of Nan* and *Snow*, have it suggested in a certain way, if not actually stated. The tragedy of Nan arises out of heredity, out of the curse laid, not by the gods but by society, upon an innocent girl. In *Snow* heredity is hinted at continually. Bronka's sister, we are told, ended her life tragically, and not only so, but precisely in the same manner as the heroine before us. At once we feel the connexion between the two, and thus appreciate subconsciously the relationship between the characters on the stage and forces beyond the theatre.

There are, of course, other methods of obtaining this feeling of universality. The means are literally innumerable by which dramatists ancient, Elizabethan, and modern have carried their plays out of the limitations of the actual and the particular to other planes of existence. Some of these means are intimately connected with the very source of the tragic spirit itself, such

118

as that impression of waste which Professor Bradley has discerned in all the Shakespearian tragedy. This impression of waste gives power and dignity to the whole tragic impression in the presentation of the vastness of the universe.

Our investigation, therefore, of this aspect of tragedy has led us toward the realization of a truth that may be thus formally expressed: whenever a tragedy lacks the feeling of universality, whenever it presents merely the temporary and the topical, the detached in time and in place, then it becomes simply sordid or never aspires to rise above melodrama. The cardinal element in high tragedy is universality. If we have not this, however well written the drama may be, however perfect the plot, and however brilliantly delineated the characters, the play will fail, and be classed with *Arden of Feversham* rather than with *Hamlet* and *Othello*.

(ii) THE SPIRIT OF TRAGEDY

PITY AND TERROR. This universality explains one thing about tragedy: it shows to us that part at least of the emotion which we gain from reading a great drama arises from the fact that we are led into contact with a series of events which themselves are majestically and subtly related to the universe without. This, however, is only part of the emotion that comes to us. It is this question of the emotions aroused by tragedy that we may now consider in greater detail.

Aristotle has decided that the object of a tragedy is to arouse " pity and terror." [1] The theme of tragedy is always an unhappy one. It frequently introduces misery, torment physical and mental, and crime. The old medieval notion of tragedy as a falling from prosperity to unhappiness has this general truth in it, that all tragedy of all nations has always had about it an element of pain and misery. There are two questions which here may arise: (1) Are " pity and terror " truly the emotions which a dramatist should seek to produce in a tragedy? and (2) If tragedy thus deals with misery what pleasure do we gain from it?

[1] On Aristotle's words and on the κάθαρσις which tragedy effects see Butcher's *Aristotle's Theory of Poetry and Fine Art* (1895), pp. 240 ff., and *cf. infra*, pp. 122-124.

The answer to the second of these two questions obviously depends upon the answer which we shall find for the first, and therefore Aristotle's statement may have primary consideration. " Pity and terror "—we cannot quite be assured what Aristotle meant by these words, but, taking them at their ordinary English value, we may well meditate whether they express exactly the genuine tragic emotions. Terror, assuredly, is frequently called forth by a great drama, although terror is not the chief emotion in an audience; but as regards pity, we may truly feel doubtful whether in a high tragedy it may to any great extent enter in. Tragedy, after all, is not a thing of tears. Pathos stands upon a lower plane of dramatic art, just as sentimentalism is lower than a genuine humanitarian spirit. Pathos is closely connected with pity, and neither is generally indulged in by the great dramatists as the main tragic *motif*. The air of Æschylus is stern and hard. The characters he has introduced are above us, mentally and morally, because of their loftiness and their nobility; and we may hardly express pity for what we feel is loftier and nobler than ourselves. We can pity a man or an animal, but we cannot pity a god. There is no call for " sympathetic tears " on behalf of Prometheus or Orestes, precisely because in the grandeur of their being they are greater than we are. We do not sympathize with Othello to the extent of feeling pity, because Othello is a force beyond our ken, primitive perhaps, but strong and majestic. We do not weep at the death of Cordelia, because she has a hardness in her nature which forbids our tears.

If we take, then, the great tragedians by themselves—Æschylus, Shakespeare, Alfieri, Ibsen—or study individual works of theirs, we shall be struck by this firmness and hardness in their characters and their plays. There is always something stern and majestic about the highest tragic art.

With Shakespeare we do sometimes descend to pathetic scenes, and it is exceedingly difficult to determine whether this is due to that spirit existing in the early seventeenth century which gave rise about 1608 to the romantic tragi-comedies of Beaumont and Fletcher, or whether it is because Shakespeare felt the necessity of pathos both as a species of relief from too high tension and as a kind of contrast to the genuine tragic sternness. After the misery and horror of Lear's wandering on the storm-swept heath, after Gloucester's eyes have been torn out *coram populo*, we suddenly find ourselves borne into that scene of essential pathos when the aged king awakens to discover his daughter bending over him. That would appear to be almost the only passage in *Lear* where Shakespeare has deliberately striven to arouse our pity and our feelings of tenderness. All is as rock around; this one scene forms a relief to the tremendous effect of the preceding acts and a moment of respite ere we pass to the even more tremendous conclusion. Magnificent passage though it be, artistically conceived and placed, it is nevertheless, when considered alone, seen to be on a lower plane of tragic expression than the rest of the play. The same phenomenon may be studied in Shakespeare's other dramas. Desdemona, weak and uninteresting, is made an object for our pity: in *Hamlet* the mad scene of Ophelia is pathetic in its aim. Both the pathos of Desdemona and the pathos of Ophelia form reliefs to the tragic tension of the dramas in which they appear.

Considering thus the relations between genuine tragic expression and pathos, we can well realize why there is such a chasm between the serious plays of 1630–40 and the tragedies of Shakespeare, and why modern plays such as *The Second Mrs Tanqueray* fall below the level of the highest tragic art. Some of these dramas are excellently constructed, magnificent in their technique; but the appeal in them is directed to the softer parts of our natures. One wonders whether this truth regarding tragedy was not in reality truly divined by the classic and the neo-classic critics when they fought with all their strength against romantic colour and variety. Although the neo-classicists never expressed it in so many words, although they confused the issue by reference to the " ancients " and by the theory of imitation, they may have felt that the rules they devised would preserve for tragedy that sternness and that statuesque grandeur which romantic notions only too soon can destroy. The later romantic playwrights all spoil their work by neglecting this hardness of texture. Ford's plays are beautiful, but they are not high tragedies; Coleridge's *Remorse* fails to thrill us, in spite of its dark caverns lit by one flaring torch and its prisons oozing forth mouldy damps. In our own age most of our dramatists seem incapable of creating real tragedy because they lack the requisite grandeur of temper and aim. It is interesting in this connexion to note that the two modern playwrights who have come nearest to capturing the authentic tone of high tragedy are Eugene O'Neill and Sean O'Casey, both of whom show in their work a certain hardness, amounting almost to coarseness of treatment. Both are stern; both are rough-handed. Neither seems capable of indulging in mere sentimentality, while pity in each is transcended by some emotion higher and sterner. In *The Silver Tassie* a passion is sounded which forbids the weak indulgence of maudlin pathos; there we are carried to a height where anger, even disgust perhaps, the sense of waste and injustice have all right of entry, and which leaves the pathetic far below. The very vastness of the theme, as in all true tragedy, presupposes an emotion richer, profounder, stronger than is provided in the sentimental play of tears.

Tragedy, then, we may say, has for its aim not the arousing of pity, but the conjuring up of a feeling of awe allied to lofty grandeur.

TRAGIC RELIEF. (*a*) *The Theory of Katharsis.* Up to this point we have considered only the aim of high tragedy so far as that aim affects its general spirit; it may now be fitting to turn from this spirit or aim to a consideration of what may be styled the tragic relief. This forms the second of the two questions proposed at the beginning of this section. Tragedy, it is admitted, deals with pain, sometimes with vice, often with misery, often, if not necessarily, with death; whence, we may ask ourselves, can arise our pleasure in witnessing this pain and this desolation?

The earliest specific answer to this problem is that offered by Aristotle, in which he affirms that by arousing pity and fear tragedy effects a *katharsis* ('purgation') of these and kindred emotions. Concerning the meaning of the word *katharsis* there has been controversy in plenty. In early Renascence times (1548) Robortelli thought that the Greek philosopher intended to imply that by witnessing tragedy we become accustomed to the terrible and are thereby aided in our thorny way of life,

while Giraldi imagined that the 'purgation' applied, not to
the pity and fear themselves, but to emotions similar to these.
Lessing opined that in life we lack balance; that there is in
our natures either too little or too much pity and fear; and
that Aristotle believed the tragic representation capable of providing for the minds of the spectators a kind of mean. The
earlier commentaries, however, do not really matter. Modern
scholarship has shown that the word *katharsis* is in truth a
medical word used here metaphorically, and that its exact sense
is that of 'purgation' in the significance of 'aperient.' As
Mr F. L. Lucas has demonstrated, Aristotle uses it almost with
the modern idea of ridding ourselves of repressions, and uses
it, too, with the object of replying directly to Plato's Puritanic
strictures on the art of poetry. It may be that in his words
there is some truth, but we may believe that in itself the theory
is far too moralistic to be a complete answer to our question.
After all, we do not go to witness a tragedy with the idea of
taking a mental medicine (although for many playgoers tragedy
certainly has the bad taste we associate with all good medicine),
and it is to be questioned whether, even unconsciously, we
share in any real effect of purgation. There seem, too, to be
other things of far greater importance in the tragic spectacle,
and perhaps we may, with Mr Lucas, reject Aristotle's thesis
as a piece of very special pleading, without permanent significance.

(*b*) *Heroic Grandeur*. When we consider our emotions carefully, perhaps we shall find that the first and undoubtedly the
greatest reason for our pleasure derived from the witnessing
of a painful drama, the prime tragic relief, is the presence
in some one or other of the characters of a lofty nobility, a
note of almost heroic grandeur. From the very spirit of the
drama, then, comes a great part of the recompense for the terror
and awe which thrill us. We gain pleasure in reading or in
witnessing *Hamlet* from watching Hamlet's honesty and inherent goodness of soul. We see him baffled by circumstance,
but we are willing to witness that because we know that his
nobility, the inner goodness of his being, will triumph over
evil and over death. So, too, with the figure of Cordelia.
Cordelia dies; we might for a moment, in reading *Lear*, be

tempted to question the necessity for her murder, but this thought will never come to us while we are seeing a theatrical performance of *Lear*, nor will it come to us if we read *Lear* aright. We do not think whether it is just or unjust that Cordelia should die. The question of justice does not affect us at all. For in comparison with Cordelia's self—with what she actually is—her death is as nothing. Death itself has ceased to be of moment. Indeed, we might say that death never really matters in a tragedy. Comedy assumes that life is eternal and death a dream: tragedy assumes that death is inevitable and that its time of coming is of no importance compared with what a man does before his death.

Although the examples already given are both from Shakespeare, we shall find that Shakespeare is by no means alone in thus presenting nobility of characterization as a tragic relief. The predominating feature of Greek drama is this high nobility and sublime tone. Orestes, Œdipus, Prometheus—all the outstanding persons of the Greek drama—are majestic in their heroic proportions. We have seen that they can excite no pity in their grandeur; on the contrary, their grandeur is so exaggerated that they seem to stand above us as demi-gods, with a nobility greater than the nobility of this earth. When we thus consider the persons of the Greek and of the Shakespearian tragedy it will at once be apparent that the heroic drama of Restoration England, ridiculous as it may be in characterization, simply exaggerates to an extreme degree the heroic note present in the persons of Æschylus and Shakespeare. We have already seen that this heroic tragedy had thus exaggerated the perfectly natural inner conflict of Shakespeare's heroes, turning it into a thing of love and honour; so here we find that Dryden's Almanzor and Montezuma are merely intensified portraits painted on the same lines as Othello and Œdipus. Although not one of those heroic tragedies ever rises to the height of pure tragic expression, we may find that, as a class, the heroic drama will serve to point out many characteristics of true dramatic productivity. The heroic tragedy is but true tragedy carried to excess, with all its elements magnified and made more obvious.

(c) *The Feeling of Nobility*. Here, however, arises an exceedingly serious and difficult problem. We have mentioned as heroic figures in the Greek drama Orestes, and in the Shakespearian drama Macbeth. Both of these, in their several ways, commit atrocious crimes; and we find that this question of nobility must be considered in close connexion with the related question of morality. Morality is, after all, a word of no absolute meaning, varying from religion to religion, from race to race, from nation to nation, from age to age, from individual to individual. This is granted, perhaps, by nearly all but the extreme religionists of the various sects, but even with such an admission it cannot be denied that there are certain common instincts in humanity, partly derived from social conventions, by which we agree as to the righteousness and unrighteousness of definite actions, particularly those of a more violent character. Murder, for example, especially murder of one nearly allied to the criminal, is commonly regarded with abhorrence by all; and if that murder be presented in a tragedy, committed by the hero of the play, then the dramatist, if he is to preserve the dignity and nobility of his work, must first of all provide ample *motif* for the committing of the crime and display in the mind of the hero emotions sufficiently powerful to counterbalance the disgust we otherwise might experience. We have to feel, that is to say, that the playwright himself is imbued with what we may call the noblest feelings of the human heart. If he treats his theme merely as a fitting opportunity for the introduction of sensational incidents then his drama, if it aims at the tone of tragedy, will be nauseous to us, or, if it does not, will fall within the lower class of melodrama. The *Choephoræ* of Æschylus provides a fitting example of the higher treatment of such a theme. There the Greek dramatist has presented Orestes with continual doubt and horror in his mind. Orestes feels terror and detestation of himself before he murders Clytemnestra; he feels horror as he moves toward his fell purpose; after it has been carried out the Furies, half personifications of his own thoughts and emotions, goad him on to madness. The *motif* of his crime is excellently and fully represented: the crime, in spite of the *motif*, is engaged in with absolute terror and shame.

With a more modern and more sensitive audience even such

a *motif* might not have appeared sufficient, and this, perhaps, was felt by Alfieri when he came to treat of the same theme. In his *Oreste* the hero dashes within the scene, mad with rage not so much against his mother as against Egisto. He plunges his sword into the breast of Egisto, but in his madness he also unwittingly slays Clitennestra. Blinded by his frenzy, he does not see what he has done; and, entering upon the stage with Pilade and Elettra, he exults in the slaughter of his father's murderer: [1]

Or.   Oh, perchè mesto,
Parte di me, se'tu ? non sai che ho spento
Io quel fellone ? vedi ; ancor di sangue
È stillante il mio ferro. Ah, tu diviso
Meco i colpi non hai ! pasciti dunque
Di questa vista gli occhi.

Pil.   Oh, vista ! Oreste,
Dammi quel brando.

Or.   A che ?

Pil.   Dammelo.

Or.   Il prendi.

Pil. Odimi—A noi non lice in questa terra
Più rimaner : vieni. . . .

Or.   Ma qual ?

El.   Deh, parla !
Clitennestra dov'è ?

Or.   Lasciala : or forse
Al traditor marito ella arde il rogo.

Pil. Più che compiuta hai la vendetta ; or vieni ;
Non cercar oltre. . . .

---

[1] A translation of the Italian is given at the foot of each page.

Ores.   Oh, wherefore sad,
Thou sharer of my thoughts? Knowest thou not
That I have slain him? See; the blood is yet
Dripping from my sword. Ah, thou hast not
Shared in my triumph! Feast then thine hungry eyes
On this rich sight.

Pyl.   That sight! Orestes,
Give me thy sword.

Ores.   For what?

Pyl.   Give me thy sword.

Ores. 'Tis here.

Pyl.   List. In this land no longer can we stay.
Come. . . .

Ores.   But what?

Elect.   Oh, speak! Pylades, speak!
Where is Clytemnestra?

Ores.   Let her be:
Perchance she lights that wretch's funeral pyre.

Pyl. Thou hast more than ta'en revenge; but come this way,
Inquire not further. . . .

Or.	Oh, che di'tu ? . . .
El.	La madre

Ti ridomando, Pilade.   Oh, qual m'entra
Gel nelle vene !

Pil.	Il cielo . . .
El.	Ah, spenta forse ! . . .
Or.	Volte in se stessa infuriata ha l'armi ? . . .
El.	Pilade ! oimè ! . . . tu non rispondi ?
Or.	Narra ;

Che fu ?

Pil.	Trafitta . . .
Or.	E da qual mano ?
Pil.	Ah ! vieni. . . .
El.	Tu la uccidesti.
Or.	Io parricida ? . . .
Pil.	Il ferro

Vibrasti in lei, senza avvederten, cieco
D'ira, correndo a Egisto incontro. . . .

Or.	Oh, quale,

Orror mi prende !   Io parricida ?—Il brando,
Pilade, dammi : io'l vo' . . .

Pil.	Non fia.
El.	Fratello . . .
Pil.	Misero Oreste !
Or.	Or, chi fratel mi noma ?

Empia, tu forse, che serbato a vita,
E al matricidio m'hai ?—Rendimi il brando,

Ores.	What is't thou say'st? . . .
Elect.	Once more

I ask, my mother, Pylades?   Oh, what
A chill invades my heart!

Pyl.	The gods . . .
Elect.	She's dead! . . .
Ores.	In maddened rage has she then slain herself? . . .
Elect.	Pylades! Ah me! . . . thou answerest not?
Ores.	Tell me;

What is't?

Pyl.	Stabbed . . .
Ores.	By whom?
Pyl.	Come ; let us go. . . .
Elect.	Thou hast killed her.
Ores.	I? A parricide? . . .
Pyl.	Thy sword

Has pierced her breast, as thou, unconscious, blind
In thy rage, dashed upon Ægisthus. . . .

Ores.	Oh, what

A fear enfolds me!   I have killed her?   That sword,
Pylades, give it me.   I must . . .

Pyl.	It shall not be.
Elect.	My brother . . .
Pyl.	Wretched Orestes!
Ores.	Who calls me brother?

Thou impious woman, perhaps, who hast to life
And to the murder of my mother saved me?—

> Il brando ; . . . Oh, rabbia !—Ove son io ? che feci ? . . .
> Chi mi trattien ? . . . Chi mi persegue ? . . . Ahi ! dove,
> Dove men fuggo ? . . . ove mi ascondo ?—O padre,
> Torvo mi guardi ? a me chiedesti sangue :
> E questo è sangue ; . . . e sol per te il versai.

El. Oreste, Oreste . . . Ahi, misero fratello ! . . .
> Già più non ci ode ; . . . è fuor di se. . . . Noi sempre
> Pilade, al fianco a lui staremo. . . .

Pil.   Oh, dura
> D'orrendo fato inevitabil legge !

This last scene is perfect in its restraint and in its power. It betokens not only the genius and the nobility of Alfieri's thought and character, but shows how the theatre will always adapt itself to the needs and desires of the different ages. The treatment of Æschylus was the treatment of a Greek; putting ourselves back in the ancient world, we can appreciate its nobility and its grandeur; but, as Alfieri felt, it is a treatment not precisely fitted for the world of to-day.

From these two plays of Æschylus and Alfieri we might turn to the cognate drama of Sophocles, where at once we see a decided weakening of tone. Whereas Orestes in the other two plays had been filled with shame and remorse, here he displays no horror at the deed he has committed. The construction is skilful, the characterization is fine; but the feeling of nobility is absent, and the play of Sophocles descends dangerously near to that fatal rock in dramatic art, sensationalism. In exactly similar manner may be compared the two tragedies of *Medea* written by Euripides and Seneca respectively. By Euripides Medea is coarsely drawn; she has not that high sublimity and that heroic grandeur which is so noticeable in the creations of Æschylus; but, at the same time, the Greek dramatist has endeavoured by all means in his command to excite for her the sympathies of the audience.

> Give me that sword, that sword; . . . Oh, Furies!—What
> Have I done? . . . Where am I? . . . Who is by me? . . . Who
> Torments me? . . . Oh, where, where shall I fly? Where
> Shall I hide my miserable self? . . . My father!
> Dost thou glare at me? Thou asked'st blood;
> And here is blood; . . . for thee alone I spilt it.

Elect. Orestes, Orestes . . . Oh, miserable brother! . . .
> He hears us not; . . . his sense is gone. . . . Ever must we,
> Dear Pylades, stand by his side. . . .

Pyl.   Cruel
> Inevitable law of fearful destiny!

She is a lonely woman, a woman suddenly cast into affliction. All her primitive furies are awakened, and the deed which she commits seems to flow from a natural cause. We may say that the Medea of Euripides is a slightly sentimental creation, but in her is expressed a nobility, a primitive nobility, where crude horror at her own crime mingles with her hate and with her desire for revenge. We turn to the Medea of Seneca and at once we discover that we have to deal with an entirely different being. Medea here is nothing more than a melodramatic villainess. We seek in her in vain for any truly noble element. Thrills we get, horror and dismay are cast upon us, but nothing that would show that the Roman author felt the terror of her crime. Seneca fails in the highest test.

There is hardly any necessity to refer here to Shakespeare. He too has chosen his villain heroes, but in every one of them there is depicted a high nobility. Macbeth sins doubly, trebly:

> He's here in double trust :
> First, as I am his kinsman and his subject,
> Strong both against the deed ; then, as his host,
> Who should against his murderer shut the door,
> Not bear the knife myself. Besides, this Duncan
> Hath borne his faculties so meek, hath been
> So clear in his great office, that his virtues
> Will plead like angels trumpet-tongued against
> The deep damnation of his taking-off. . . .[1]

Everywhere he sees the horror of his deed. It makes him start with terror when he first conceives it; it gives him visions of blood-smeared daggers as he goes about his fatal purpose; it sears all the rest of his days with the thought-stains of conscience.

There is something of horror, perhaps, that stays the hand of the hesitating Hamlet. He accuses himself of cowardice; " religion," he says, retards him. He cannot stab this drunken king in cold blood. Othello too sees all the hideousness of his murder; he feels " the pity of it," and slays Desdemona with heroic terrors gnawing at his heart. It is " the cause," not a selfish jealousy, that nerves him to smother his wife. In killing her he kills himself:

> Put out the light, and then put out the light !

---

[1] *Macbeth*, Act I, Scene VII.

Nowhere in Shakespeare's genuine work is there a loss of this high morality, this feeling for all that is best and most lofty in the human conscience, and the same impression is created in our minds by the plays of Æschylus, Sophocles, and Ibsen. Goethe's words again express the truth : " If a poet has as high a soul as Sophocles, his influence will always be moral, let him do what he will."

This is not a question of didacticism. None of the great dramatists have preached, though all indirectly have been stern moralists. Æschylus, Sophocles, Shakespeare, Racine, Alfieri, Ibsen—all are alike in sharing a certain aloofness. They stand apart from, never descend into, their creations. On the other hand, although all of these have seen the triviality of the lesser ' poetic justice ' which led astray so many of the minor playwrights, and although they all present in some way or another their realization of the narrowness of that conception of tragedy which makes death a punishment and life a reward, nevertheless they have all indicated in general outlines a broader and a grander justice. Lear's sufferings, for example, in one way may be regarded as the punishment meted out for his pride, but the misery which falls upon him is out of all proportion to his fault, and in his suffering he is made to rise to a new nobility. Lear was never more a king, says a critic, than when he stood shorn of the outward trappings of royalty and enhaloed with that fresh majesty which became a man. Cordelia too suffers for her pride, but before her also a new world is opened in her suffering. Again, it is only after the murder of Duncan that Macbeth understands the sadness of life, realizes the uselessness of all he has done, sees, by contrast with the sere and yellow leaf, all the beauty and the grandeur he has abandoned. Death for him is no punishment; his punishment has already come. In a general sense, therefore, we may say that *Lear* and *Macbeth* are didactic plays, but not in the way that Lillo's *London Merchant* or Holcroft's *Road to Ruin* are didactic. Herein truly lies the reason why all great tragedies present a problem, but never give a solution. We are faced in them with terror, awe, nobility, suffering idealized; the problem is given to us, but the solution remains. Although we feel that the great dramatist, such as Shakespeare or Æschylus, as opposed to Seneca, is on the side of the noble, on the side of the good, he never deserts his mission of creative artistry to descend, through his characters or *in propria persona*, to preach a moral or a lesson. He leaves that part to the minor writers, or to those who, misled by false theory, find no art valuable but such as serves a didactic purpose. The elusiveness of Shakespeare is simply the elusiveness of high art; it is not a characteristic peculiar to himself : he shares it with pre-Christian Greece and with modern Europe.

(*d*) *The Sense of Universality*. From the nobility of the characters and from the implied, though never directly stated, moral aim comes the greater part of the tragic relief; but this is not all. Part, too, comes from that very sense of universality which has been stated to be the fundamental characteristic of all high tragedy—some form of contact with infinity. If we are religious we shall say it is a contact with forces divine; if we are atheistic we shall say it is a contact with the vast, illimitable forces of the universe. Everywhere in high tragedy there is this sense of being raised to loftier heights. In older drama it had naturally a more distinctly religious note; in modern drama it will more probably tend toward the introduction of scientific forces—evolution, racial characteristics, heredity, even of abstract social forces and convention. Just as *Ghosts* is a tragedy of heredity, so *The Tragedy of Nan*, which also, as we have seen, touches on the same theme, is largely a drama of social conventions. Many modern tragedies depend not on certain personalities presented in isolated surroundings, but on individuals placed in the midst of social powers from which they derive their joys and their sorrows. We may have plays where the whole *motif* is drawn from such a source. *A Doll's House* is one; *The Second Mrs Tanqueray* is another. Here the personalities are set in the peculiar circumstances which cause the tragic development of the plot because of their contact with, and their reaction to, the rules of their society.

This use of universality as a means of tragic relief, at once raising and making trivial the actual emotions of the characters before us, is almost indistinguishable from that sense of waste which, as we noted, is most marked in the dramas of Shakespeare. We feel that the dramatist has become great as nature itself, ruthless as nature is. By their strength and by their sternness these tragic writers appear in union with the vast forces of the physical universe, and the very presence of their minds above and beyond the play and its characters gives us comfort and recompense and relief, just as the vast presence of a cruel and compunctionless nature provides a relief when we contemplate the misery and the pettiness of life.

(e) *Poetical Effect*. There are, besides, other elements in high tragedy which serve to take from the utter darkness of the story unfolded before us. There is the presence of the creative artistic power of the dramatist himself, and, particularly in the Greek and Elizabethan plays, the rhythm of the verse, to reave away our minds for a moment from the gloomy depths of the tragedy. A more detailed consideration of the use and of the value of verse in tragedy we may leave till later, but here it may be observed that verse in many cases acts as a kind of anæsthetic on our senses. The sharp edge of the pain is removed in the plays of Æschylus and Shakespeare, and though it becomes more poignant in some ways, yet it is reft of its crudeness and sordidness by the beauty of the language. This effect of verse is obviously lacking in the realistic prose plays which appeared in such numbers during the nineteenth century. We may not condemn these prose dramas, many of them among the masterpieces of the world's art, but perhaps the ultimate value and even necessity of verse in high tragedy is indicated by them.[1] Not only do they seem to lack something which is present in the blank-verse dramas and in the lyrical tragedies of past ages, but in themselves they appear continually to be straining toward what is for them a perfectly illegitimate semi-poetic utterance. Sometimes this endeavour to pass from pure prose levels is successful, but more often it clashes rather pitifully with the general atmosphere of the play, as in Mr Masefield's *Tragedy of Nan*, where the old gaffer seems disassociated from the other characters in the tragedy. The same disharmony is present also in the figure of the Nurse in Przybyszewski's *Snow*. This endeavour, unconsciously

---

[1] In his essay on *Tragedy* Dr Smart comes to the same conclusion: " It seems to follow that tragedy in its most perfect form is poetical, and the greatest tragic works are poems " (p. 27).

practised, indicates and registers a dissatisfaction on the part of the dramatists with the peculiar medium they have adopted. Just as in the novels of Dickens or in Kingsley's *Westward Ho!*, when the theme takes on a deep colouring of passion, the writers have fallen into a spurious half-rhythmic movement, so in these prose dramas, unless in the hands of the absolute genius, there are frequent lapses from what is the true spirit of the play.[1]

(f) *Vanity of Vanities*. Among the various explanations given of the source of the tragic pleasure that put forward by Schopenhauer is not the least interesting. In effect his thesis runs as follows. Life is a thing of misery, and the wise man is he who finds, ere death inevitable comes, a calmness of spirit expressed in resignation and in renunciation of the all too fleeting and tormenting joys of existence. Tragedy is the form of dramatic art in which this serious and miserable side of life is emphasized. All men vaguely, and the wise men consciously, realize the utter vanity of living, and in tragedy we are given prime representation of the worthlessness of all things. After the terrible clash of contending wills, after the wretched conflict between man and an unseen fate, comes a moment of peace before the darkness sweeps down to cover all. Vanity of vanities—has Schopenhauer here truly seized on one of the main emotions resultant upon the witnessing of tragedy? Perhaps, in the end, we must answer yes. The final sadness of *Hamlet*, the despair uttered tormentedly by *Macbeth*, the grim wretchedness of *Othello*, the mood evoked in a serious strain—although not in a tragedy—by Prospero's lovely likening of the world to a dream—these assuredly seem to be arguments for this conception. And when we turn to modern drama is the mood not much the same? With a savage curling of the lip, Mr Sean O'Casey demonstrates the littleness and the wretchedness of life, while Synge, hymning a higher harmony, teaches that death is as nothing to the spirit, that it is better even to " cease upon the nothingness " than live tortured by haunting memories and the drabness of the present.

[1] On the more harmoniously artistic ' poetic prose ' used by Synge and Maeterlinck see *infra*, p. 142. This, of course, is by no means to be confused with the unconscious lapse from prose melody into blank-verse measures.

And, like this insubstantial pageant faded,
Leave not a rack behind—

this mood of quiet resignation, this emphasis on the visionary nature of reality, this calmness in face of death, are all inherent in the spirit of tragedy. Those who mourn over Cordelia or grudge Desdemona's end are misinterpreting the fundamentals of the tragic expression.

This conception of the true spirit of tragedy has been trenchantly expressed, too, by Schlegel. " When," he says,

when we contemplate . . . the relations of our existence to the extreme limit of possibilities; when we reflect on its entire dependence on a chain of causes and effects; when we consider that we are exposed in our weak and helpless state to struggle with the immeasurable powers of nature, and with conflicting desires on the shores of an unknown world, and in danger of shipwreck at our very birth; that we are subject to all manner of errors and deceptions, every one of which is capable of undoing us; that in our passions we cherish our own enemy in our bosoms; that every moment demands from us the sacrifice of our dearest inclinations, in the name of the most sacred duties, and that we may at one blow be robbed of all that we have acquired by toils and difficulties; that with every extension of possession the danger of loss is proportionately increased, and we are only the more exposed to the snares of hostile attack: then every mind which is not dead to feeling must be overpowered by an inexpressible melancholy, against which there is no other protection than the consciousness of a destiny soaring above this earthly life. This is the tragic tone; and when the mind dwells on the consideration of the possible, as an existing reality, when that tone is inspired by the most striking examples of violent revolutions in human destiny, either from dejection of soul, or after powerful but ineffectual struggles; then *tragic poetry* has its origin. We thus see that tragic poetry has its foundation in our nature, and to a certain extent we have answered the question why we are fond of mournful representations, and even find something consoling and elevating in them.[1]

Perhaps Timocles was thinking of the same thing when, according to Athenæus, he declared that a spectator at a tragic performance " is reminded that all his calamities, which ' seem

[1] *A Course of Lectures on Dramatic Art and Literature*, translated by John Black (1840), pp. 43–44. Minturno approaches the same view when he says that from tragedy " we learn not to place too great a trust in worldly prosperity, that nothing here below is so durable and stable, that it may not fall and perish, no happiness but may change to misery."

greater than mortal man has ever borne,' have happened to others, and so he bears his own trials more easily." [1] After all, life is a foolish thing, and a thing dark and often full of torment; here in tragedy its very darkness is intensified that our own gloom may thereby be made the lighter.

(g) *Malicious Pleasure.* There are other reasons adduced by various critics for the pleasure we thus receive from witnessing or from reading a tragedy. Many of these have no real value, but concerning a few others a word may be said. First, there is Mr Lucas' view that tragedy, so far from being a purge, is a true banquet—a banquet of experience which we indulge in freely because of the fascination it offers of watching life in some of its most poignant moments. Mr Lucas believes that the motto of tragedy lies in Hamlet's words: " What a piece of work is a man! " This conception unquestionably bears within it an element of truth, but it is much to be questioned whether truly the final impression is that suggested in such a motto. The sense of greatness is there, but once more we must return to Schopenhauer's theories, and discern, not merely the greatness, but the futility and the littleness as well. Then there are those who enter more deeply into psychological effects. Some, such as Fontenelle [2] and Shelley, believe that pleasure and pain are sisters, and that in meeting with the one we discern the form of the other. Maybe this psychologically is true, but it is indeed difficult to agree that when an assembled audience in the theatre is swayed and torn by the brilliant performance of some terrible tragedy it extracts real pleasure in this way out of the painful scenes. More apposite possibly is the theory that in the august pity which is evoked by a great tragic drama there is a real hint of self-pity; that the fictitious creatures of the playwright's imagination for whom our emotions are called forth are likened to ourselves; with their fortunes we identify ourselves even while we remain separate and detached. The Egyptian *ka*, hovering over its own dead corpse, might, not unfittingly, be considered a parallel. That there is indeed something of this impression in the mind of an average spectator may readily be acknowledged; the spectator

---

[1] Athenæus, vi, 233 b–d.
[2] *Réflexions sur la poétique* (1685).

is human, and here in front of him is presented a series of
great actions in which, as it were, the most tragic moments
of humanity are concentrated. To escape from the mental
association of his own self with these events of a magnitude
so great as to embrace within itself many particulars were truly
a difficulty. Yet this but comes back full circle to that from
which we started. It only renders more intense the impression
of nobility and of littleness combined, of things that seem to
matter and of a vanity exceeding all vanities.

Changing ground, we approach those who, rejecting such insistence upon majestic thoughts, plead that there is evidenced
in a tragic performance the primitive pleasure derived from
watching pain. Some speak of the sadistic emotions, explain-
ing, as Segni did in the Renascence, that it is always pleasing to
man to hear related the torments of another;[1] some turn to the
masochistic idea, thus approaching those who liken pleasure to
pain and say that we take a genuine delight in torturing ourselves. It is needless to say that in its crudest form this conception, save for certain peculiarly minded individuals, cannot
be pressed far; yet possibly there exists in us just sufficient
of the savage to make us take a kind of unconscious delight in
witnessing the sorrows of a Hamlet or of an Othello. The
very fact that we can see how Othello is being hoodwinked,
how Hamlet is losing his opportunities, gives us a strange thrill
of pleasure. We realize that, great and noble and majestic as
these heroes may be, we have the better of them in one way
at least. We stand for a moment alongside the dramatist-
creator, and smile at the puppets. Possibly there is not much
of this in our pleasure at witnessing a tragedy, but unless
there were an element of it we probably could not bear to see
a play of misery through. We have long passed the stage when
real pain in others might be a laughable thing, when a fierce
delight could come from watching another's distress; but
perhaps in the world of the theatre, where we know that the
figures are unreal, we retain enough of the spirit of the boy
who loves to see a butterfly feebly struggling on a pin, or of
the savage who has not an atom of pity for his conquered

---

[1] This view appears in a variant form in Rousseau's *Lettre sur les
spectacles* (1758).

enemy, to gain a secret and an unacknowledged pleasure from what are truly our most primitive emotions.

The truth is, of course, that no single answer to this question can possibly be adequate in itself. When there is provided for us in the theatre that " emotion proper to tragedy " our passions are so moved and our very beings so aroused that a myriad of fleeting thoughts and impressions, inextricably intertwined and vaguely oriented toward one central emotion, captures us, so that images of greatness and worth, of futility and vain questing, of the triumph of will and the dominion of fate, appear so confusedly and yet harmonized by art as utterly to defy any logical analysis.

(iii) STYLE

THE LYRICAL ELEMENT IN TRAGEDY. On account of its importance, although it has come up in connexion with the spirit of tragedy, we have left the problem of style to be treated by itself. In dealing with it we must always bear in mind that this problem of style is intimately related to the problems of action, of conflict, and of tragic relief.

A glance at the origin and development of tragedy may help us here toward a solution. The drama in Greece rose out of a song; in England it was nearly related in origin to a religious chant. As it has progressed both in ancient days and in Elizabethan England, there has clung to it a certain strain of lyricism, which expresses itself at times through the actual dialogue, at times breaks into more formal melody. "The Greek tragedy," says Coleridge, " may be compared to our serious opera," and opera in truth is but the extreme development of what is inherent in nearly all forms of tragic development. In England, when men as yet were ignorant of classical example, the serious mysteries tended to assume lyric measures; later, when the drama developed in the hands of Marlowe, Shakespeare, and the later Elizabethans, blank verse was taken over as the inevitable medium for tragic expression. Song, moreover, was continually introduced, and this has appeared as a handmaid to tragedy in almost all the succeeding centuries.

The origin of tragedy was a song; its development has been

137

along lyrical lines. In viewing this, may we not well ask ourselves whether lyricism, the singing strain in some form or another, is not the most fitting medium for all true tragedy? Our query may take the form of a double question: is this lyrical element in Greek and in early English tragedy something that the playwrights have felt to be necessary, something that truly has an intimate relationship with the inner core of the tragic spirit, or is it the mere traditional remnant, conservatively retained, of the source of the species, something that no one has had the courage to fling off even after it had served its legitimate purpose and had become useless? Lyricism was preserved in Greek drama not only in the dialogue, but even in the strophes, anti-strophes, and epodes of the chorus; but may this not have been an element retained, like the chorus itself, because of religious prejudice? Shakespeare has kept a lyrical element in his blank verse and in the songs which he occasionally introduces; but may not this again be due to the conventions inherited from the days of the mysteries and strengthened by Renascence enthusiasm for the example of the ancients?

Before we come to answer these questions directly a further glance at the history of this lyricism in tragedy may not be inopportune. It is evident that the Elizabethan dramatists struck a mean, adhering to the new blank verse brought from Italy by the Earl of Surrey, a type of verse rhythmical in utterance, yet nearer to the language of real life than any species of verse of the riming type. With occasional lapses into decasyllabic couplets here and there, and with the infrequent introduction into the dialogue of poetic forms such as the sonnet (as in *Romeo and Juliet*), blank verse dominated the whole of tragic endeavour in England from Sackville and Norton's *Gorboduc* to Shirley's *Traitor* and *The Cardinal*. As drama advanced, however, there may be observed two reactions to this employment of blank verse. In the rimed couplets and in the heightened style of our own late seventeenth-century heroic tragedy, and in the rime of the French drama, we may trace an attempt to increase the lyrical element, although at the same time to restrict the true lyric note by an exaggerated decorum and a false regularity of expression. This increased lyrical element is to be seen still further developed in the plays produced in Spain under Calderon; there the measures are not so monotonous as those of Dryden or Racine, and the song quality is, as a consequence, more in evidence. Opposed to this there is to be discovered a development toward the opposite extreme. In the verse of Fletcher and his companions we can trace a sense of dissatisfaction with the Shakespearian blank verse, an endeavour to work back to the language of ordinary life, where " the pitch of poetry," in the words of Symonds, has been lost. Still more revolutionary were the prose dramatists. The verse of *Arden of Feversham* is continually breaking down from the levels of poetry, and the tendency marked in this play was caught up by the *bourgeois* dramatists of the eighteenth century. Lillo set the fashion with *The London Merchant*, and his example was followed by Moore and Holcroft in England, by Diderot and others in France, by Lessing and Kotzebue in Germany, and by Ibsen and Strindberg in the North, until prose was established as one of the chief media for the expression of modern serious drama.

The question, then, before us takes a slightly altered form: it is not merely a decision between verse and prose that is demanded, but a choice of one of three media—rimed or excessively lyric measures, blank verse, and pure prose.

BLANK VERSE AND RIME. As regards the first two little need be said. Except perhaps for certain particular types of drama, rimed verse appears too far removed from actual life to be a suitable medium for tragedy. The development of the drama in Greece is highly instructive here. The chorus, which, because of the origin of the Athenian stage, was retained as an integral part of the structure of his plays by Æschylus, was in the hands of Sophocles and Euripides gradually driven out of the scheme of tragedy. With the last-mentioned playwright, indeed, the chorus became merely the medium through which was presented to the audience a series of often detached and independent songs. Had any other great dramatists arisen after his time it is highly probable that the chorus would have been still further degraded, and that the dialogue would have stood by itself. The development of Shakespeare's tragic productivity proceeds on lines strictly analogous to those taken by the Greek drama as a whole. Exaggerated lyricism in his art is a sure sign of youthful workmanship; in the later and greater tragedies the language is brought as near to real life as the requirements of the blank verse will allow.

Racine, certainly, and Calderon have succeeded to some extent in expressing high emotions through the medium of rimed verse, but generally their efforts may be regarded as mere *tours de force*. The Restoration drama, even in the hands of a genius such as Dryden, fails not only because of its exaggerated emotions, but because of its tinkling dialogue. There are beautiful masques in rime, but the masque after all never rises to the dignity of high tragic expression. Tragedy must always have some close relationship to life; if we remove it overfar from worldly existence it ceases to thrill us with a sense of awe and of grandeur. The *Prometheus Unbound* of Shelley is a beautiful dramatic poem, but it could never, because of its intense lyrical note, startle and surprise us like *Hamlet* and *Macbeth*. Blank verse is rhythmical; it allows of the expression of the most poetical of thoughts; and yet, because of its structure, it remains close to real life. In listening to it we are not startled by the artificiality of the expression. In blank verse we hear the language of ordinary life rarefied and made more exalted. In the choice between it and rimed verse, therefore, we may unhesitatingly decide for the former, declaring that an undue lyrical element is unfitted for the expression of the highest tragic spirit; but the decision between verse as a whole and prose as the most suitable medium for tragedy remains to be taken.

BLANK VERSE AND PROSE. It may be best to put forward here a dogmatic statement and then to consider several reasons that may be adduced to prove its soundness. In general, it may be said, it would appear that the Elizabethan dramatists were right in employing verse in their tragedies, and that the more modern prose development is uninformed, an experiment dangerous and antagonistic to the spirit of high tragedy.

That which is appealed to most in a tragedy is the emotions. Tragedy does not often direct itself to the intellect as such; it deals always with the deepest moments of human feeling. There are few tragedies of pure thought; even *Hamlet*, which is more philosophical than the majority of the Elizabethan dramas, has emotion constantly threading the intellectual framework of Hamlet's character. It has been proved, however, by the practice of long ages and of diverse races, that the emotions invariably find their fittest literary expression in rhythmical form. There is a certain natural melody in passion of any kind, and tragedy, in dealing with the passions, will therefore find its true utterance in rhythmical words. It is possible here, perhaps, to make an exception for some modern plays in which the emotional element seems to be continually and consistently repressed, and where consequently prose might be considered a more fitting medium. We could not, for example, very well picture *Strife* in verse form as it stands; but even here not very much can be said for non-rhythmical utterance in serious drama. Prose undoubtedly drags the play in which it appears down overfar into the levels of ordinary life; and even in dealing with such a theme as *Strife* it is to be considered whether the dramatist would not have secured a profounder impression by lifting his whole conception above these restricting levels. Hardy's *Dynasts* is an example of a similar theme created on a broader plan, the actuality of the forces being lost in deeper and richer considerations. *Strife* is an interesting drama in which something of the tragic spirit is evoked, but it is not high tragedy. It cannot thrill us like the great masterpieces of tragic art; and that, it would appear, is due almost entirely to its excessive actuality, to its refusal to express those broader truths, those ultimate ideas, which dominate all great tragedy.

POETIC PROSE. Modern playwrights, however, are faced by a serious difficulty, for the blank verse which was natural, right, and creative in the Elizabethan age seems now to have grown stale and outworn. The nineteenth- and twentieth-century tradition in the ' poetic play ' has yielded hardly anything of worth, and it appears unlikely that there will be any recrudescence of a vital dramatic expression by means of this form in the future. Already, on the other hand, there are signs that some dramatists, unconsciously feeling the want of that medium which so greatly served Shakespeare and his contemporaries, are striving toward a dramatic language which contains in itself something of the poetic quality. Appropriately enough, these signs have first made their appearance in Ireland, where the Celtic spirit, allied to a peculiarly imaginative yet simple utterance, has provided the basis for a kind of dialogue, conventional certainly, yet instinct with that vitality always present in theatrical speech which, instead of being artificially distinct from the ordinary terms of conversation, is a sort of concentrated ideal of common parlance. When, for example, in Synge's *Deirdre of the Sorrows* we find the heroine speaking thus,

> Let us throw down clay on my three comrades. Let us cover up Naisi along with Ainnle and Ardan, they that were the pride of Emain. . . . There is Naisi was the best of three, the choicest of the choice of many. It was a clean death was your share, Naisi; and it is not I will quit your head, when it's many a dark night among the snipe and plover that you and I were whispering together. It is not I will quit your head, Naisi, when it's many a night we saw the stars among the clear trees of Glen da Ruadh, or the moon pausing to rest her on the edges of the hills,

we recognize a prose utterance bearing a subtle melody of its own and not merely the borrowed rags of blank-verse measures. When, too, we find Ulf, in Lord Dunsany's *Gods of the Mountain*, " almost chanting,"

> I have a fear, an old fear and a boding ! We have done ill in the sight of the seven gods; beggars we were and beggars we should have remained; we have given up our calling and come in sight of our doom; I will no longer let my fear be silent: it shall run about and cry: it shall go from me crying, like a dog from out of a doomed city; for my fear has seen calamity and has known an evil thing,

again we recognize the same aim on the part of the dramatist. A similar 'lyric' note is struck in Mr Sean O'Casey's *Silver Tassie*, where the second act is only a long chant of impassioned prose. A cognate tendency, too, is traceable in that strange language in which M. Maeterlinck has expressed his tragic view of life. None of these is the result of an unconscious lapse from prose rhythm into the movement of blank verse; in each there is a deliberate evolving of a special kind of prose music, with a form harmonious and proper to itself. Herein, perhaps, lies a hope for the tragic drama of the future. Blank

142

verse has served its day; the rhythmic prose may, in the future, take the place that it occupied in the seventeenth century.

THE UNIVERSALITY OF RHYTHM. In speaking, then, of ' verse ' in tragic drama, this new ' poetic prose ' may be put alongside of the special form of dialogue used by the Elizabethans; and, thus broadening the significance of the term, we may well say that, as a means of raising the events of a drama above the levels of real life and as the natural expression for emotion, verse claims the close attention of every tragic dramatist. Before he casts off verse, possibly because of some hastily conceived critical theory, he must consider well whether verse be not one of the necessary and integral parts of true drama, or at least whether in abandoning verse he will not be forced to give to his drama something else as a recompense for its loss. Verse, too, has other forces. The figment of the music of the spheres has at least a symbolic truth about it. Through rhythm and melody we seem to reach some universal chords of human feeling. By mere rhythm alone we certainly touch vibrations otherwise impossible of realization. A foreign prose work may be unintelligible to us, but a foreign symphony will be interpreted by us as easily as by a native of the land that gave it birth; and even a foreign poem, well recited, may awaken feelings and emotions in our hearts beyond the unintelligibility of the words. Rhythm, after all, is a common heritage; it strikes deep at primeval and general instincts of mankind. It is, moreover, not confined to man; it is universal to the whole of nature. The songs of the birds possess a melody pleasurable not only to themselves but to humanity. There are symphonies of sounds and of colours appreciated by the entirety of the natural world. Such a consideration of the force of verse obviously leads us back to our primal consideration of universality. Herein lies one other main means of securing the broader atmosphere demanded by tragedy. Verse will aid not only in removing tragedy from the levels of actual life, but in giving to it that universality demanded by the highest art.

VERSE AS A TRAGIC RELIEF. Finally, verse may be considered as a species of tragic relief. This, in the section devoted to the spirit of tragedy, has already been tentatively hinted at. It may here be formally stated that verse undoubtedly takes

143

away some of the horror and the gloom and the despair of
the tragic spirit. Again a return must be made to that word
' sordid.' When we speak of a sordid tragedy we do not refer
so much to the subject-matter as to the treatment of the
subject-matter, to the lack of something which may take away
part of the pain. Verse, introducing that melody which is
but symbolic of a higher and more universal symphony, this
quality of lyricism, is probably among the greatest of the re-
lieving media. After all, the story of *Othello*, if it were told in
plain prose, would be but a sordid story of a faithful wife and
a deceived husband ' avenging his honour '; *Hamlet* would be
but a sordid tale of a murdered king and a semi-incestuous
attachment. The lyricism, however, with which these plays
are invested helps to raise them above the level of actuality,
and to relieve the horror which otherwise we should feel in
them. When Othello comes to the height of his jealous hate
and enters staggering and blind with passion, Iago looks at
him, and his words take on a gorgeousness of colouring that is
surely intentional on Shakespeare's part:

> Not poppy, nor mandragora,
> Nor all the drowsy syrups of the world,
> Shall ever medicine thee to that sweet sleep
> Which thou owedst yesterday.

The poetry is not strictly in accord with Iago's character,
although Shakespeare may have had a purpose here too, but
it is in accord with the genuine tragic *motif*. It is a rush of
music to still the horror and pain the scene might otherwise
have aroused in our hearts. If we can but imagine in the place
of these lines of poetry a sneer of Iago's cynicism we may be
able to appreciate their value and force. Possibly for the same
reason may have been introduced that remarkable speech of
Iachimo in Act II, Scene II, of *Cymbeline*:

> 'Tis her breathing that
> Perfumes the chamber thus : the flame o' the taper
> Bows toward her, and would under-peep her lids,
> To see the enclosed lights, now canopied
> Under these windows, white and azure laced
> With blue of heaven's own tinct. . . .
> On her left breast
> A mole cinque-spotted, like the crimson drops
> I' the bottom of a cowslip.

Shakespeare probably realized that the situation he had devised —the innocent girl lying in her bed, the cunning Iachimo issuing from his trunk—was both improbable and horrible. It was horrible because of the meanness and the duplicity shown in it; it was improbable because of the sudden heavy sleep of Imogen, necessary for the development of the plot, but distinctly unnatural. To counter both, to attract the attention of the audience and to allay their suspicions and their disgust, he bursts into lyrical utterance, sacrificing character for the sake of dramatic effect. The same phenomenon may, of course, be discovered in many other dramatists apart from Shakespeare. The Greek playwrights knew of the device, and many of their most poignant and most terrible scenes are clad in the richest of their poetry. In later days Otway, when dealing with a particularly terrible theme in *The Orphan*, contrived thus to soften and relieve the pain he had aroused. The last scene of the fourth act, when Monimia learns the truth from Polydore, is the most poetical of his tragedy, and the fifth act opens with a song.

In dispensing with verse, therefore, the adherents of the realistic prose drama appear to be abandoning a legitimate method of securing atmosphere and of giving pleasure. Verse is seen to be not merely a traditional remnant of choral song or cathedral chant; it is something closely connected with the inner spirit of tragedy itself. If verse and the opportunity for securing lyricism be neglected then other qualities must be deeply stressed in an endeavour to atone for the loss. Occasionally it is not possible so to stress these other qualities; often their introduction seems unnatural and strained. The ordinary prose tragedy fails partly because of a lack of melody, partly because prose, by its very nature, prohibits the introduction of many of those features which in the poetic drama seem but natural and just.

(iv) THE TRAGIC HERO

THE IMPORTANCE OF THE HERO. So far attention has been paid to the final aim, to the medium and spirit of tragedy; there remains the question of that which is commonly the means by which the dramatist expresses both aim and spirit —the tragic hero.

It is to be observed that commonly tragedy differs from comedy in selecting some one or two figures who by their greatness and by their inherent interest dominate the other *dramatis personæ.* There may be comedies where one figure so absorbs all, or nearly all, the attention of the audience, but such comedies are both rare and inclined to approach toward more serious realms. We have, for example, some of the plays of Molière, *L'Étourdi* and *Le Misanthrope* especially, and the *Volpone* of Ben Jonson. A close analysis of the atmosphere of these comedies, however, would reveal the fact that they are slightly abnormal.[1] They appeal not only to the risible faculties, but to the more serious part of our being as well. They draw near, that is to say, the dominion of the tragic spirit. Normally comedy of any kind depends upon interplay of character, where no one person is of so much more importance than another that he becomes a solitary hero. This fact will be made more evident by comparing the interest of the tragedies and comedies written by Shakespeare, as typical of Elizabethan output, and by Otway, as typical of Restoration productivity. In *Hamlet* the hero stands well-nigh alone; in *Lear* it is the King and Cordelia who absorb nearly all the attention; in *Othello* it is the Moor and Iago; in *Macbeth* it is the Thane and his wife. It is not that the other characters are badly drawn, but they are, from the point of view of construction, given hardly any important speeches, and, from the point of view of characterization, placed on a level far below the principal figures. A reference to Shakespeare's comedies marks the completely different conception. Take *Much Ado about Nothing*, in which there are Claudio and Hero, Benedick and Beatrice, Leonato and Antonio, Dogberry and Verges; or *A Midsummer Night's Dream*, where there are the two pairs of lovers—Lysander and Hermia, Demetrius and Helena—the fairies Oberon and Titania, and the artisans Bottom, Quince, and their company. We note here not only that the characters are more on a level, none assuming importance far above the others, but that there are various quite distinct points of dramatic interest. The tragedies,

[1] See *infra*, pp. 218-219.

on the other hand, are simpler and more concentrated. Otway's plays present much the same features. In *Venice Preserv'd* we have as the centre of interest Pierre, Jaffier, and Belvidera, all the other characters being subordinate to them; in *The Orphan* the attention is thrown exclusively on Polydore, Castalio, and Monimia. *The Souldier's Fortune*, on the other hand, has Captain Beaugard and Courtine and Sylvia, Sir Davy and his wife, Sir Jolly Jumble and the servant Fourbin; *The Atheist* has old Beaugard, his son and Porcia, Courtine and his wife, Daredevil the atheist, Theodoret and Gratian. While in tragedy, then, the interest is placed on one or two main characters, in comedy it is distributed over a body of diverse figures. It is because of this that we may discuss in such detail the character of the hero or the heroine in tragedy, whereas in comedy such a discussion would lack not only value, but meaning. Tragedies often are called after the name of the one chief figure—*Œdipus* and *Medea* of Greek times, *Hamlet, Lear, Othello, Macbeth* of Shakespeare, *The Orphan* and *The Cenci* of later days; comedies hardly ever. It is the hero who gives significance and tone to a tragedy.

THE TRAGIC FLAW. In considering this tragic hero we may begin again with Aristotle. Here the Greek critic has been more explicit than he was on the former subjects already dealt with. The tragic hero for him is " a person neither eminently virtuous or just, nor yet involved in crime by deliberate vice or villainy, but by some reason of human frailty [δι' ἁμαρτίαν τινά]." That is to say, the tragic hero, while not a paragon of goodness, must in Aristotle's opinion have noble qualities in him, but he must at the same time be capable of indulging in some error, due either to ignorance of affairs beyond his knowledge or to human passion. Aristotle, in the *Poetics*, has proceeded to indicate a couple of lines of development [1] in the presentation of this hero, but his division is rather logical than strictly critical, and we may find the characteristics of the hero in tragic drama somewhat more extended, both in Greek and in modern works, than he has presented them.

UNCONSCIOUS ERROR AND THOUGHTLESS FOLLY. There is, first of all, as Aristotle has noted, the hero who acts wrongly

---

[1] There is a third, but this seems hardly to lead toward tragedy.

through an unconscious error. This is the human frailty (ἁμαρτία) derived from ignorance. The typical example (given in the *Poetics*) is the Œdipus of Sophocles. This conception of the hero is distinctly non-Shakespearian, although, in a modified form, it has been adopted by several English writers. It was a legitimate type in ancient Athens because of the religion of the time, but with the loss of that religion it appears slightly out of place and can be treated in modern times only with the greatest of care. A resuscitation of the hero who errs in ignorance is visible in the seventeenth-century drama just after the time of Shakespeare. It is very probable that this resuscitation was caused by the strange errors of the Beaumont and Fletcher romantic tragi-comedy, which often introduced characters who acted after the Greek model, although not often toward tragic ends. At the Restoration the type found a magnificent expression in *The Orphan*. Here one of the two heroes commits a deed of tragic import because of his ignorance of a certain set of facts, the only departure from the model of *Œdipus* being that the crime committed was in itself an odious one, even allowing for ignorance of the facts which made it truly tragic. The tragedy certainly arises from the fact that Polydore did not know that Monimia had married his brother Castalio, but the tragic act was not carried out wholly in ignorance. It was led up to by Polydore's lust, a genuine ἁμαρτία, and by Castalio's feigned libertinism. We have thus in *The Orphan* a play of two atmospheres or conceptions, the Greek idea being modified by the more modern element of direct human frailty, based not on a mere lack of knowledge. While dealing with this play, *The Orphan*, it may be noted in passing that the theme, generally thus modified, was distinctly popular at the time of the Restoration, and has appeared sporadically in later drama of the eighteenth and nineteenth centuries. It is responsible for all the ' Fatal Marriages ' and ' Fatal Innocencies ' of the period 1660–1700, just as it is responsible for the tragic motive of Lillo's *Fatal Curiosity* in the mid-eighteenth century.

CONSCIOUS ERROR. There is, besides this type, the hero who acts wrongly with conscious intent. Aristotle has noted this also, instancing the example of the *Medea*. Phædra in the

Hippolytus of Euripides and the same character in the play of Seneca might also be adduced as similar figures from the Greek and Roman drama. This conception was adopted by Shakespeare and by many other Elizabethan dramatists. *Macbeth* has its villain hero; *Othello* has a similar central figure, although here the tragedy has characteristics of the first type as well. The crime of the Moor springs out of a conscious act, while, on the other hand, he was misled concerning the true facts of the case. In the presenting of a character of this stamp, as has already been pointed out, the playwright must in some way or another display clearly the horror and the detestation aroused by the crime committed. With the romantic dramatists this may be done by showing a change of character after the execution of the deed of violence, as in *Macbeth*. Perhaps Shelley had the same idea in mind when he presented the peculiar figure of Beatrice Cenci. With the classical playwrights, on the other hand, the abhorrence can be shown only immediately before or immediately after the crime, as in the Æschylean presentation of Orestes. But where there is no expression of horror and detestation, as in the *Hippolytus* of Seneca, the tragedy inevitably falls to a plane of lower and purely melodramatic creation, for tragedy, as we have seen, must not only thrill with the sense of awe, but must also uplift with the sense of majesty. It is possibly the absence of this essential which takes from our pleasure in reading or in seeing *The Cenci*. In spite of the loud praises of the Shelley-worshippers, it would appear that in this drama there is not that high feeling and nobility of soul which is present in the works of Sophocles and Shakespeare. Shelley fails as Ford fails, not for the same reasons certainly, but in a precisely similar manner.

Akin to the Polydore type is the Shakespearian hero who brings disaster on his own head through some thoughtless act which springs from his own character. Lear hardly commits a crime, either consciously or unconsciously, but his rejection of Cordelia is an action that takes its rise directly from his own character and temper, and it is the immediate cause of his future sufferings. Coriolanus, in a similar way, passes to his ruin through his pride and his aristocratic contempt—failings that make him lose sight of all other human considerations. So, too, Antony is lost in his love and goes to destruction with a kiss on Cleopatra's lips. Perhaps the Oreste of Racine's *Andromaque* might be regarded from a cognate point of view.

IMPOTENCE AND AMBITION OF THE HERO. Again, there is the hero who is faced by a task greater than his powers. Here we have, certainly, a ' human frailty,' but it is one that is expressed in wrongful action of no kind whatsoever. Hamlet is of the kin neither of Œdipus nor of Medea. We can realize that the web of tragedy which envelops him has been spun from his own personality, that his hesitation and delay have brought about an almost general catastrophe; but he is not a villain in any sense of the word, and he does not actively precipitate the tragic action.

As a species of subdivision of what may be called the Hamlet type we find the heroes of Marlowe. In Marlowe's plays, certainly, the ambition of the protagonists brings about their ruin, but the basis of the tragic action appears to lie more definitely in the opposition of a human force of extraordinary dimensions to a force beyond it and more powerful than it. The doom of the hero is thus again brought about by a human frailty, the desire for knowledge or for " dominion infinite," but the tragedy of the play lies in the defeat of that desire by supernatural powers. By a slight change of stress from the typical Greek treatment of the theme, the Prometheus of Shelley's play approximates closely to this Marlowe type, and the Cain of Lord Byron has the same characteristics.

THE FLAWLESS HERO. Here may be discussed the question of the flawless hero. In the period of the Renascence both Castelvetro and Rossi [1] decided that not only might the man with a genuine ἁμαρτία figure in tragedy, but the central position might be occupied by one unsullied by moral blemish and innocent of having committed any serious error. For these writers the saint could be a figure suited for tragic treatment. The same view is upheld by Dr Smart, who, in his essay on *Tragedy*,[2] quotes the examples of the Gospels and Richardson's *Clarissa*. Now, it is exceedingly hazardous to

---

[1] In *Discorsi . . . intorno alla tragedia* (1590), p. 12.
[2] English Association *Studies*, vol. viii.

argue from one type of literature to another; the novel, as we have seen, has an aim and utilizes methods entirely different from those associated with drama, while the Bible is read normally not with those emotions called forth by non-religious literature. Of tragic dramas in which the hero is utterly flawless there are but few examples, and such as exist seem to show that Aristotle was right in recognizing this character as unsuitable for tragedy. Romeo, perhaps, belongs to this *genre*. As presented by Shakespeare, he indulges in no fatal error, the reasons for his destruction lying entirely in outward circumstance. The two lovers could have acted in no other way than they did. They are not in the position of Œdipus, ignorant of the meaning of their own actions; they go into their marriage with open eyes, and only fate or chance destroys the promise of their love. A Gervinus may endeavour to explain that their error is marrying without their parents' consent, but such a view seems artificial and forced, an argument designed in order to discover at any hazard an ἁμαρτία in Romeo's character. The truth really is that in *Romeo and Juliet* we seem to have a pure tragedy of fortune, and we accordingly fail to experience the passions called forth by a Hamlet and an Othello. Difficult indeed is it to explain to ourselves the exact effect produced upon our minds. It is not, as some have thought, that the error in the other tragedies is a moral error, for which the characters are made to suffer. After all, those who say that Hamlet is destroyed because he delays are asserting that his real duty was that of a murderer or, at best, of an executioner; this conception arises only because of an illogical desire to apply moral significance to the tragic error. Nearer the mark, possibly, is the explanation that in both *Hamlet* and *Othello* we are presented with heroes whose misfortune it is to be placed in circumstances impossible for them adequately to cope with, whereas in *Romeo and Juliet* we have simply a story of ordinary love, a common thing enough, running counter to social prejudice. Hamlet is led, because of his nature, inevitably onward; pure chance, the misfortune of a moment, brings death to the lovers. A happy ending to *Hamlet* is inconceivable; *Romeo and Juliet*, we feel, might easily have closed as a tragi-comedy, with an awakening in the tomb and a parental reconciliation. There are no tragic throes for Juliet and her Romeo; their passion is a joyous thing, and the darkness of their death corresponds not to any of that darkness of spirit seen in Hamlet, in Othello, in Lear.

THE HERO SWAYED BY TWO IDEALS. As a completely separate type, although one that has certain elements in common with the others already enumerated, might be taken the hero who is torn between two duties. This, to a certain extent, is but a variation of the hero who acts wrongly through some flaw in himself or through some mistake, the only difference being that he is faced with two alternatives, neither of which is wholly bad, but of which one represents the power of common duty and law, and the other the power of passion and emotion. Here the tragic action may be brought about by a conscious or unconscious deed springing from some ἁμαρτία, but the interest of the play lies rather in the inner struggle between two desires or ideals in the mind of the hero than in the wrong action committed. This type is to be found in its crudest and most exaggerated form in the heroic tragedy of the Restoration. However dull Dryden's dramas may appear, we realize that there are in his heroes the elements of tragic greatness. Examples are to be discovered likewise in the rimed tragedies of neo-classic France. The type dominates nearly all the *dramatis personæ* of Racine, sways the tragedies of Voltaire, and, carried thence, appears in almost every classical tragedy produced in England in the eighteenth century. In Shakespeare it is apparent in the conception of Antony, although a comparison of Shakespeare's drama with the cognate play of Dryden, *All for Love, or The World Well Lost*, will show how Shakespeare has humanized and softened the too sharp stress of the conflict, so heavily marked in the Restoration tragedy.

THE FLAW ARISING FROM CIRCUMSTANCES. Finally, there is perhaps one other species of hero that might be considered, again a subdivision of the wrongly acting character. In this type the hero accepts a life of crime not because of some flaw in his being, but because of circumstances which operate harshly against him, and in his crime he remains honest and pure-souled. A typical example is to be discovered in *Die*

Räuber of Schiller. Here Charles de Moor is driven to become an outlaw because of the action of his father, who in his turn has been cheated by the younger son, Francis de Moor. It is Francis who is the villain, who pursues Amelia and immures his old father in a dungeon. Charles becomes the instrument of vengeance, liberating his father and deciding at the close to give himself over to justice. As is obvious, this type owes something to the sentimental villain-heroes, or ' good-bad ' men, of the eighteenth century, but in it the sentimental note is raised and purified. It is distinctly a modern conception, and, taken over by the romantic dramatists, also makes its appearance in a number of nineteenth- and twentieth-century plays.

THE POSITION OF THE HERO IN THE PLAY. Before passing from these definite types of heroes it may be noted that beyond their several varieties there are two very differing positions which any of these may hold in the plays in which they appear. Any of these heroes may be placed in a tragedy either in an active or an inactive capacity. There is, on the one hand, the hero who sways the whole course of the drama. Orestes thus dominates both the tragedies of Æschylus and of Alfieri; Macbeth is the motive force in Shakespeare's play. Here almost everything that happens on the stage arises out of the thoughts and the emotions of the hero himself. Hardly any other character may be said to influence the development of the plot. There is, on the other hand, the hero who, like Lear, is " more sinned against than sinning." Lear gives the initial motive-power to the play in which he appears, but that first scene when he apportions his kingdom is almost a prologue, and in a non-romantic drama would assuredly have been told to the audience by narration. After it is over Lear is wholly acted against. The conduct of the piece passes entirely out of his hands into the hands of his daughters. This latter position of the hero has been but sparingly utilized by the great dramatists, because of the sense it gives of the powerlessness of the hero himself. It was only a Shakespeare who could present a Lear majestic and exalted in the midst of his affliction and misery.

THE TWIN HERO. One other consideration must also be

touched upon. In some dramas, particularly of the Elizabethan period, there is not merely one hero, but two, and the
tragic emotion arises out of the clash or conflict of their personalities. Who shall we say is the hero of *Othello*? Othello
himself, until the very last act, does absolutely nothing; it is
Iago who drives the plot forward and attracts nearly all the
attention of the play. In this tragedy we seem to see indeed
two chief figures: Iago by a terrible ἁμαρτία engaged in a
grim game of deceit, and Othello by a different species of human
frailty moving slowly onward to his destruction; this is not a
mono-hero play such as is *Hamlet* or *Lear*. The same situation arises in *Venice Preserv'd* and in *The Orphan*. Jaffier and
Pierre are both heroes, and the misery and the awe in the play
arise out of both the weakness of the former and the ruthless-
ness of the latter. In *The Orphan* a tragic situation could not
have been developed out of either Polydore or Castalio alone.
It is when they are put in juxtaposition that they are brought to
destruction and misery.

THE HEROLESS TRAGEDY. Within recent years there has
been a marked development of a peculiar type of tragic endeavour which probably indicates at one and the same time
an extension and development of the sphere of tragedy and a
progressive movement proving the continued presence of a
genuinely creative element in this sphere. Often we meet
with plays which, like Mr Galsworthy's *Strife* and *Justice* or
Mr O'Casey's *Silver Tassie*, seem to be entirely lacking in a
hero of adequate proportions. In *Strife* we cannot say that
the hero is either the leader of the men or the leader of the
masters. In *Justice* the hero is assuredly not the pitiful, weak-
willed clerk. And in *The Silver Tassie* he is not the war-
wrecked Dublin footballer. In none of these plays does one
single figure, or one single pair of figures, loom up sufficiently
large to take dominating importance in our minds, and we
have, therefore, no hero or heroes in the older sense of the word.
Yet each of those plays definitely summons something of a
tragic impression; indeed, *The Silver Tassie* seemed, in the
theatre, to be one of the outstanding modern experiments in
the realm of tragedy. Now, it appears that this tragic impression does not derive merely from our watching a human being

caught in the web of circumstance and cruelly tormented. There is something more than that, and at first sight it may appear difficult precisely to explain the source of our emotions. A moment's reflection, however, reveals the fact that in each of these plays the chief persons are regarded merely as symbols, or as parts, of humanity. This aspect of the modern drama has already been discussed cursorily in the section devoted to universality in tragedy; here it may receive a little further attention. Taking *The Silver Tassie*, we might almost say that humanity has been guilty of a tremendous ἀμαρτία; it has allowed the primitive passion for war to seize upon it and to find full expression; and, as a result, it has been wounded and torn. The person who takes the chief *rôle* in the play is, therefore, not in himself the hero; he is such only by virtue of the fact that he is a man. This is shown clearly in the expressionistic second act, in which he plays no part at all, although the theme of the act deals with that which provides the very basis of the tragedy. The same is true of *Justice*. Humanity has, by one of its fatal errors, produced a code of laws calculated to act unjustly in certain instances. The poor Falder is, then, merely one part of the greater protagonist, which is humanity itself.

This tendency is visible everywhere in modern tragic productivity, not only in these definitely heroless dramas, but in those tragedies where some attempt has been made to present an outstanding central figure of some kind or another. In these latter there is nearly always evidenced a desire on the part of the dramatist to soften the sense of independent individuality. *Abraham Lincoln* is an historical play with one central figure, but Lincoln is carefully made into a symbol of something apart from himself. He is hardly a man as the Henrys and the Richards of Shakespeare were men; he is a force symbolized in a man. So *Mary Stuart*, in the hands of former dramatists, was a tragedy of personality. With Mr Drinkwater it has become a drama of a particular class of temperament, symbolizing in the Scots Queen a class ever at war with social forces and with social ideals, whether in the sixteenth century, in ancient Egypt, or to-day. So obviously did Mr Drinkwater desire to emphasize this point that he has not let this Mary Stuart drama stand by itself. The prologue has been introduced for no other purpose but to display the fact that Mary is connected in spirit with our own days, that she was no unique personality, but stands as a high symbol of a certain type of mind and of soul. Probably no clearer example could be found of the tendencies of present-day art and thought. One may suggest also that the expressionistic movement of recent years, as exemplified, for instance, in the plays of Herr Toller, is merely another aspect of this main tendency. In *Masses and Men* (*Masse-Mensch*) the title of the drama itself draws deliberate attention to this purpose in the playwright's mind.

How far all this differs from earlier example is seen at once when we take for comparison any typical Elizabethan play. *Othello* again will serve. Here at once we realize that Othello's error is peculiar to himself; it does not depend at all upon social conventions. Humanity outside himself has little or nothing to do with his emotions or with his fortunes. The dramatist may suggest that Othello's case may be paralleled elsewhere, but that is entirely a different thing. The treatment of the hero as merely part of a tremendous whole, over which, perhaps, he wields but small or no control, is peculiar to the modern stage.

THE HEROINE. Mr Drinkwater's presentation of Mary Queen of Scots leads us to the question of the presentation in tragedy of the heroine. Already it has been noted that tragedy differs from comedy in being often almost entirely masculine. The use of the words masculine and feminine is, of course, fraught with peculiar difficulties, for they may refer not only to the sexes, but to the qualities which, in past centuries, have been associated with the sexes. Thus we may say that *Tamburlaine* is a purely masculine play because it introduces hardly any women characters; but at the same time we may say that *Macbeth* is masculine because, although Lady Macbeth is one of the main forces in the drama, she is not of that type of mind which we usually call feminine. The connotations of these words, obviously, have changed considerably during the last few generations, but, reservations being made, they may be utilized thus to signify spirits and temperaments of differing values.

TRAGEDY

Tragedy, it was said, differed from comedy in that it might often be wholly masculine; this statement might be carried still farther and take the form of a pronouncement that tragedy almost invariably stresses the masculine at the expense of the feminine elements. The reason for this is quite evidently the hardness and sternness which we have already noted in the highest tragic art. The central figure, then, of all great tragedies will be a man, or else a woman who, like Lady Macbeth or Iphigenia or Medea, has in her temper some adamant qualities and severity of purpose not ordinarily associated with the typically feminine. The feminine element, on the other hand, is rarely lacking in any great tragedy; its absence mars the dramas of Marlowe. This feminine element, however, does not often have any great influence on the development of the play directly, although indirectly, by influence on the mind of the hero, it may have much. Ophelia is thus a weak, wholly inactive character, yet it is evidently her death which changes Hamlet from a man of deep philosophy and of profound, if unrealized, purpose into a careless creature for whom nothing is of any consequence or interest. In the same way Desdemona plays no direct part in *Othello*; she is essentially feminine, weak, deceptive,[1] purposeless, and thus does not actively forward the plot. Only indirectly, by her influence upon Othello, does she carry on the tragic movement. Cordelia, in *Lear*, is of more importance, but she shares with Lady Macbeth certain qualities which we commonly call masculine; she is, in many ways, simply a replica (more hastily sketched in, it is true) of her father.

The corollary to this truth is seen in those dramas begun by Banks in the middle of the Restoration period and continued by Rowe and others in the eighteenth century. These 'she-tragedies,' as sometimes they have been called, have rarely an atom of tragic greatness, although some of them are affecting. *Vertue Betray'd, or Anna Bullen*, of Banks, *The*

---

[1] The word deceptive is deliberately employed here. For me the tragedy of *Othello* rises out of the deception and self-deception of the chief characters, and Desdemona, by her deception of her father, by her deception of her husband, and by her last pitiful deception of those who witnessed the final tragedy, stands related to the general atmosphere and purpose of the play. This conception is developed in *Studies in Shakespeare*.

Tragedy of Jane Shore of Rowe, and *Mary Queen of Scots* of St John, are all pathetic and touching, but they are not tragedies. They never reach that sternness of majesty which is an inevitable concomitant of this highest type of literature. It is this insistence on the feminine, and, along with the feminine, the pathetic, which has marred the plays of Fletcher, Webster, and Ford; it is partly this which takes away from the grandeur of *Venice Preserv'd* and *The Orphan*; it is this which has led several modern dramatists, misled by sentimental notions, hopelessly astray. The feminine in high tragedy, we may repeat, must either be made hard, approaching the masculine in quality, or else be relegated to a position of minor importance in the development of the plot. The only exception to this lies, possibly, in those heroless plays already referred to, where the tragedy arises not so much out of individual characters as out of the clash of varying temperaments and the operation of social or external circumstances; and even here the atmosphere of loftiness and hardness is usually preserved.[1]

(v) TYPES OF TRAGEDY

FEATURES OF GREEK TRAGEDY. In thus analysing the characteristics of drama from Æschylus to modern days all the main types of tragedy have been touched upon. There would remain here, therefore, little more to do than to sum up some of the results which have been obtained, as these particularly apply to the tragic endeavour of the various ages. As practically none of the main types of tragic endeavour is unrepresented in English, it may be well to confine all remarks here to the development of tragedy in this language, with but occasional reference to the practice of other lands.

(*a*) *The Chorus and the Unities.* Of the Greek drama much has been said and written, and the details of its technique and development need not here be entered upon. There is much

---

[1] This view may seem to run counter to the fact that, both in ancient and in modern plays, women characters have often assumed an important place in the tragic action ; but when we analyse the appearances of an Antigone, a Clytemnestra, a Bérénice, a Phèdre, a Hedda, or a Rebecca West, we shall, I think, find that their treatment is governed by the methods outlined above.

that is permanent in the tragedies of Æschylus, Sophocles, and
Euripides, but there is also much that has a purely temporary
value. The chorus, for example, is essentially an incidental
feature. It is part of the traditional origin of the Greek stage,
and in the hands of Euripides it was, as we have already seen,
relegated to a subordinate position. That it was not necessary
for the expression of true tragic emotion has been proved not
only by the romantic genius of Shakespeare, but by the classical
genius of Racine. On the other hand, the chorus marked that
lyrical quality in tragedy which later iconoclasts were inclined
too recklessly to neglect. The spirit of the chorus, that of
which it was the expression, is a permanent thing, well-nigh
necessary in all high tragedy, but the form of the chorus is
purely temporary and topical. Quite apart from this lyrical
element, too, the chorus presents features of a kind essential
to tragic expression. Countless commentators have noted the
chorus-like words of Enobarbus in *Antony and Cleopatra*, and
perhaps such figures as the Fool in *Lear* and Horatio in *Hamlet*
bear a similar quality. In other words, the fundamental
comments made by the chanting crowds which appeared on
the Athenian stage have been passed over in Elizabethan and
modern drama to individual characters who sometimes, like
Lear's Fool and Horatio, have an integral part in the working
out of the tragic theme and sometimes, like Enobarbus, remain
apart.

As we have seen, the unities also present features of a temporary sort, with, however, a suggestion, not lacking in importance, regarding eternal dramatic truths. Strictly observed,
the unities are either absurd or dictated purely by the external features of the stage; in a broader sense, they are rules
from which no great dramatist may ever swerve. The unity
of action, intimately associated as it is with the unities of
place and time, thus accords with the hardness, the restricted
passion, and the concentrated emotion demanded by high
tragedy.

(*b*) *The Stage.* The Greek drama and its conventions,
therefore, may have much to tell us. Even from the conjec-
tures of the most absurd of the neo-classic critics there may
be gained genuine elements of dramatic truth. The main

difference, however, between the Greek theatrical world and that of to-day does not lie in the chorus or in mere dramatic technique, but in the stage; and a consideration of the Greek theatre, capable of holding 30,000 spectators, raises at once the problem as to the most suitable medium for the presentation of tragedy. On the one hand there is this vast amphitheatre, with the actors far removed from the audience, with little opportunity for ordinary scenic effects, and on the other there is the *théâtre intime*, where a small body of spectators is brought into close contact with the actors, and where scenic effects can be employed and illusions of all kinds created. The true answer to this problem would seem to be that both the *théâtre intime* and the Greek amphitheatre can produce fine plays, each of separate and quite distinct beauty; but, at the same time, there is something of vastness and of majesty in the plays produced on the Greek stage which is impossible in the plays written for a *théâtre intime*. There may be delicacy in the latter; there may be more poignant and subtle situations; there will certainly be more intricate character-drawing; but there will usually be lacking the statuesque effect, the grandeur, and the exalted tone of the other. History has shown to us that the finest dramas have been produced for heterogeneous audiences—the aristocrats and the artisans of Athens, the apprentices and the peers of Elizabethan England. When the audiences tend to break into separate groups, when the theatre is patronized not by all, but by a class, then the drama produced for that theatre becomes weak and effeminate. Drama, it would appear, is not wholly a thing of pleasure in its highest forms; in the ages when the theatre is merely a place of amusement, to-day and in Restoration England, then the average play-writing is poor and uninformed. Only in the periods when the theatre mingled pleasure with some species of reflection, some humanitarian, national, or religious ideal, was fine drama produced. Æschylus, Sophocles, and Euripides reflect the age of Periclean Athens; Shakespeare reflects the age of Drake and of Raleigh; Schiller and Ibsen reflect the age of broader ideals. Disillusionment gave birth to the plays of the later seventeenth century and to the plays of to-day. The *théâtre intime* is the result of the desire of one class to abstract itself from the rest, to divorce the highest drama from the whole of humanity. It would seem that the hope of a genuine dramatic revival lies rather in the elevating of the tone of the vaster theatres than in the attempt on the part of some of our dramatic enthusiasts to further the theatre of the refined and circumscribed audience.

The Greek drama, therefore, teaches us that while mere slavish imitation of past models can lead toward nothing but dull and ineffective productivity, romantic dramatists may be wrong in throwing over entirely the precepts and the example of the classicists. While it may be admitted that, with the exception of Milton's *Samson Agonistes* and Shelley's *Prometheus Unbound* (a dramatic poem rather than a drama), there are few adequate imitations of the Greek drama in England, and while it may also be admitted that in details of dramatic technique the Greek drama has nothing to teach us, we must nevertheless realize that there are elements of permanent dramatic truth not only in the works of Æschylus, but in the apparently ridiculous theories of a Castelvetro and a Rymer.

EARLY ELIZABETHAN TRAGEDY. The next type of tragedy which we have to note is the tragedy of the earlier Elizabethans, a type by itself in however many diverse forms it might be expressed. The first tragedies produced in England which can be deeply analysed are those of Shakespeare, but Shakespeare's achievement was, as is well known, raised upon the previous and less exalted endeavours of his predecessors, and this fact renders a glance at the history of the development of the tragic idea in England absolutely necessary here. In England, as in Greece, the drama sprang out of the religion of the people. By innumerable gradations it moved forward to the vast cycles of the mystery and miracle plays. Moralities then took their rise, probably with the development of more professional companies of actors. These moralities, again by innumerable gradations, passed into forms that approached toward truer dramatic shape, and then, grafted on to the new growth of humanistic sentiment, developed ultimately into the marvellous flourish and fruit of the Elizabethan stage. With this development went a corresponding progress in the conception of the tragic spirit. For the Middle Ages tragedy was essentially a falling from happiness or great estate into unhappiness or misery. Chaucer's lines from the Monk's prologue already quoted, express summarily the typical medieval view. Dante's great poem was a " divine comedy," because it passed from the torments of Hell to the happiness of Heaven. Thus, for the Middle Ages, tragedy, as dealing with persons of high degree, with " him that stood in greet prosperitee," harmonized exactly with the Aristotelian idea that tragedy should deal with the hero of " high fame and flourishing prosperity." At the same time there arose almost unconsciously the feeling that tragedy should deal with these exalted deeds and persons in an exalted manner; hence verse in some form came to be the natural concomitant of all true tragedy, and this, likewise, joined forces with the verse plays of Seneca and with the then less well-known verse plays of ancient Greece. So far the Athenian and the medieval ideals coalesced. Medieval criticism, however, had one peculiarly characteristic feature: it expressed in the most extreme form the moral attitude toward literature. Swayed by strictures against the drama, and, indeed, against all poetry which found expression from the time of the Fathers of the Church to that of Girolamo Savonarola, it attempted everywhere to discover some utilitarian end for every type of art and every piece of artistic workmanship. Moral considerations, therefore, met with the new humanistic ideals, and developed a type of literary criticism confused and heterogeneous, but none the less influential upon the development of dramatic literature. This clash is to be seen most clearly in the pronouncements of some of the late sixteenth-century theorizers. " Tragedy," says Puttenham, who may be taken as a representative of many others, " deals with the doleful falls of unfortunate and afflicted Princes, for the purpose of reminding men of the mutability of fortune and of God's just punishment of a vicious life." Here, in this one sentence, we find ideas culled from ancient Greece and from medieval Europe mingled together and confused with no sense of their inherent incongruity. There is the Aristotelian idea of magnitude; there is the medieval idea of fall from happiness into unhappiness; there is the pagan idea of fortune; and there is the Christian idea of moral punishment. The confusion is interesting and valuable, because from just such a confusion grew the drama of the Elizabethans.

As regards the general idea of tragedy at this time, we may sum up briefly by saying that, in the belief of all, tragedy consisted in the fall of the great; that all were agreed as to the advisability of having five-act dramas (Horace here is responsible, and Seneca); that all were convinced of the value of a poetic form for tragedy; that, consciously or unconsciously, no one would have denied the necessity for a ' moral ' in all tragedies; and that, perfectly unconsciously, the conflict of the old moralities was operating on the minds of the critics and the dramatists toward the stressing of an element neglected to a large extent in the Greek drama. Apart from these general suppositions and beliefs, the classicists parted company from the popular, so-called romantic, playwrights. Whereas the classicists held for the three unities, the popular playwrights, looking to native example, disdained or violated them; whereas the classicists, with Sidney, regarded tragi-comedy as a ' mongrel ' creation, the popular dramatists, looking back to the crude admixture of sadness and mirth in the mysteries, patronized this form above all others; whereas the classic dramatists and critics, following Horace, cried for declamation and for decorum, the popular writers strove to stress action, to make their tragedies vigorous, to deny nothing to the eyes of the spectators.

The Senecan influence had been working in Europe years before it passed to England. As early as 1315 was penned the *Eccerinis* of Albertino, a Latin drama modelled on the strict Roman form. In 1515 came the Italian *Sofonisba* of Trissino. Only in 1559 did there appear in England the first translation of a Senecan drama, and it is from about this year that we can trace the growth of the classical species here. Sackville and Norton's *Gorboduc* was acted only two years later, in January 1562. This *Gorboduc*, the first regular English tragedy, is the initiator of a long line of Senecan dramas, chill and uninteresting, but valuable to us because of their variations from the strict norm. *Gorboduc* has a native mytho-historical theme, not a classical subject, and the structure is closer to the old chronicle-history manner than to the Roman type. Love passion was introduced into the composite *Gismond of Salerne*,

and a native note into Thomas Hughes' *Misfortunes of Arthur*.
In these plays the unities are commonly broken, and English
historical or quasi-historical themes are treated as well as stories
borrowed from Italian *novelle*, but the whole is set in a framework
of rigid and impossible declamation, and every turn of the plot
is coloured by the medieval idea of a moral aim. There is the
confusion here in creative art, such as it is, which was visible
in the critical pronouncement of Puttenham quoted above.

Meanwhile, playwrights who had been tutored in the
morality tradition were attempting in some crude manner to
adapt that tradition to other themes and other styles. Most
of these early plays, such as Edwardes' *Damon and Pithias*,
R. B.'s *Apius and Virginia*, and Preston's *Cambises*, are
" lamentable tragedies, mixed full of pleasant mirth." Shakespeare in later years might make fun of those crude attempts,
but in them lay the stepping-stones of tradition from the
productions of medieval days to his own works. Often not
much of the morality tradition has been lost in these primitive
dramas, but there are hints at the future development of the
species. Nearly every one of them possesses its Vice and its
personifications, but at the same time there is visible an endeavour to create something more in keeping with the newer
age than anything that had gone before.

Along with this native, or semi-native, development of crude
tragedy we must also note the development of the chronicle
history, often with elements serious and tragic. Even from
very early times there had been a tendency in the morality to
substitute for a pure abstraction some typical and well-known
royal figure. Bale's *King Johan* is a good example of this.
From the presentment of history for the object of enforcing a
moral lesson to the presentment of history in and for itself was
obviously but a step. Although one Latin history play, the
Ricardus Tertius of Thomas Legge, is thoroughly Senecan in
manner, it is perfectly obvious that Senecan methods would
hardly harmonize with the freer development of the events of
a king's reign. History evidently demanded a more natural
and less trammelled mode of expression. In dealing with a
king's career little could be concealed, and it was inevitable
that the unities should be broken. As history, moreover, was

never wholly tragic, and as thus high and low tended to appear in the one play, the impulse given to the development of tragi-comedy in such works as Pikeryng's *Horestes* or Preston's *Cambises* was here deeply strengthened. With the rise of patriotic sentiment in the latter half of the sixteenth century, these history plays became exceedingly popular, and even although they do not belong to the strict tragic type they must be duly taken into consideration when we are dealing with the elements which went to make up the Elizabethan drama.

In all of these various primitive types we see a struggle, sometimes conscious, but more commonly unconscious, toward the attainment of a truly national and truly unified drama. No one, however, had apparently considered carefully what would suit the tastes of the age. The classicists were severe and unwilling to depart overfar from their ancient laws and precepts, even if here and there they had to make concessions to popular predilections; the other dramatists, although they occasionally borrowed hints from Seneca, were rough and unformed in their conceptions and in their manner. It is now perfectly obvious that the only hope for the rise of a national drama lay in a conscious union of the two forces, the native elements providing variety and vitality, the classical elements providing unity and harmonious construction; but this fact may not have been so apparent to the critics and the play-wrights of the age. Dramas like the anonymous *Locrine* and *Selimus* seemed to be tending in the right direction, but they too were unformed, and it was left to the so-called University Wits to make the classical tragedy popular and the popular tragedy unified in construction and conscious of its aim.

Many of these University Wits confined their work to comedy, and hence may barely be mentioned here; although to them all, comedy-writers and tragedy-writers alike, is due the development of a freer and a sweeter blank verse; while to Lyly, who wrote only fantastic comedies, we owe the introduction of a finer, if conceited, prose style, and to Greene and Lyly alike those delicate romantic-realistic portraits of women which were taken over by Shakespeare in his early years and were later modified by him. By the time that these University Wits appeared the London world was ripe for the origination of the new drama. The private shows at the Inns of Court and elsewhere still continued, and were to continue till the closing of the theatres in 1642, but the centre of theatrical interest was now the professional actors, playing in regular theatres modelled partly on the old inn-yards where of old they had performed, partly on the ancient mystery platform-stage, and partly on the Roman amphitheatres.

The audience was now a mixed body of spectators, embracing all classes from the courtiers to the rudest groundlings, all passionate and all accustomed to sights of blood, all demanding a rich, full-blooded drama, and all prepared, with the fiery enthusiasm born of the Renascence, to listen to the finest out-bursts of poetical frenzy, but not prepared, under any con-sideration, to witness anything artificial or stilted. The actors were men of the one histrionic profession, bent on making a livelihood and determined to sacrifice no opportunity of gain by adhering to theoretical prejudices, classical or otherwise. The stage conditions were medieval, admitting ample change of scenery, allowing for the episodic treatment of themes, if that should be deemed necessary. Already, even in the Inns of Court performances, it had been amply proved that the unities in their stricter forms were not in English taste, and that Renascence enthusiasm and passion had burst aside the fetters of the more precise humanistic movement. The stage conditions, likewise, which permitted this multitude of shifting scenes, demanded a long description, which the audience would willingly listen to only when it was couched in the fullest of poetical forms. From the presence among the actors of famous clowns, added to the vital tradition of the medieval Vice, influenced too by the general atmosphere of the primitive English liturgical drama, came the demand for tragi-comedy. Tragedy, pure tragedy, could be produced only when it was of a bombastic, exaggerated kind, so thrilling and so gripping the imaginations of the spectators that they would be willing to sacrifice for a time that mirth which for them seasonably spiced the most serious of plays.

MARLOWE. The man who, as is well known, finally estab-lished the tragic type in England was Christopher Marlowe. In his works, crude in construction as they appear when set in comparison with Shakespeare's later triumphs, we find for the first time a conscious striving to reach a form of tragedy that should be not so amorphous and so purposeless as the previous attempts in classical, popular, or chronicle-history styles. Marlowe's dramas fall naturally into two groups: the first, consisting of *Tamburlaine*, *Dr Faustus*, and perhaps *The Jew of Malta*, stands apart from the later *Edward II*, a history play which shows a quite separate tragic aim. It is the first group that is of paramount importance as forming a type of tragedy by itself, hardly touched in its pure form by any other writer.

The first point we note about these early dramas is that their author has drunk deeply of a source unknown to the preceding dramatists. *Il Principe* of Macchiavelli had appeared at Florence in the year 1513, and from the date of its publication, in an ever-increasing wave of admiration and of abuse, its fame and notoriety spread through Europe. In England Marlowe, because of his independent and almost rebellious attitude toward life, was one of the first to embrace its doctrines and the doctrines which had sprung from it. Macchiavelli had made a god of *virtù*, expressing in imperishable prose that desire and that ambition which had operated in almost every Italian state, raising humble *condottieri* to principalities and dukedoms, and retaining them there by diverse selfish and cynical actions. Macchiavelli had denied all morality except that morality, if so it may be called, which operated for the good of the individual man. There is no action too ignoble for him to condone, in his advice to his prince, so long as it leads toward making his position in the State more secure. Marlowe probably had in him some of this dominating egoistic power, and it is this that he has fixed on in his first three tragedies. There is an element of conviction in the prologue to *The Jew of Malta* which rings true; the lines have been written by one who sincerely believed in the principles of *The Prince*:

> And let them know that I am Machiavel,
> And weigh not men, and therefore not men's words.
> Admired I am of those that hate me most. . . .
> I count religion but a childish toy,
> And hold there is no sin but ignorance. . . .
>   O' the poor petty wights
> Let me be envied and not pitied !

This Macchiavellian strain may not have been taken up in its purer form by later dramatists, but great elements of it served to enter into the structure of many of the major Elizabethan tragedies. It presents the quality of boldness and of strength which was demanded on the English stage.

Virtù, will, ambition, call it what we please, always tends to overlook class. The majority of the Italian dukes and princes of the fifteenth and sixteenth centuries were base-born men who had won their positions by sheer personal merit, confidence, or villainy. In Marlowe's dramas, similarly, the heroes are not of the class that had formerly appeared in tragedy. Tamburlaine is certainly a king when we see him on the stage, but he has been raised to empire from mere peasanthood. Barabas is only a moneylender, and Faustus is an ordinary German doctor. Thus the old medieval conception of tragedy as the descent from greatness to misery was being supplanted by the Renascence ideal of individual worth. The more ancient tradition continued to endure for centuries, but, as in the dramas of Shakespeare, it was being modified gradually by the Marlovian ideal.

In the same way, we find in Marlowe's tragedies a change in the tragic aim. The kernel of his dramas lies not so much in the falling of a great person from happiness as in the struggle of some brave, ambitious soul against forces too great for it. The moral conception of tragedy for Marlowe was gone. The whole interest centres on the one personality; the attention of spectators and of readers is fixed on that personality and on the greatness and nobility which is connected with it. Tamburlaine is obviously the master of those about him. Faustus is one in whose hands infinite knowledge has been put. The Jew moves as a kind of super-mind among a mass of puppets whose lives he sways continually. There is the same sense of intellectual majesty in all Marlowe's heroes which is to be felt in Hamlet.

There are several other striking departures on Marlowe's part from contemporary procedure, one of the most important being his more poetical use of blank verse; but with these we need not deal. One other point, however, may be noted; and that is the tremendous advance which he made in *Dr Faustus* in his conception of an inner struggle as bearing a great part of the tragic interest. There is no struggle in the soul of Tamburlaine or in the soul of Barabas, but what makes *Dr Faustus* really great is the hint at conflicting desires within the mind of the hero. Here it may not be uninteresting to observe that of all Marlowe's dramas *Dr Faustus* comes nearest in conception, character, and plan to the older moralities. In it we can trace the union of the morality with the new Renascence ideals, all modified a trifle by reminiscences of Seneca. From this union later tragedy was to spring.

Marlowe, of course, has many weaknesses, some due to his own youth, some due to the fact that he was a pioneer who had to hew out a way for himself without any master to guide or stay him. In structure he is decidedly of the older age, inheriting the native chronicle tradition of separate episodes loosely strung together. *Tamburlaine*, after all, is not really a drama in the ordinary sense of the word; it is merely a dramatized semi-epic of one man's fate. *Dr Faustus* is marred as a tragedy by its detached nature; it is simply a string of odd scenes connected inorganically together. *The Jew of Malta* lacks balance entirely, although how far this may have been due to later ' improvements ' is not now determinable. A more serious defect in all Marlowe's early dramas is the absence of subordinate characters. All Marlowe's persons, by their very greatness, stand alone. They have no one to fight against. They are lonely figures set in a world of Lilliputians, with the gods alone as their masters. The only drama of Shakespeare's which to any extent presents this phenomenon is *Hamlet*, but even here, although no character but Hamlet rises to tragic proportions, there are *dramatis personæ* of interest and of individuality. Even more noticeable is the lack in Marlowe of women characters. In the typical Renascence attitude expressed by the dukes and the princes of Italy in social life, by Macchiavelli in philosophy, and by Marlowe in drama, there was but little place for women. Women were winning their way to an independent life in the time of the Renascence, actively through the work of persons as diverse as Vittoria Colonna and Veronica Franco, theoretically through the women characters of drama, but the philosophy and the attitude toward life expressed by a Macchiavelli and by a Marlowe were distinctly masculine in character. Marlowe shared not at all the spirit of Greene and of Lyly. Zenocrate in *Tamburlaine* is but a figurehead; no women but the Duchess and Helen enter into *Dr Faustus*; Abigail in *The Jew of Malta* is little more than a shadow. It has already been seen that tragedy is more masculine than comedy, and that, moreover, there can be great tragedies with an almost entirely masculine cast. On the other hand, the study of great drama will prove to us that, while the general temper of a tragedy is masculine, women figures tend to make the atmosphere of a play more natural and general, and that the consistent elimination of women in the works of Marlowe proves in him a lack of sympathy with the whole of life. Combined with this lack of interest in women characters is Marlowe's complete lack of a comic spirit. The comic portions of *Dr Faustus* are inexpressibly dull, and those of *The Jew of Malta* rise little above buffoonery. *Tamburlaine*, the very type of his art, serious throughout and masculine in conception, lacks at once that contrast and relief which is presented in the tragedies of Shakespeare.

The general spirit of the Marlovian dramas, then, is of tremendous historical importance. That conception of Renascence *virtù* battling onward to success and then falling unconquered before fate gave to English tragedy a theme of greatness and strength which before was wanting in it. Marlowe's drama is an inhuman drama, but, before Shakespeare could arise, men had to be taught to look for this strength and purpose in tragedy. On the other hand, all of these early dramas of Marlowe can be regarded as little more than experiments. They are not truly great; they merely point the way toward the greatness of the future. By reason of their limitations, by reason of their lack of structural power, above all by reason of their want of more subtle characterization, they fall below the level of true tragedy.

SHAKESPEARE. With Shakespeare we move upon another plane. - The Shakespearian type of tragedy has not been taken over in its entirety by many dramatists, largely because of the vastness of its conception, but it forms a species of drama which has, in parts, found many imitators, and which has exercised an incalculable influence on all succeeding English tragic endeavour. In speaking of this Shakespearian type of tragedy we must confine ourselves almost entirely to the four major dramas. *Romeo and Juliet*, as we have seen, stands apart, as being a tragedy of fate and of outward circumstance. The major dramas are all formed on another plan, borrowing elements now from Seneca, now from Marlowe, and now from the more primitive native English plays. It may be noted in regard to these four plays that, although they have all elements in common, they seem all to be in the nature of experiments. *Hamlet* is peculiar in having but one figure of tragic magnitude; *Othello* in being formed on a peculiar plan and in dealing largely with intrigue; *Lear* in reverting technically to the chronicle-history tradition and in adopting an actionless hero; and *Macbeth* in transforming a villain into a hero. In all of these dramas, however, there are features which bind them together into one group. In every one there is an outer and an inner tragedy, the outer sometimes working in direct contrast to the inner. The outer tragedy is laid down on lines of the utmost sensationalism, dealing with murder and torture and bloodshed; the inner tragedy is quieter and more poignant, involving usually a struggle between emotion and intellect, or between emotion and traits of character which have arisen out of habit and custom. So in *Hamlet* it is a struggle between the emotion of revenge, and perhaps also of love, warring against a certain quality which Hamlet himself names as " religion " and which we might call moral scruple; in *Othello* it is passionate love warring against jealousy; in *Lear* it is petty pride warring against a tenderer sympathy; in *Macbeth* it is kingly ambition warring against the emotions that have arisen out of conscience. The same phenomenon is visible likewise in *Antony and Cleopatra* and in *Coriolanus*.

Apart from this, the two most noticeable characteristics of the Shakespearian type are the hint at supernatural forces operating unseen but surely, and the peculiar relationship which the hero bears to his surroundings. The supernatural element, which is displayed in its crudest form in *Hamlet* and *Macbeth*, is weakest in *Othello*, which approaches toward the domestic type, but even there it is delicately marked. In all the tragedies it is hinted at, yet, as we have seen, rarely enunciated in a deliberate manner. The relationship of the hero to his surroundings, however, is the definitely characteristic mark of the Shakespearian species. All Shakespeare's heroes are set in positions where they, and they alone, cannot battle with fate. Hamlet, the " religious " and the lover, doomed to set the world aright; Othello, stupid and unintellectual, fiery in his passions, set opposite to Iago; Iago, unscrupulous and clever, literally tempted by Othello's imbecility; Lear, conceited and proud, unobservant and credulous, faced by his evil daughters and by Cordelia; Macbeth, emotional and weak, yet ambitious, met by the witches and goaded on by his wife; Lady Macbeth, hard and self-seeking, confronted by temptation; Coriolanus, overweening in his pride, condemned to stoop to plebeians; Antony, amorous and doting, met by Cleopatra; all of these are placed in the exact situation which they are incapable of mastering. Put Hamlet in Othello's place or Othello in Hamlet's and there would have been no tragedy, either of the Shakespearian type or any other. It is this almost fatal confronting of the hero with forces beyond his strength that marks the tragedy of Shakespeare.

HEROIC TRAGEDY. As is evident, the heroic tragedy of the Restoration is but an exaggeration of many of the elements we have noted above as characteristic of the Shakespearian species, with the omission of this fatal relationship between the hero and his surroundings. Here also there are clearly marked the outer drama and the inner, the inner being again a struggle between emotion (restricted to the one emotion of love) and intellect (narrowed down to duty), as well as the lofty nature of the hero of the tragedy, while supernatural aids to the drama are by no means lacking. The heroic tragedy needs little comment in a work that professedly deals most largely only with the finer species of dramatic productivity, but the fact that it is thus a normal development of earlier English tragic types gives it a peculiar historical and even critical value of its own.

One thing in particular, however, may be specially noted here. In the heroic tragedy there is, as it were, a return to the main element stressed in the Marlovian type—the impression of grandeur. Admiration is the effect most sought after by the Restoration dramatists. It is this, indeed, which most frequently leads them astray, for they have not the power to conceive of such higher personal qualities as are calculated to raise a lofty impression of grandeur, and they err thus in seeking for sources of that impression in false regions. They make an Almanzor whose physical prowess is so over-emphasized as to become ridiculous; they force their heroes to mouth out bombastic speeches that fail to convince us; they exaggerate the love *motif* because they think that the spectacle of a great hero forsaking all for passion will make us wonder and admire. We realize now that these things are wrong; on the other hand, these elements, false and ridiculous though they may be, are but exaggerations of those qualities which, more subtly indicated, lie at the foundation of Shakespearian tragedy.

HORROR TRAGEDY. More important intrinsically is the horror tragedy patronized by Webster and Ford. This horror tragedy will be found, on examination, to approximate very closely to the comedy of intrigue, for in both the appeal to the audience is made not by means of the *dramatis personæ*, but by means of incident on the stage. It is not, of course, a strictly separate species, for elements of horror may enter into tragedies of quite a different type, as in *Hamlet* and in *Lear*; but it stands apart in having all or most of the stress on the outward elements, with whatsoever there may be of inner tragedy closely interwoven with and depending upon the stage sensationalism. Horror from situation and incident thus dominates *The Duchess of Malfi*, *Vittoria Corombona*, and *The Broken Heart*, three plays which may be taken as characteristic of the species. Here there may be something of an inner struggle, ending disastrously, but that is not the prime point of interest in any of these dramas. Our attention is captured entirely by the development of the plot itself. The thrill of awe and of majesty hardly comes from any direct words or phrases, but from the incidents and from the situations in which the characters are involved.

DOMESTIC TRAGEDY. The domestic tragedy stands apart from all these types, not because of stress laid on one element or another, but because of its subject-matter and its special

173

tone. In dealing with this species it must be noted that the domestic tragedy can take one of two lines of development, the first leading toward true tragedy, and the second descending to a position similar to that of the sentimental drama. Tragedy, as we have seen, requires some atmosphere of what may be called majestic grandeur, and this, in many domestic plays, is entirely lacking. *The London Merchant*, for example, could never for a moment be associated with the high tragedies of any age of literary history, because of its lowered and uninspiring tone. On the other hand, many of the nineteenth-century dramas of a domestic type have about them a note which raises them above the level of the workmanship of Lillo's play. We may admit, as we shall see, the sentimental dramas, the *drames*, to an honourable place in the history of theatrical productivity but these domestic dramas of a lowered tone have attempted to achieve something which it is outside the power of tragedy to treat. We may include, therefore, in the types of high drama (1) plays of the true tragic spirit, majestic and awe-inspiring, (2) plays of the true comic spirit, fanciful and witty, and (3) serious happy-ending plays of a lowered tone; but we must regard as failures those domestic dramas which, attempting to gain the height of tragedy, lack altogether the sternness and grandeur of tragedy. One of the points which have been shown up most clearly in this analysis into dramatic productivity is that there are certain laws and characteristics in all great drama which no dramatist may transgress with impunity. There is an aim proper to tragedy, an aim proper to comedy, an aim proper to the serious *drame*; a confusion of these aims or the attempting of one aim in the medium of another leads only to failure or to mediocrity.

III

COMEDY

IN dealing with the subject of comedy an attempt will here be made to carry an investigation along the lines already laid down in the treatment of tragedy, partly for the purpose of discovering the points of connexion between tragedy and comedy, partly for the purpose of stressing the different aims and methods of these two dramatic species. While our main concern here will be with pure comic productivity, it will be necessary at least to glance at the intermediate group of serious plays which seem to belong neither to the one class nor to the other, and also at that other group of dramas which are more properly styled tragi-comedies, in which tragic and comic motives meet and mingle. Even when we are discussing the purely comic species these two groups must always be kept in mind.

(i) UNIVERSALITY IN COMEDY

THE SUPERNATURAL. As in tragedy there was a sharp distinction between melodrama, dramatized tales, and what may be styled high tragedy, so in the kindred realm of comedy there is a line of demarcation, slighter, it is true, and less to be appreciated by spectator or by reader, between a merely amusing play and what may be called fine comedy. Moreover, just as in tragedy this raising of tone was secured mainly by the element of universality, brought about by one means or another, so in fine comedy universality seems ever to be sought after by the greater dramatists. This quality of universality may, it is evident, be attained partly by methods similar to those already analysed in serious plays, but the fact that most comedy differs from tragedy in being often heroless, realistic, and consequently unpoetic, renders several of these methods completely useless.

The supernatural, in any of its cruder forms, could thus never have any entry into many types of comedy. The air of comedy is generally too cynical, too reasonable, too unemotional, to allow of any heavenly or spiritual visitants. If the gods descend to the earth in comedy, as in Dryden's *Amphitryon*, they usually do so in a frank spirit of farce. Mercury becomes a common serving-man, and Jove takes on the attributes of mankind. The weird sisters of Shadwell's *Lancashire Witches* are not as their companions in *Macbeth*. In the tragedy, although the actions and the words of the witches might be related to Macbeth's own thoughts, there is a sense of supernatural awe in their appearance; in the comedy, not only does the author express his scepticism in his preface, but he is careful to make many of his characters as sceptical as himself. Ghosts could never enter into a comedy of any kind, unless indeed those ghosts which are, in the end, resolved into mortal essence. The spirit of Angelica appears in Farquhar's *Sir Harry Wildair*, but in the last act reveals itself as the bodily form of Sir Harry Wildair's wife; a ghost is brought into Addison's *Drummer*, but once more is discovered to be nothing but an earthly shape in disguise. The high emotion, the majesty, the awe of tragedy are all absent here; sacred things are laughed at; an air of reason and of disbelief permeates the whole.

There is, it is true, one particular type of comedy which does admit of the introduction of the supernatural. Here Shakespeare's comedy of humour provides obviously the most representative examples, and at once we think of *A Midsummer Night's Dream* and *The Tempest*. In the one we meet with the supernatural in Puck, Titania, and Oberon; in the other it appears in the persons of Ariel and Caliban, even in the magical powers of Prospero. Unquestionably, the element of the supernatural acts here in the same way as it does in tragedy, raising the level of the play, creating subtly the same impression of universality. Witnessing *The Tempest*, we feel that that comedy is a drama of symbolic vastness. The world, and it, become a dream, and the figures we see on the stage representatives of a humanity shadowed forth in little. The comedy of humour, however, is a rare type. Calderon, Shakespeare, perhaps Barrie, have reached full expression within its sphere, but the commoner forms of comedy—essentially intellectual and rational in tone—have attracted most, and form our general impression of the comic as a type of dramatic creation.

That even the intellectual comedy, however, is not wanting in the finer suggestion of supernatural forces may readily be proved by a glance at the typical situations of many plays stretching from classical times to the present day. There are scores of comedies that depend for their main merriment on situations that are themselves founded on chance and on the suggestion of forces playfully baffling mankind. There cannot be, of course, the slightest enunciation here of an active fate. The fate sense, in its direct form, is utterly alien to comedy, but there may be the subtle hint of mocking gods behind the actions of the human figures on the stage. M. Bergson, of whose entertaining and profound study of *Le Rire* frequent mention will be made in the succeeding pages, has diagnosed as one of the chief sources of the risible what he styles inversion, which he connects with simple puppets on a string and with what he decides is of the essence of the laughable— automatism. Men are made into puppets; events take place in a series of extraordinary repetitions, where coincidence is not out of the question, but where at the same time there is more than a suggestion that the chance is not uninformed by some higher power. For instance, twins are born, so alike that they cannot be distinguished even by their parents. So far only Nature has had a part; such twins may be found in any large town. But at this point the gods step in. They create a couple of twin serving-men, identical in appearance, and, not content with that, they separate the pairs of brothers for long years, to make them meet again in a series of extraordinary embarrassments in the town of Ephesus. Such is the stuff of *The Comedy of Errors*. This *Comedy of Errors* has but the spirit of *Romeo and Juliet* inverted. Fate is sporting with the Antipholuses and with the Dromios, as a more solemn fate sported tragically with the unfortunate lovers. Repetition, inversion, *interférence de séries*, the three main theses of M. Bergson's chapter on the *comique de situation*, all depend in some way or another on the automatism of man in the hands of a higher power.

Here, then, is one of the first suggestions of universality in comedy. The gods are laughed at and sacred things are turned into causes of merriment, and yet a hint remains that there is more in heaven and earth than is dreamed of in any philosophy. The element of universality derived from suggestion of the supernatural, however, is by no means one of the chief in comedy as it was one of the chief in tragedy, and for the average dramatist it is an exceedingly dangerous medium. Unless in a purely fantastical play such as *A Midsummer Night's Dream*, where there is a momentary suspension of disbelief, or in *The Tempest*, where the supernatural is related to human knowledge and human skill, a touch too crude will destroy all illusion. The supernatural may be introduced most freely in the comedies of romance, and hinted at in the comedies of manners, but only with the most delicate and most hesitating of outlines.

CLASS SYMBOLISM. More potent and more common is the equivalent to the tragic hero of royalty and empire. Comedy, as we have seen, is ordinarily heroless, the mirth usually arising from the juxtaposition of a number of characters. An analysis of these characters will disclose to us that the playwright habitually endeavours to secure one of two effects, both dependent on the one idea: he will try to introduce several of a particular species or class, or he will try to suggest that a certain figure is itself representative of a class. The fundamental assumption of comedy is that it does not deal with isolated individualities. These classes thus presented in the body of comedy will obviously have broader ramifications beyond the walls of the theatre; and at once there will be raised in the minds of the audience a connexion between the particular work of art and the wider reaches of humanity as a whole. Very frequently, as we have already seen, humorous or laughable characters are presented in pairs or in groups. The artisans in *A Midsummer Night's Dream* include Bottom, Quince, Snug, and Starveling. Dogberry and Verges, Launce and Speed, the two Dromios—all of these, although foils to one another, are representative of particular classes, and their juxtaposition strengthens the assumption that their idiosyncrasies are not peculiar to themselves but shared by many another. In the comedies of manners we frequently find opposing bands of wits and of would-be wits. Not all the wits are alike; not all the would-be wits are alike; but each group has certain qualities common to all its varied representatives. The various " Schools " of the eighteenth-century comedy—*The School for Scandal, The School for Wives, The School for Greybeards*—all of them ultimately to be traced back to Molière's *L'École des Maris* and *L'Ecole des Femmes,* present characteristics of an identically similar nature.

When a person is isolated in comedy he is nearly always a type, a representative of something broader than himself, and in the highest art a representative of what are the permanent classes of mankind. " The characters of Chaucer's Pilgrims," said William Blake, " are the characters that compose all ages and nations. . . . They are the physiognomies or lineaments of universal human life, beyond which nature never steps." Blake's words might, indeed, be applied to all fine comedy. Comedy may revel in the follies of an age, but we shall find that it usually seizes upon those particular follies which are permanent in all ages. Sir Toby Belch and Sir Andrew Aguecheek are not only Elizabethans; Captain Bobadil, even the gulls Matthew and Stephen, are in a way universal; there are Mirabels among us, and Sir Fopling Flutters and Mrs Malaprops. This permanent value we shall find in all the greatest comedies of the ages. It is this that makes Molière, Shakespeare, Congreve, and Sheridan as fresh to-day as when they wrote. Only the lesser dramatists will trouble themselves with the topical, the temporary, and the particular. It is the lack of these permanent elements that makes the comedies of Shadwell, well written and well constructed, so dull beside the comedies of Etherege; Shadwell strove to reproduce his age, and, accordingly, although he has historical value, he has less intrinsic worth than many of the other writers who were his contemporaries. Comedy may set out to be a mirror of the times; but far more, in its highest form, must it be a mirror of time.

Comedy, therefore, from one point of view, is an abstract of society, or at least of certain aspects of society. If laughter is essentially the punishment of society inflicted on certain eccentric types and classes of mankind, we can see how it operates to secure a broader significance than is included in the literal words and in the actual persons on the stage. It is true that the risible has something in it peculiarly racial and national, but there are general 'lineaments' of humanity which seem to pass beyond the borders of the various lands. The virtuoso, the hypocrite, the miser, the simpleton who preens himself upon his wit—these are figures which are not peculiar to any one country, and they appear indiscriminately in the plays of Shakespeare, Jonson, Molière, and Congreve. There are, then, in high comedy two main suggestions: first, that the characters are not the characters peculiar to one age or to one place; and, second, that the comedy as a whole is but a part of, or a mere symbol of, the larger world of society beyond it. From this springs the feeling of generality, the feeling that is presented in high tragedy as well, that these facts and situations and persons are not isolated and separate, but are simply abstracts of something greater and of weightier significance than themselves.

THE SUB-PLOT. This effect of universality may, of course, be secured in many other ways than these. The use of the sub-plot which we have already noted as a feature of romantic tragedy is to be found here too. The lover pursues a witty mistress, and the servant hunts the no less witty maid. There enters in once more M. Bergson's repetition, inversion, *interférence de séries*, in a slightly differing form. Sir Martin Mar-all is a fool and betrays his own plots; so does Sir John Swallow, his rival. Warner is clever and contrives wondrous devices; he is cheated in the end by Mrs Millisent. The lovers in *A Midsummer Night's Dream* have their quarrels; so have Oberon and Titania. Olivia in *Twelfth Night* is deceived by a girl dressed as a boy; Malvolio is cheated by a fool who pretends to be a clergyman. This tendency toward repetition of the main theme, or even toward parallel plots, each working to much the same end, is to be found in nearly all the romantic comedies; it has become almost a staple part of the comic stock-in-trade. That unconsciously its value was appreciated by the dramatists is proved by the fact that, just as the heroic tragedy of the Restoration exaggerated and made mechanical the true elements of tragic greatness, the Restoration comedy-writers frequently elaborated to a ridiculous degree the qualities hinted at in Shakespeare and in his companions. What did Dryden and D'Avenant do with *The Tempest*? They made Ferdinand love Miranda as in Shakespeare, but they also created a sister for Miranda and provided a lover for her, a boy who had never seen a woman. They gave Ariel a spirit bride in Milcha, and presented Caliban with a sister in Sycorax. Not content with this, they exaggerated those scenes of the sailors, which in Shakespeare hint delicately at the connexion between the rule of Milan and the boorish republic of the mariners, and between both of these and the rule of Prospero. They made the Trinculo and Stephano scenes into a satire against democracy, and deliberately made explicit the comparison only hinted at before. This quality of repetition by means of a sub-plot is to be traced, too, in an exaggerated form in the plays of the Spanish intrigue type. Dryden's *Spanish Fryar* is as good an example as any. The Queen loves the general Torrismond, but is more or less engaged to Bertran; by subterfuge she gains her ends. Elvira, married to old Gomez, loves the colonel Lorenzo, and employs subterfuge to see her lover. A scene between Torrismond and the Queen is followed by a scene between the more comical lovers; and at once there is raised in our minds, subconsciously perhaps, a comparison between the two situations, and not only is the poignancy of the humour in the " Spanish fryar " scenes increased by their opposition to the more serious Court passages, but an atmosphere of inevitability and of generality is created by the repetition of the same theme. Still more noticeable in this play is the *dénouement*. Torrismond turns out at the end to be the son of the imprisoned monarch of the land, and therefore the real heir to the throne. Such a discovery, alone, might have appeared improbable—an isolated fact unrelated to the rest of the world, because of rare occurrence. Dryden, to counter this, has introduced an exactly similar discovery of identity. The lady whom Colonel Lorenzo has been pursuing turns out to be his sister. The two discoveries are made practically at the same moment, and the shock of the two coming together is such that it creates an atmosphere which forms a fitting background for the events of the play. Shakespeare utilized something of the same device in *The Winter's Tale*. The queen, Hermione, has been kept in seclusion for sixteen years—a situation perilous indeed for the dramatist. She is revealed in the last act, but at the same moment it is discovered that her daughter is also alive, and Perdita becomes a princess. Again the close concurrence of the two events creates a spirit, a romantic glow, which aids the playwright in arousing in the minds of the spectators a belief in the events of the play, and, incidentally, in producing this atmosphere of universality. This concurrence, of course, need not always take the form of an identical or almost identical series of events. Thus, in Fletcher's *Wit at Several Weapons* there are two plots, but not of a similar character. In the one Sir Perfidious Oldcraft destines his niece for Sir Gregory Fop. She falls in love with and ultimately marries Cunningham. In this part of the plot occurs Pompey Doodle, who, believing that the niece is in love with him, gives himself airs. The second part of the plot deals entirely with the cheats put upon his father and his cousin Credulous by Witty-pate Oldcraft. Separate as all these events seem to be, there are yet a number of characteristics which bind them together and give them a universal significance. Thus, Pompey Doodle is opposed to and connected with Sir Gregory Fop, while, on the other hand, Credulous is opposed to Pompey Doodle. The whole theme of both plots, moreover, is deception and intrigue. In the one the niece cheats her uncle; in the other this uncle is tricked by his own son. Sir Perfidious Oldcraft forms the bond between the two, and helps to make connected these worlds of deception which, in their turn, by their close opposition render probable the most improbable situations in the play. A somewhat similar series of connected and opposed situations, still more complicated, appears in Fletcher and Massinger's *Custom of the Country*. Here there are more than two plots. In the first place Arnoldo marries Zenocia, and Clodio claims the custom of the country. Arnoldo, his brother Rutilio, and Zenocia flee by boat. Zenocia is captured outside Lisbon, but Arnoldo and Rutilio escape. Here the plot divides into separate spheres of interest. Arnoldo is loved by Hippolyta, is tempted by her, refuses her offers, is cast into the hands of law officers, and is eventually released by her. This Hippolyta, moreover, administers poison to Zenocia, but brings her to life again. Rutilio, meanwhile, has apparently killed Duarte, son of Guiomar, a rich widow; the last, through a promise, shields the supposed murderer. Rutilio later makes offers to Guiomar, is refused, and is cast by her into gaol. At this moment Duarte, who has suffered no serious injury, reveals himself. Now here in these romantic events there are several situations which might have appeared improbable on the stage, and it is quite clearly to be seen that it is precisely these situations which have been duplicated and paralleled. Take the supposed death of Duarte, not impossible certainly, but unlikely. At once there is to be traced the similarity between that and the supposed poisoning of Zenocia. The two are brought to life just as suddenly and just as miraculously. Zenocia's purity is paralleled by Arnoldo's; Clodio's lust by Hippolyta's. Hippolyta makes offers to Arnoldo as Rutilio to Guiomar. Arnoldo is taken up by Hippolyta as Rutilio is by the bawd. There is here, therefore, not merely one parallel, but a whole series of parallels, each one strengthening the atmosphere of the piece and suggesting to the audience the universality of these diverse romantic themes. One further note might be made in regard to these sub-plots and their various connexions. It has been evident from the examples given above that it is not always necessary that the separate parts in the development of a comic theme should be exact parallels; the relation may be one of contrast rather than of similarity. This might still further be illustrated from Beaumont's comedy of *The Woman Hater*. The main plot here deals with the love of the Duke for Oriana, sister of Count Valoret. The lover sees his mistress at the house of Gondarino, who slanders her and leads her to a house of ill-fame. One of the two sub-plots deals with the rascal Palmer's forcing of the prostitute Francissina upon Mercer, a foolish but inoffensive tradesman. Quite obviously in this play there is no parallel; but the purity of Oriana, apparent after the lengthy series of intrigues and duplicities, stands in close contrast to the impurity of Francissina, also immersed in a series of intrigues and duplicities. The contrast, instead of weakening the spirit of the play, gives it a peculiar unity, which possibly might have been lost had the main plot stood in isolation.

EXTERNAL SYMBOLISM. This play, *The Woman Hater*, also presents an example of the use of a certain kind of symbolism, closely related to the symbolism utilized with such effect in tragic themes. The second sub-plot has for its subject the courtier Lazarillo, one who adores strange viands, and it treats of his following the rare fish-head in its wanderings from house to house. This fish-head is the link between the various otherwise disconnected portions of the play. It carries us from palace to hovel, and in its way succeeds in raising a connexion between the Duke, Francissina, and Mercer. It is an external object which has a force beyond itself, a generalizing force, which at one and the same time unifies the play and gives it a sense of universality. This employment of an external object is naturally not of such wide occurrence in comedy as it is in tragedy, but it makes its appearance sporadically throughout the history of this type of drama, and must be included in any analysis of the characteristics of the species. Possibly along with it might be mentioned the utilization of some scene or locality which bears a symbolic relation to the events of the play. Thus, in *The English Traveller* the house which is reputed to be haunted serves as a means of linking together the two plots of the play and of suggesting something besides; in *As You Like It* the forest of Arden, unseen by sensual eyes on the Elizabethan stage but present to imaginative vision, serves as a symbol of the emotions raised in that comedy.

STYLE AND PATHETIC FALLACY. Finally, there are two other methods which must be taken into our account. The first of these is style, and the second is that device which may be named pathetic fallacy. Of the latter examples have already been given from *Much Ado about Nothing* and from *The Merchant of Venice*. Nature, certainly, is not made to sympathize with man's emotions so frequently in comedy as in tragedy, and the marked instances given above are both, it will be noticed, from comedies of a serious, almost tragic, cast; yet the device is not unknown even in plays of the most artificial and most satirical kind. It can be traced all through the

184

lighter productions of Shakespeare, and even makes its appearance in the midst of the town laughter of the drama of the Restoration. In style, too, there are marked differences between the tragic and the comic species. Whereas verse has until recent days been acknowledged as the prime medium for serious plays, prose has ever tended to be the medium for comedy. At the same time blank verse has been freely used not only in Elizabethan comedies, but in comedies of the Restoration and later periods. Song too appears in these, as in tragedies. This sporadic utilization of verse and frequent introduction of song probably marks a desire on the part of the playwrights to rise beyond the level of mere prose. Prose, certainly, is the fitting medium for comic dialogue, and the fact that it was not always retained tends to prove the existence of this subconscious desire.

Comedy, then, like tragedy, must have some universality; it must have some ramifications and connexions beyond the theatre. That universality is attained generally by the classes of the *dramatis personæ*, by the types and by the peculiar nature of the sub-plots, but the dramatists throughout the centuries have made constant, if not always organized and deliberate, use of other devices lying ready to their hands.

(ii) THE SPIRIT OF COMEDY

CLASSIFICATION OF DRAMA. It has already been noted in the first part of this inquiry that there is no sharp line of demarcation between tragedy and comedy, that the two have been freely used together by all but the most precise and the most artificial of the pseudo-classicists, and that there are certain types of tragedy and of comedy which have intimate relations one with another. This being so, it becomes exceedingly difficult to determine accurately not only what are the main characteristics of comedy itself, but whether certain plays are to be included in the one category or in the other. We may easily determine that *Othello* is a tragedy and that *The Way of the World* is a comedy; but there are countless dramas which appear to lack the distinguishing characteristics of the one type or of the other. There are, for example, a number

185

of what may be called problem plays, dating from the days of Shakespeare to our own times, which end in a fairly happy manner, and which yet have none of that sparkle and gaiety which is usually accepted as the prime quality of the comic muse. There are, again, problem plays which end unhappily, but not with death; where gloom hangs over the production from the beginning to the end, but where there is nothing on which we can lay our hands and say, "This is truly tragic emotion." There are the plays of the poetic justice order, where good characters are saved and evil characters are duly disposed of by execution or by murder. There are amorphous plays, such as *The Winter's Tale*, where death comes to characters of perfect honesty and goodness, but where the end is not predominatingly tragic. There are, too, plays, mostly of the time of the early seventeenth century, where a genuinely tragic *motif* runs parallel to a *motif* as genuinely comic. There are plays, such as some of Shakespeare's tragedies, where odd comic scenes, not developing into an ordered sub-plot by themselves, are interposed at infrequent intervals, destroying, according to the neo-classic critics, intensifying, according to the romantic critics, the terror and the awe of the more serious portion. Among these, then, with infinite gradations, there are to be found not any clearly marked divisions, but a whole series of classes, the one merging almost imperceptibly into the other. If we accept for the moment the usual concomitant to a tragedy, the unhappy ending, and the usual concomitant to a comedy, the happy ending, and if at the same time we adopt the use of the term *drame* for a play not sparklingly amusing but yet no tragedy, and if we confine tragi-comedy to those plays where true tragic elements run parallel to true comic elements, we may be able to frame a very rough classification of the majority of plays, always remembering the fact noted above, that the one class can almost imperceptibly fade into the other. This rough classification, imperfect as it may be and of no practical utility for exact critical purposes, may serve at least as a guide in the following investigation.

(1) The tragedies unrelieved by comic elements: *Othello, Œdipus Tyrannus, Ghosts.*

(2) The tragedies with a slight introduction of mirth, never formed into a regular under-plot, and presented mostly for the sake of relief or of contrast: *Macbeth, Hamlet.*

(3) The tragi-comedies where tragic and comic elements have an almost equal balance: *The Changeling.*

(4) The tragi-comedies where a comic under-plot holds a subordinate position: *The English Traveller.*

(5) The tragi-comedies where the comic is the main theme, and the tragic forms an under-plot: *The Winter's Tale, Much Ado about Nothing.*

(6) The poetic justice plays, where good characters are preserved and evil characters are destroyed: *The Conquest of Granada.*

(7) The *drames* which end happily: *The Road to Ruin.*

(8) The *drames* which have not a completely happy solution: *The Merchant of Venice.*

(9) The *drame*-comedies, where a serious plot mingles with comic elements: *Secret Love, The Spanish Fryar, Caste.*

(10) The satiric comedies, where the ending may be, and usually is, of the poetic justice order: *Volpone.*

(11) The comedies, where the ending is happy and where the dialogue and the theme are wholly laughable: *The Way of the World, The Merry Wives of Windsor.*

It is primarily this last category with which we have now to deal, although elements from the others will necessarily enter into our investigation.

From this classification it is seen that, just as tragedy does not depend wholly on an unhappy conclusion, comedy does not depend primarily on the ending of the play; that is to say, a play ending happily, even brightly, is not necessarily a comedy. The comic spirit is embodied in the midst of the dialogue and the situations. A happy ending may be advisable, but it is not the distinguishing characteristic.

DISTINCTION BETWEEN 'DRAME' AND COMEDY. M. Bergson has undoubtedly seized upon the fundamental point of difference when he indicates that the *drame* invariably deals with personalities, while true comedy deals with types and with classes. The plays of Kotzebue, so popular in England at the close of the eighteenth century, are *drames* because, however weak the characterization may be at times, there is at least an attempt to secure individuality of expression. *Measure for Measure* is a *drame* largely because the main figures are not types but persons. *Volpone*, although there is little that is laughable in it, is not a *drame*, because Volpone himself, Corbaccio, Lady Politick Would-be, and the rest are pure types not in any way individualized. *Volpone* we may call a serious or satirical comedy. At the same time there are other characteristics of the *drame* beyond the mere presentation of the *dramatis personæ*. Again, M. Bergson has hinted at another distinction when he lays down the rule that comedy depends upon insensibility on the part of the audience. As soon as we begin to sympathize then we entirely lose the spirit of laughter, and we begin to sympathize when we see before us not types but personalities. If we felt pity for Mercer in *The Woman Hater* then the whole play in which Mercer appeared would cease to have any comic pleasure for us. This partly explains the loss for us to-day of an appreciation for what was risible a couple of centuries ago. Undoubtedly, as man passes from the primitive savage stage of his history to a more developed plane his emotions and his feelings are increased, and that for which he would never have felt pity before becomes an object of tears and of commiseration. Bear-baiting and cock-fighting were sports of the sixteenth and seventeenth centuries, but they would not be sports to the majority of people in the twentieth century. Undoubtedly later ages will look back with surprise and horror on our own popular sport of chasing a wretched fox with full panoply of hound and horn. This increase of sensibility, the product of emotion and of feeling, rapidly kills the available sources of the comic, and may explain not only the lack of appreciation we feel in many Elizabethan comedies, but also the fact that so few true comedies are produced in modern times. Sensibility has always been connected with a moral note, which is expressed usually by means of a problem. A problem of one kind or another lies at the back of every *drame*. It colours *Measure for Measure*, just as it colours any of the modern plays of the same cast. There is never a problem in pure comedy, because the events on the stage, universal as they may be in significance, are never wholly related to the actual conditions of life. In comedy, as personalities are artificialized into types, so the situations are removed so far from the situations of actual life that there is no direct relation established between the two. Any of the marriages in seventeenth-century comedy would, if brought down to the levels of ordinary existence, cease entirely to be comic; and here again arises a question of the appreciation of the older comedy. With the rise of sentiment and of feeling, modern readers and spectators are enabled to get beyond the artificiality and to reduce that artificiality to mortal essence. Just as they get beyond the barriers of the type, so they get beyond the barriers of the situation. It is this that accounts for Addison's strictures on Etherege; it is this that explains the thesis of Macaulay's article on " The Restoration Comedy."

Comedy, then, as such, we find separated from the *drame* by the substitution of type for individual, insensibility for emotion, pure artificiality for moral sentiment (the relating of art to life and the consequent presentation of a problem). We can trace the merging of the one into the other very clearly in the giant person of Falstaff. Falstaff is a comic figure; but, in Shakespeare's hands, he grows out of his world, and, ceasing to be a type, develops into a formal entity of his own. He is individualized, and so steps out of the bounds of comedy into the bounds of serious drama. It is this that accounts for the dissatisfaction we feel at the close of the second part of *Henry IV*. Had Falstaff remained a mere type as Pistol and Bardolph are types, we should have felt no sorrow at his rejection; but as Shakespeare has made him a personality and has treated him as if he had been a purely comic type we feel the incongruity of the situation, and for once are hardly inclined to accept without a murmur the words and the actions of the dramatist-creator. The clash of the two moods or methods produces an apparent disharmony. For the Falstaff of *The Merry Wives*, on the other hand, we feel no pity, because in *The Merry Wives* he is merely a type. The dramatist here could have done anything to him and we should not have cared.

189

SATIRE AND COMEDY. *Drame*, thus, as well as tragedy, has been separated from comedy proper: tragedy as being distinguished by an unhappy ending and a plot arousing the feelings of awe and of majesty; *drame* as dealing with emotion and with personality. There remains for us still the analysis of the characteristics of comedy itself. Already there has been raised a problem in *Volpone*. *Volpone* is a comedy, yet it is not wholly laughable. Is laughter, then, not necessary for comedy? Is the risible not the *sine qua non* in this type of drama? The problem raised by such a question as this is undoubtedly a vital one, and hits deep at the essential qualities of the comic species. Here obviously there must be made some distinction between satire and pure laughter.[1] Satire may certainly be laughable, as, for example, in the opening lines of Dryden's *Mac Flecknoe*:

> All humane things are subject to decay,
> And, when Fate summons, Monarchs must obey:
> This *Fleckno* found, who, like *Augustus*, young
> Was call'd to Empire and had govern'd long:
> In Prose and Verse was own'd, without dispute
> Through all the realms of Non-sense, absolute.
> This aged Prince now flourishing in Peace,
> And blest with issue of a large increase,
> Worn out with business, did at length debate
> To settle the Succession of the State;
> And pond'ring which of all his Sons was fit
> To Reign, and wage immortal War with Wit,
> Cry'd, 'tis resolv'd; for Nature pleads that He
> Should onely rule, who most resembles me:
> *Shadwell* alone my perfect image bears,
> Mature in dullness from his tender years;
> *Shadwell* alone of all my Sons is he
> Who stands confirm'd in full stupidity.
> The rest to some faint meaning make pretence,
> But *Shadwell* never deviates into sense.

These words, assuredly, may call more than a smile to our lips, and, if recited in a theatre, might give rise to a roar of merriment; but fundamentally their object, save in certain witty turns of phrase, is not primarily to arouse a laugh or even a smile. Their object is to cast derision upon some person or upon some thing. The satirist, however, is not a

---

[1] There is an interesting study of satire in J. Y. T. Greig's volume on *The Psychology of Laughter and Comedy* (1923).

moralist in the sense that Steele is a moralist. The true moralist appeals nearly always to the feelings and not to the intellect, and the satirist rarely plays upon the emotions. The satires of Juvenal are hard, presenting to the reader a series of pictures addressed to the reason. We are not called upon to sympathize with anything or to feel emotions of any kind in *Volpone*. Swift's satires appeal entirely to the intellect. Thackeray is a satirist because of his extraordinary piercing eye and brain. Nor does the satirist attack vice simply from the moral point of view. Steele will inveigh against duelling; Moore will attack gambling; Holcroft will attack horse-racing—all through the medium of the emotions and because the sentiments of the writers have been aroused by pity for one ruined, or by religious feelings. The satirist lashes vice largely because of its folly; and he lashes, besides vice, objects which are not necessarily in the least immoral. Thus Swift may include vice in his satirical pictures in *Gulliver's Travels*; but he passes far beyond vice as such. His real object, as it is the real object of every satirist, is to ridicule follies. It is only because follies when exaggerated often become vicious and immoral that the writer of satire becomes in many cases apparently a moralist. Wycherley is no moralist in *The Plain Dealer*, although he has frequently been made out to be such. What he attacks is not the immoralities of his time, but the follies—the fops and the simpletons and the would-be wits.

The division between satire and pure comedy is, as is evident, excessively slight. Satire may be so mild that it can barely be detected under its mask of laughter, for satire fades in some of its forms imperceptibly into both wit and humour. Still, the fact remains that we really do not laugh at the satirical as such; we laugh at the purely comic qualities with which it is accompanied or in which it is enclosed. The purest of comedy, however, usually rules satire in any form out of its province. The appeal of this pure comedy is solely to the laughing force within us. When comedy is thus separated from the moral sense and even from satire which lashes follies, including vices among these follies, it is evident that there is little truth in the old claim that " Comedy is an imitation of the common errors of our life, which he representeth, in the most ridiculous and scornefull sort that may be. . . . [So that] there is no man liuing, but by the force trueth hath in nature, no sooner seeth these men play their parts, but wisheth them in *Pistrinum*." [1] This is purely the argument of a poetry-lover who has had to meet the attacks of a misopoetic moralist. To us to-day it is plain that there is not the slightest hint of this in the purest comedy. If we regard types as types, if we do not sympathize with their good qualities, then we have no hope of scorning their evil qualities. Bardolph is laughable, Pistol is laughable, Sir Martin Mar-all is laughable; but we assuredly never for a moment wish any of the three " in *Pistrinum*." The satiric spirit may at times become sufficiently strong in a comic dramatist to make him ridicule certain follies, but this is apart from his main aim, which is to make the audience laugh. Of direct morality in comedy, as in tragedy, there is absolutely none.

THE SOCIAL ASPECT OF COMEDY. At the same time, of indirect morality of a sort there is a considerable amount in certain kinds of comedy. Morality ultimately springs from social conventions, and laughter is predominatingly social. We do not laugh overmuch when we are by ourselves, or, if we do, we imagine the jest shared with some other person or persons. A witty remark read in solitude in a play may attract our intellect, but we do not laugh at it; a humorous character may appeal to us, but it will not make us laugh as the same character would do in a theatre. Laughter is essentially a social thing, and the richest laughter rises out of the group-mentality. Laughter, however, as we have seen, is in most of its forms directed against eccentricity of some one type or another. To such an extent is this true, indeed, that M. Bergson has declared that insociability on the part of the object of laughter is a necessary condition. While this may be rather a straining of a particular thesis, it must be admitted that in the majority of cases it is true. Laughter, then, becomes an attack by society as a whole, or by a particular portion of society, on what it regards as anti-social, something out of the way and possibly provocative of harm.[2] This laughter, however, is never

---

[1] Sidney, *Apologie for Poetrie, ed. cit.*, p. 45.
[2] That this closely approaches satire is obvious. The distinction might be made that, while satire is conscious, this cognate characteristic of the comic spirit is largely unconscious.

directed against anything masterful or more powerful than the ordinary. The laughter of society goes out only toward that which falls lower than the average mentality or the average custom. Just as greatness in the *dramatis personæ* of a tragedy presupposes a lack of pity in the audience, so greatness of type in a comedy rules out the possibility of laughter arising at that type, except, indeed, in the few cases where that type is a wit, when the laughter is not at, but with, him. When the mentality or the habits of the type vary from the ordinary levels of social conventionality, and when that type is felt to be not greater than the average, then laughter is really aroused, and is, in fact, the unacknowledged reproof of society. A miser is anti-social, but because of his meanness he becomes lower than the usual level, and is, if presented as a type, a laughable figure. If he is presented as a person, on the other hand, the laughter cannot possibly be raised; we could never dream of laughing, or of having the opportunity for laughing, at Simon Eyre. So conceited folly is anti-social, and society will laugh with indifferent merriment at the clownish airs of a Pompey Doodle and at the self-assurance of a Sir Martin Mar-all.

From this point of view, comedy as the artistic medium for the expression of laughter, having these distinctly social qualities, may be regarded from a quite definitely utilitarian standpoint; but, for the most part, this social quality in laughter has not only been largely lost in more fully developed communities, but is never consciously in the mind of any particular dramatist at the moment of creation. Comedy exists not for any purpose it may have, but in and for itself; it does not even require to have any of that sense of high morality which we found to be necessary in tragedy. It may be that the morally purer comic dramatists are those who will most be remembered, because of our sensibility and our feeling of moral fitness, but laughter exists independently of any outward considerations, religious, moral, or other. It is the laughter we look for in comedy, not the sense of moral right or of moral wrong, not the purpose or the significance of the play.

THE SOURCES OF THE COMIC. The source of the risible is a subject on which have been written not a few theses, brilliant as well as dull. Fundamentally different these theses are, but in each of them is some indication of the truth. In probably not a single one of them are all the reasons of our laughter fully analysed. Aristotle evidently believed the risible to lie in degradation; men, he says, are in comedy made worse than they are and consequently become objects of merriment.[1] Ben Jonson, too, noted that "what either in the words or sense of an author, or in the language or actions of men, is awry or depraved does strangely stir mean affections, and provoke for the most part to laughter." Kant, and after him a whole series of critics and of philosophers, from Schopenhauer to Hazlitt, have discovered the secret of laughter to lie in the incongruity of two facts, two ideas, two words, or two associations. "The essence of the laughable," declares the last-mentioned writer, "is the incongruous, the disconnecting of one idea from another, or the jostling of one feeling against another." This comes to practically the same as Sidney's judgment that "laughter almost ever commeth of things most disproportioned to ourselves and nature."[2] M. Bergson, going farther and taking this view in his philosophical sweep of the subject, has devised another theory based in reality on both those referred to; namely, that the conditions of comedy are insociability on the part of the object of laughter, insensibility on the part of the laugher, and a certain automatism in the situation, in the words, or in the character that appears ludicrous.[3] This theory M. Bergson has traced out along the three lines of repetition, inversion, and *interférence de séries*, seeing in each a certain reduction of the living thing to a machine-like *raideur* or inelasticity.

There is much that can be said for the brilliant French philosopher's theory; yet it seems not quite comprehensive. The truth lies in a higher harmony, with the introduction of perhaps one or two other explanations for special species of merriment. Degradation, incongruity, automatism, of course, may mean much or little, may include much or little, according

[1] This view he puts forward not only in the *Poetics*, but also in the *Nicomachean Ethics*. Plato's theory, enunciated in the *Philebus* and since elaborated by later critics, that the comic is fundamentally malicious should be taken into account here. The same view is expressed by Jonson, in his *Discoveries*, by Molière, and by Hobbes.

[2] *Ed. cit.*, p. 66.

[3] The comic for Bergson always derives from "something mechanical encrusted on the living."

to the interpretation we put upon the words; but if these words are taken at their ordinary value the theories to which they give the titles would, even when taken together, hardly seem to explain all the manifestations of the laughable. There is, for example, the laughter that arises at times out of an exceedingly solemn and serious situation, not because of some incident or word or person that may appear incongruous, but because of some mood working within us. There are not, I presume, many people who on some such occasion when they themselves felt serious and even sad have not broken into a smile, if not into open laughter. It may be that there is subconsciously an incongruity presented either between the normal mood of man and this exceptional solemnity, or between the solemnity and some unacknowledged idea or reminiscence which comes dimly to the consciousness and arouses the laughter; but it would appear more probable that the merriment comes straight from the sacred or solemn occasion itself, that the smile or the laugh is an unconscious attempt of our only half-conscious selves to escape from the bonds of the solemn and the sacred. This merriment at sacred things or on solemn occasions is a spontaneous merriment; it is aroused apparently by none of those springs of the risible which have been indicated above. This spontaneous laughter must, naturally, be carefully distinguished from the laughter that may arise as a secondary result of it. The contrast of the spontaneous laugh and the solemnity of the occasion may cause others, through the sense of incongruity, themselves to burst into merriment, merriment that is clearly explainable under the theory of Hazlitt. The essential source of the spontaneous laugh would seem to be a desire for liberation, liberation from the restraints of society, and as such it is entirely the opposite of the social laughter analysed by M. Bergson. What is it that makes us laugh at a reference to the indecent? There may, of course, be a double reason for merriment expressed at a ' smoking-room ' story, or at a Restoration comedy. There may be wit in the utterance, or there may be incongruity of a rougher sort; but even a tale or a dialogue that is not essentially witty or incongruous may cause merriment. There is nothing here of automatism; other reasons must be sought for if we are to explain it aright. Mr Sully has suggested that the reasons for this laughter lie in a breach of rule or of order and in a loss of dignity, but even these do not seem to meet the case. The real cause would appear to lie in the sense of liberation which the laugh itself involves. It is the liberation of the natural man from the ties and conventions of society. In the same way, we may explain the laughter which greeted in the Middle Ages the appearance of the Devil-character of the mystery plays. There could be little sense of incongruity in this and none of automatism; it was the laugh of liberation, just as the Feast of Fools was a whole festival of merriment, celebrating liberation from the too strict bonds of the Church.

INCONGRUITY. Degradation, incongruity, automatism, and the sense of liberation are all sources of laughter, and these are by no means exhaustive. Of them all, however, undoubtedly the greatest is incongruity. It is the incongruity of Jove in Amphitryon's shape, of Mercury in the form of a serving-man, that provides the prime comic essence of Dryden's play. It is the discrepancy between the idea and the object which provides the cause of laughter in *L'Étourdi*. It is the incongruity between two ideas that presents to us the twin qualities of wit and of humour.

In another chapter it was stated that mere eccentricity is not comic unless it be opposed to or contrasted with something that is normal. No comedy can be a true comedy unless there is presented alongside of the humorous situation, words, or character something that is more or less ordinary. A comedy full of eccentric types ceases largely to be a cause of merriment. This explains the fact that in all our finest comedies we find as a central pivot a pair or a quartette of *dramatis personæ* who, although not closely individualized, are by no means absurd, and around them a body of mere eccentrics—characters who take their colouring from their contrast with the central figures. In *Twelfth Night* the Duke, Sebastian, Viola, and Olivia form the centre of the picture; Sir Toby Belch and Sir Andrew Aguecheek are ridiculous because seen in their light. In *A Midsummer Night's Dream* Theseus and Hippolyta are the centre; the artisans are absurd in comparison with them. It is noticeable in this connexion that in nearly every comedy of

196

the older period we find two sharply differentiated series of names given to the *dramatis personæ*. In the plays cited above Aguecheek, Belch, Snout, Bottom, Starveling have ' humours ' names; Viola, Olivia, Theseus, and the rest have ordinary names of mankind. *The Way of the World* has Mirabel and Millamant, beside Witwoud, Petulant, Waitwell, Foible, and Mincing. *The Provok'd Husband* has Manly and Lady Grace, and around them Sir Francis Wronghead, Count Basset, John Moody, Mrs Motherly, and Mrs Trusty. In modern times this tendency toward the introduction of ' humours ' names is not so apparent, but the same division is there. Thus, in Mr Lennox Robinson's *The Far-off Hills*—to take but one example—the normality of the young nephew and his middle-aged aunt is opposed to the eccentricity of nearly all the other figures in the comedy.

The endeavour to institute a comparison between two sets of characters is of the essence of the comic conflict; it is a feature of modern drama just as it was a feature of the drama of ancient Rome. The *Eunuchus* of Terence has Chremes and Phædria, Antipho and Chærea, with the opposed characters of Gnatho and Thraso and Parmeno. *Heauton Timorumenos* presents Clitipho and Clinia as opposed to Chremes and Menedemus, Dromo and Sostrata. So in modern times we find the average intelligence placed in strict juxtaposition to the equivalents of the old fathers and the cheating servants and the vaunting soldiers of the ancient stage.

Beyond the mere enumeration of the causes of merriment we must note that laughter can be caused both consciously and unconsciously, and that it may take on varying shapes and forms in accordance as it is mingled with non-humorous matter. Wit is thus, as we have already seen, purely conscious; the wit sets himself to raise a laugh. He plays with words; his fancy works swiftly, and out of the movement of his fancy he orders phrases and ideas in such a manner that others laugh along with him. The absurd, on the other hand, is purely unconscious. We laugh at *l'étourdi*, but he himself is quite innocent of the cause of our merriment. This distinction between wit and the absurd is, naturally, an important one, for it completely separates the spirit of *Twelfth Night* from

197

the spirit of *The Way of the World*; the two, to all intents and purposes, belong to separate and almost unrelated types of literary composition. In many ways *Twelfth Night* is far more nearly allied to some species of early tragedy than to the later Restoration comedy.

HUMOUR. A distinction must also be made between wit or the absurd and what is usually known as humour. The word ' humour ' has, of course, had an exceedingly varied history from its inception as of the kin of ' humid,' through its Jonsonian sense in the seventeenth century, to its modern, rather indefinite signification. Humour is not the same as the ludicrous; humour in some of its forms barely makes us smile. We can readily in concrete examples separate it both from wit and from the absurd, yet it is difficult to place our finger on the precise points wherein it differs from these. " Humour," decides Hazlitt, " is the describing the ludicrous as it is in itself; wit is the exposing it, by comparing or contrasting it with something else." This, from the point of view of comic creation, is certainly true; but it does not explain why one character or one phrase is styled humorous and another witty; nor does it explain wherein lies the difference between the ludicrous and humour. M. Bergson, proceeding farther, discovered in humour the inverse of irony. In irony we pretend to believe what we do not believe; in humour we pretend to disbelieve what we actually believe. This carries us considerably nearer the goal of definition; but even this theory is not of universal application. It may explain some—nay, many—forms of humour, but it leaves quite a number totally unaccounted for. The most thorough and the most far-reaching analysis yet presented to us is undoubtedly that given by Mr Sully in his *Essay on Laughter*. His words may be quoted in full.

> These contrasts [between ordinary laughter and the laughter that arises from humour] point clearly enough to certain positive characteristics of the moods of humour. A quiet survey of things, at once playful and reflective; a mode of greeting amusing shows which seems in its moderation to be both an indulgence in the sense of fun and an expiation for the rudeness of such indulgence; an outward, expansive movement of the spirits met and retarded by a cross-current of something like kindly thoughtfulness; these clearly reveal themselves as some of its dominant traits.

Humour is, says Mr Sully, distinctly a sentiment, yet at the same time it is markedly intellectual.

These qualities of restraint, of reflection, of pity, of kindliness are assuredly the distinguishing marks of the humorous temperament. The presentation of the ludicrous can be cruel and coarse, as in the comedies of Shadwell; wit can be biting and cynical, as in the comedies of Etherege and of Congreve; humour is always mellow and generally refined. It is certainly intellectual in that it appears only after a large and comprehensive view of the world; its greatest exponents have nearly all been men of intense intellectuality; but, at the same time, they have been men of feeling. If insensibility is demanded for pure laughter sensibility is rendered necessary for true humour. Humour, we shall find, is often related to melancholy of a peculiar kind; not a fierce melancholy, but a melancholy that arises out of pensive thoughts and a brooding on the ways of mankind. Had Congreve written of Don Quixote he would have made of the Knight de la Mancha a figure larger than, but on the same scale as, his own Petulant or Witwoud. He would have had not the slightest sympathy for the eccentric medievalist. Cervantes, on the other hand, being a humorist, has laughed, but his laughter is tinged with and mellowed by sympathy and even by a certain melancholy of spirit. So far M. Bergson's theory is right—that the humorist often takes delight in poking fun at that which he holds most sacred or at that for which he has a secret sympathy. The absurd character puts forward all his follies, unconsciously, to the world; the man of wit sneers and mocks at everything which is different from himself; the humorist is himself an eccentric who sees the fun of his eccentricity. This fact is very clearly to be seen in the humorous stories of such nationalities as the Scots and the Irish. The Scotsman and the Irishman delight in telling tales against themselves or against their own country, not because they despise their countries, but because they love their countries, even although a sense of humour displays to them their native eccentricities. Humour, therefore, is a union of unconscious with conscious laughter. Wit is the laughter of the ordinary man or of the intellectual man directed at others abnormal; humour is the laughter of the eccentric directed against himself.

In this brief survey of some of the main theories regarding the laughable we have found, first, that there are three cardinal reasons for an object's being ludicrous—degradation, incongruity, automatism; and alongside of these a number of subsidiary causes, such as the sense of liberation; second, that the objects of ordinary comic laughter are unconscious of their ridiculousness; and, third, that there are two species of the risible, wit and humour, which lie apart from the rest in being conscious and, in the case of humour, sympathetic. In the world of the theatre these various species of the laughable are presented in five main ways—through the physical attributes of the *dramatis personæ*, through the mentalities of these *dramatis personæ*, through the situation, through the manners, and through the words. A rapid survey of concrete instances may close this section.

LAUGHTER ARISING FROM PHYSICAL ATTRIBUTES. The laughter that arises from merely physical attributes of the *dramatis personæ* in a comedy is obviously of the lowest possible kind. The music-hall comedian and the clown in the circus know how to raise coarse laughter by this means; but no great comedy will depend upon it for more than an infinitesimal part of its merriment. The principle of degradation provides for physical deformities of a laughable type. Bardolph's nose is a deformity that is meant to cause laughter in *The Merry Wives of Windsor*, and it succeeds to a certain extent. This source of the comic, however, is seriously restricted not only by the fact that even the most unintelligent will recognize its low character, but by the fact that pity forbids us to laugh at genuine deformities. We could not laugh at a blind man or at a man on crutches, unless in such a case as, for example, that of an elderly man suffering from gout hopping in rage over the boards of the theatre. Here, however, the merriment arises not merely from the deformity as such, but from the facts that the man for a moment has been made into a mere object without the control of his own limbs, and that we realize the ' deformity ' has arisen from the over-indulgence of the victim himself. Deformity of another type appears in, let us say, the affectedly ridiculous dress of Malvolio or of the Gallicized fops of the Restoration period. These, taken along with Bardolph's nose, may lead toward a certain generalizing in regard to this type of the laughable. We laugh not so much at the mere physical deformities as at the deformities brought about by mental action or by foolish habit. Bardolph's nose arises from his propensity for drink, just as does the gouty foot of the old gentleman; Malvolio was not ridiculously garbed by nature, but by himself.

The principle of degradation, also, is to be seen partly in certain characters, partly in certain situations, of a type such as is presented in *The Spanish Fryar*. There the jealous, conceited little moneylender is beaten and ill-treated; he has suffered a loss of dignity, and the degradation arouses our merriment. Of the same type is the degradation of the shrew or of the ' tamer tamed '; a degradation, however, that is not wholly physical, but arises partly out of the situation.

Physical incongruity is also a rich source of rather coarse merriment. The laughter or the smile that may come from the sight of a very tall woman alongside of her very diminutive husband is due to this. The sight of Titania, frail and ethereal, beside the ass-eared Bottom is equally risible, and for the same cause. It is because of this that in the music-halls of to-day we frequently find the comedians going in pairs; one excessively tall man going with an abnormally tiny one. Falstaff sails forward in his bulk with his little page following him, the contrast arousing our mirth because of the incongruity of the pair.

An example of physical automatism might be taken from *Sir Martin Mar-all*. There Sir John Swallow and Moody are placed on the top of several stools, one set on the other. They who have had most say in the moving forward of the plot have suddenly been made no better than machines, objects incapable of movement unless the other characters come to their assistance. The situation in itself is laughable, but the greater part of the merriment arises out of the physical positions of the two characters. Of a similar nature is the powerlessness of Katharina in *The Taming of the Shrew*: by her husband she has been reduced from a thinking being, independent and capable of action, into an automatic machine.

In surveying these scattered examples of laughter arising

from physical causes, it is evident that we cannot always diagnose exactly the immediate source of our laughter, or, rather, that that laughter may take its rise from a variety of causes operating all at the one time. Thus physical appearance, character, situation, and words may all influence us, and automatism join with the sense of degradation. This is particularly true of physical attributes and of character.

LAUGHTER ARISING FROM CHARACTER. In character we may find one of the richest and highest media for the arousing of laughter possible to the dramatist. Although comedy does not deal with personalities and with individualities as does tragedy, yet types of character form its basis. It is the presence of character that largely differentiates true comedy from farce.

Mental deformity is obviously one of the handiest themes for the comic playwright. This deformity may or may not be a vice, but it must be a folly. The stupid conceit of Sir Martin Mar-all or of Malvolio, the porcine stupidity of Dogberry and Verges, the irritating and irritated vanity of Petulant, all in a variety of ways give the dramatists opportunity for the introduction of the risible. M. Bergson has related all of these to his theory of the automatic, averring that our laughter comes, not from the sense of the mental deformity, but from the sense that the particular figure is, as it were, in the hands of his deformity, that none of those persons mentioned above are men, but merely machines in the control of their 'humours.' It does not, of course, precisely matter which name we give to it, but the truth probably lies between the two theories. It is possible that our laughter arises from a double source, and that the automatism and the deformity are both present to our minds subconsciously in the very midst of our laughter. Mr Sully has well pointed out in connexion with this laughter arising out of the sight of mental deformity that our laugh is not by any means a moral laugh. Our merriment is not by any means confined to vices; it is directed against eccentricities, against extremes of any kind. It is applied, therefore, as heartily to virtues in an exaggerated form as to vices.

Mental incongruity is another prime source of merriment, either incongruity within one character (inner conflict) or between two characters (outward conflict). A typical scene

202

of the inner incongruity is presented by Shakespeare when he brings in Sir Hugh Evans, stripped and preparing for a duel with Dr Caius. We know Evans for a mild and inoffensive schoolmaster, and the sight of him here, alternately lunging at an imaginary enemy and falling on his knees for fear, is truly laughable. More commonly, as we have seen, the incongruity is presented not as an inner conflict, but as a contrast between two eccentric figures. The comic characters in the plays of the manners school usually enter in pairs. Petulant is opposed to Witwoud; Sir Martin Mar-all is opposed to Sir John Swallow. So in Shakespeare there are Autolycus and the Clown; Stephano and Trinculo; Touchstone and Jacques. Here obviously there is a very mixed cause for our laughter, the characters contributing something in themselves, much more in conjunction, with words and situation playing almost equal parts.

Mental automatism may perhaps be differentiated in a way from mental deformity. Sir Martin Mar-all's conceit is a true mental deformity, but his mere repetition of certain phrases —" In fine " being the most famous—is not exactly a deformity, but a piece of sheer mechanical utterance. The charwoman's " Me teeth are raging " in *The Far-off Hills* may be taken as another example. It is possible, of course, that no strict division can be made between the two, but there is apparently a slight variation between the confusion of words, such as we find in Mrs Malaprop, due to true mental deformity, and this automatic repetition of familiar, if often meaningless, phrases.

LAUGHTER ARISING FROM SITUATION. The situation, however, as forming the basis of the plot of any comedy, presents to the dramatist possibly the very fullest opportunity for the introduction of the laughable. The physical person and the character are nearly always shown not isolated, but in the midst of some other persons, in a situation itself of an amusing character. On the other hand, it must be remembered that mere comedy of situation will lead to nothing but farce; that, although an audience looks to situation far more than to character or to words, situation offers an opportunity only for the introduction of a very limited kind of laughter.

Countless are the situations based upon the principle of

degradation. Several examples of these have already been cited above. Stripping the dignity from a set of circumstances, dragging down the seriousness of a situation to trivial realms, will always awaken our merriment. It is amusing to watch the situations in which Falstaff finds himself with the " merry wives "; it is amusing to see the pert Malvolio divested of his dignity and immured in a mad-cell. We could pass through the whole range of English comic drama and discover but a small percentage of comedies which have not in one way or another made use of this device.

The situation of incongruous circumstances is no less common. When Theseus is faced with the play of Pyramus and Thisbe the situation is incongruous. There is a certain incongruity in the second act of *The Way of the World* when we discover Mirabel walking off with Mrs Fainall, and Fainall with Mrs Marwood, both for the purpose of upbraiding their mistresses. This incongruity evidently may arise out of the events themselves, or out of the conflict between the character and the events, or out of the contrast of two persons, who may be both eccentric, or one eccentric and the other normal, or both normal. The example given from *The Way of the World* may be taken as representing the last-mentioned. Incongruity arising out of the normal and the eccentric occurs in the famous serenade scene of *Sir Martin Mar-all*; and a scene of two eccentric characters in conflict is that duel episode already mentioned in *The Merry Wives of Windsor*. The variations in which any of these may actually appear are, quite obviously, infinite.

A situation involving M. Bergson's theory of automatism depends, on the contrary, almost entirely on the events. The characters are in the grip of the machine, powerless to alter or to shape their destiny. In this way the repetition of the same or of a similar scene leads toward a sense of the mechanical. There is this effect in the second act of *The Way of the World*, just as there is in several scenes of *The Comedy of Errors*. Here, too, enters what M. Bergson has styled the *interférence de séries*, the placing of one theme upon another. This method of securing laughter has not, probably, been so fully utilized in comedy as it has been in the novel, possibly because of the difficulty of presenting in comedy the two series in an equally elaborated form. Mark Twain can obtain a finely ludicrous effect in *The Innocents Abroad* from the superimposition on the relics of ancient Rome of the modern American vitality and temperament. National humour and the genuinely absurd in situation and in character are in this book too, but the main source of the laughter in it comes from its general scheme. This *interférence de séries* has certainly been used by a number of comic dramatists, but always in a somewhat modified manner. It appears in the first part of *Henry IV*, where the Falstaff scenes are, as it were, superimposed upon the scenes of genuine heroism. It appears similarly in the contrast between the artisans and the noble Theseus in *A Midsummer Night's Dream*, and it appears in *Much Ado about Nothing*, where the Dogberry and Verges episodes are run into the episodes of Leonato and his company.

The sense of liberation occurs in comic situation also, but, because of its often cynical and blasphemous effect, tends to appear only in restricted periods of dramatic output. The indecent situations in the Restoration comedy are laughable when regarded from this point of view; they are nauseous if regarded from the standpoint of strict morality. Dryden's satirical references to the Church and to Deity in *The Spanish Fryar* are amusing if we do not look upon them from the definitely religious aspect. Both the one and the other are escapes—escapes from the trammels of civilization and of the Church. The natural man attempts in them to free himself for a moment from the fetters that have changed him from a savage to a clothed being in the midst of a series of laws and customs and conventions. Situations of this kind, however, are dangerous, and nearly all dramatists, except the *naïve* playwrights of the Middle Ages and the cynical playwrights of the age of the Restoration, have neglected them. They may occur in modern drama, but only in an exceedingly restricted and circumscribed form. As civilization advances it is probably more and more careful to prevent these sudden moments of liberation through reference to things which it habitually conceals.

LAUGHTER ARISING FROM MANNERS. Along with the physical appearance, with the character, and with the situation goes what we may style manners. There is a *comique de mœurs* as well as a *comique de situation* and a *comique de caractère*. The manners, of course, are often expressed through the medium of the situation and of the words, and they themselves are reflections of character, but very often they stand separately in a different category from the others.

Deformity of manners might be instanced by a lack of *savoir faire*. The awkwardness of a certain type of character in a circle of easy and refined figures is amusing; just as the awkwardness of a Society lady in a circle of more natural but less polished working-class women is amusing. The lack of ease displayed by a Conservative addressing a Labour club and by a working man addressing a circle of more educated persons have both in them, when stripped of political or sentimental feelings, something of the ludicrous. The manners are not exactly deformed, but they are below the level, or out of the level, of the particular society or of the particular part of society.

Incongruity, of course, is present here as well, and it is difficult to say exactly where the one begins and the other ends. The introduction of the sailor Ben in Congreve's comedy, for example, is incongruous, and most of our merriment arises from the sense of this incongruity; part, however, certainly comes from the sense that his manners are not the manners of the people with whom he comes in contact. The laughter of the primitive peasant or of the civilized man at the manners of a foreigner may depend to a certain extent on incongruity, but more perhaps on the very difference in the manners themselves. The numerous introductions of foreign types, therefore, in comedy rely for their humorous effects partly on the one and partly on the other.

Added to this there is automatism. Here the effect may take one of several forms. The mechanical manners may be due to character, as in the case of Ben. They may, on the contrary, be due only indirectly to character; they may be taken directly from imitation of other manners. Sir Martin Mar-all is comic because he has attempted to adopt the airs and the actions of the French; Sir Harry Wildair, in a similar way, although he is no fool as the other is, has something ludicrous about him because of his imitated customs. The manners of a character, however, may derive wholly, not from his own character or from any conscious imitation, but from the society in which he has been brought up. A lawyer who cannot escape from the atmosphere of the law; a doctor who cannot escape from the spirit of medicine; a professor who cannot escape from the university environment; the old man who cannot see anything good in the newer age—all of these are amusing because in each case the man has become a machine at the mercy of those feelings and manners which have been placed upon him by his surroundings.

LAUGHTER ARISING FROM WORDS. Finally, among the species of the unconsciously humorous in the theatre, there is the laughable that arises from the dialogue—*le comique de mots*. This comic spirit derived from the words in a play shares in point of importance a position equal to that held by character and by situation. The word reveals the character; it explains and intensifies the ridiculousness of a situation. Comedy of a type may exist without words, like the mimetic pantomime, where physical appearance and gesture made up for the silence of the piece; but such comedy must by its very nature be not only temporary, but largely farcical. The gesture can express but an infinitesimal part of the thoughts and of the desires of the figures upon the stage.

The deformed word, if we may speak of such, finds its typical example in the speeches of Mrs Malaprop, but Mrs Malaprop is only one of a number of characters who, before her, spoke in a similar strain. This deformity of language, naturally, combines with incongruity and other forms of the laughable for its full effect. The most amusing of Mrs Malaprop's phrases are those where there is not merely a simple deformation of the word, but where the deformed word has itself a significance wholly incongruous, where there is raised a contrast between the idea (the word that was meant) and the object (the word as it was uttered). The merely deformed is not always even amusing, either in words or in persons, and the finer dramatists have always endeavoured to add to the effect by blending together this and some other forms of the comic.

Incongruity of words is, as must be evident, still more ridiculous than mere maltreating of them. Unconscious incongruity must here, of course, be carefully distinguished from conscious incongruity, which is wit. The introduction of, let us say, a hearty swear-word in a company of refined and delicate maiden ladies will have an incongruous effect, but it may be perfectly unconscious in the sense that it springs naturally from the lips of some character innocent of the dissonance he creates. So there is incongruity of words and of situation in Farquhar's *Constant Couple*, where the words of one sphere of life are uttered to a person of another sphere, the one character not understanding the meaning of the other. Wit and unconscious word-humour may, of course, meet together, as in that scene of *The Double Dealer* between Careless and Sir Paul Plyant:

> CARELESS: Alas-a-day! this is a lamentable story; my Lady must be told on't; she must, i'faith, Sir Paul; 'tis an injury to the world.
> SIR PAUL: Ah! would to heaven you would, Mr Careless; you are mightily in her favour.
> CARELESS: I warrant you; what, we must have a son some way or other.
> SIR PAUL: Indeed, I should be mightily bound to you if you could bring it about, Mr Careless.

There are here quite a number of reasons for our laughter at such a passage. There is the innuendo in the situation itself; there is the wit of Careless, conscious and assured; and there is the incongruity in the words of Sir Paul between what he says and what he actually thinks.

Incongruity of words, in a manner somewhat similar to the above, is also utilized largely by comic dramatists in a very special form. Countless are the situations in comedies ancient and modern where two humorous characters have failed to understand one another. There is not here the contrast between wit and the ridiculous, but between two ridiculous elements, the real fun arising out of the incongruity of the words utilized by each. Examples of this are common from the days of Shakespeare to the days of Sheridan.

Automatism in the use of words is closely bound up with

what is generally known as *le mot de caractère*, the word that expresses the mentality of a particular person, but it may at times be differentiated from that. As we have seen above, the " In fine " of Sir Martin Mar-all is in a way such a mechanical phrase, and his insistence on the " plot " is another. Occasionally in a comedy one word or one phrase occurs again and again in varying senses and forms, as if it were a machine with a motion of its own driving over the characters themselves. Mere automatism of this sort, however, is rare, and usually, as in the example of character and of situation noted above, it is bound up with incongruity and with kindred sources of the risible.

WIT. This consideration of the unconscious humour of words leads us to a glance at the conscious variety of the same species. The *bon mot*, as we have seen, depends upon incongruity, but it is sharply differentiated from the unconscious incongruity of words. *Bon mot*, *esprit*, wit—these are the moods and expressions of a highly intelligent man playing with his fancies, and with the discrepancy and incongruity of his fancies, for the delectation of himself and of others. The playwright, of course, the creator, may be exercising the faculty of wit all through the composition of his particular work; but wit in the theatre appears only in certain clearly defined characters of a highly intellectual and fanciful cast of thought. The prime example of such is the figure of Mirabel. His *bons mots* do not depend on situation, and only indirectly do they express his own character. Fainall and he play with words as they would play a game at cards:

> FAINALL: Not at all; Witwoud grows by the knight, like a medlar grafted on a crab: one will melt in your mouth, and t'other set your teeth on edge; one is all pulp, and the other all core.
>
> MIRABEL: So one will be rotten before he be ripe; and the other will be rotten without ever being ripe at all.

All these words and fancies are independent of time and of place and of character. They are the deliberate gambollings of a mind swift and rich in fancy, tutored by long practice to ease and facility of expression.

Although this wit is one of the highest excellences in a comedy it must be confessed that often, especially when it appears in excess, it may ruin the true comic spirit in the theatre. The dangers in its use lie in the facts that the *esprit* or *bon mot* may be placed in the mouths of characters wholly unfitted to give expression to genuine wit, and that the dramatist, in his continual endeavour to keep up the sparkle and brilliance, may become in the end merely wearisome and monotonous. We cannot fail to appreciate the diamond-like quality of *The Way of the World* or of *The Importance of being Earnest*, but in both we feel there is something lacking. There is lacking not only true delineation of character, but situation of a truly amusing kind. All the wit is on the surface; it does not penetrate deeply into the core of the drama. What is the plot of *The Way of the World*? There is none. What are the characters? Mere puppets, the mechanical mouthpieces for the utterance of the conceits of the author. What are the situations? Weak and uninteresting, relieved only by the brilliance of the dialogue.

Wit, therefore, we may say, although it is one of the highest types of comic expression, when presented in an exaggerated form kills the play in which it appears. It carries the artificiality which is present in all high comedy to a point of absurdity, so that we can feel in no way the connexion between the figures on the stage and real life. Comedy in this presents the same phenomenon as was presented by tragedy. Just as in tragedy there was a union of high ideality and a profound realism, so in comedy do we find an intense artificiality in the presentation of types and of situations, but at the same time an ever-present relationship established between that seeming artificiality and the world outside the theatre. *The Way of the World*, therefore, although it is probably the most brilliant comedy of wit we possess, fails when placed alongside of the truly richer and more profound drama, *Love for Love*.

HUMOUR IN COMEDY. Humour, likewise, has been found to differ from the unconsciously ludicrous, and from the conscious play of fancy as expressed in wit. Wit is brilliant; humour never so. Wit is clear and refined and cultured; humour is whimsical. Wit is modern in its expression and aristocratic in its tone; humour has always some half-wistful glance at the past and is generally humble in its utterance.

COMEDY

Humour gives always to comedy a mellowed note that stands in strange contrast to the hardness and insensibility of the play of wit. In it, as we have seen, sentiment and intellect are united; a spirit of kindliness meets with a spirit of satire. " The fault of Shakespeare's comic Muse," says Hazlitt, " is that it is too good-natured and magnanimous. . . . I do not, in short, consider comedy as exactly an affair of the heart or the imagination, and it is for this reason only that I think Shakespeare's comedies deficient." This criticism is penetrating, but it tends to lose sight of the fact that there are in comedy many totally divergent species, dependent in their turn upon the diverse types of the ludicrous. *The Taming of the Shrew* depends on the ridiculous situation and is a farce; *Volpone* depends on the satire; *The Way of the World* depends on the *bon mot*; *Love for Love* depends on manners and on character; *Twelfth Night* depends on humour. This comedy of humour is as important a species as any of the others, and, moreover, it has to be judged on its own standards, not by reference to other different types of comic productivity. The fact that kindliness and a certain broader aspect of mankind (Hazlitt's " good-natured and magnanimous " elements) appear in it should not blind us to its real excellences. The fact that its serious undertone often reaves away from it the spirit of pure laughter must not make us rule it out of the realms of comedy proper.

Humour, naturally, may appear in comedy in many different ways. The humour of character is to be discovered in its fullest form in the person of Falstaff. Falstaff is highly intellectual; at the same time there is in him just sufficient of emotion and of whimsicality to turn him from a wit into a humorist. He is fat and he laughs at his fatness. There is more than a hint that he runs away at Gadshill solely for the pleasure of indulging in the exquisite joke of the lie. He poses continually for the sake of arousing laughter. He does not make fun exclusively of others; he himself is the butt of his own wit. It is quite sufficient to compare Falstaff with any of the heroes of Congreve to see the vast gulf that lies between the two. Mirabel would never dream of laughing at himself; he is too self-assured, too unemotional, ever to dream of such a thing.

It is Falstaff's main pleasure and joy in life so to indulge in pleasantry at his own appearance and at his own habits.

Humour may be displayed also through the media of the situations, of the words, and of the manners. The situation in which Bottom finds himself is not amusing because of the character of Bottom, for he is not Falstaff; it is amusing because of the whimsicality with which it is presented, the mirth arising out of the manners and out of the situation. *Twelfth Night* presents examples of the same or a similar type. Shakespeare, indeed, has so plumbed the depths of this species of comedy that no more detailed analysis of it need here be given.

SATIRE. Finally, we come to that even less amusing species of the comic spirit—satire. Satire, as has been pointed out, can be so bitter that it ceases to be laughable in the very least. There is nothing to laugh at or even to smile at in the severity of Juvenal. There is more bitterness than laughter in *Volpone*, save for that scene where the English Lady Politick Would-be enters with her affected airs and her vanity. Satire falls heavily; it has no moral sense; it has no pity or kindliness or magnanimity. It lashes the physical appearance of persons, sometimes with unmitigated cruelty. It attacks the characters of men, as in *The Alchemist*. It strikes at the manners of the age with a hand that spares not. Witness the follies and the vices laid bare in the last-mentioned play of Jonson's; or glance at the terrible pages of Swift's last voyage, to the country of the Houyhnhnms. It continually presents duplicity and vice, and delights to witness that duplicity and that vice overturned in the end. Mosca and Volpone, Corbaccio and the rest, are sent screeching to their doom.

There is always a certain vulgarity in true satire; and there is always a sense that the poet before writing has looked into his own heart. He is horrified at the vices he sees in himself. This note is deeply stressed in Jonson's plays; it is apparent in Swift; and it occurs in a very marked form in Wycherley's *Plain Dealer*. Most commonly satire perceives underneath the specious disguise of social conventions and nominal morality the native brutality and ignorance of mankind; and in exposing this brutality and this ignorance to the view of the world there is a special coarseness and roughness in its treatment. This explains the hideousness of Wycherley's play, as well as the awful nature of Swift's last works. Pure comedy largely grows out of the acceptance of social conventions and the presentation in an amusing form of any variations from the normal custom. Satire lashes the customs of society as well as the eccentricities of individuals.

In this rapid glance at the nature of comic motives as expressed in comedy there are several important points which have become apparent. (1) There are at least four main types of comic expression used by the dramatists; the unconsciously ludicrous, the conscious wit, humour, and satire. (2) These may be mingled all together in one individual comedy, the highest forms of comedy usually combining at least two or three. (3) The laughable may, and indeed generally does, depend not on one source of merriment, but on several, so closely intertwined that it is almost impossible to disentangle them and to analyse them separately. (4) Comedy does not necessarily depend upon laughter, although laughter is assuredly its most common characteristic. Both in humour and in satire the purely risible may be entirely, or almost entirely, absent.

(iii) TYPES OF COMEDY

These considerations may serve us toward the making of a rapid analysis of the separate types of comedy. These varying types, because of the diverse and sharply differentiated species of the laughable, are much more clearly marked than the corresponding types of tragedy; but it must never be forgotten that they may and generally do fade almost imperceptibly into one another. In general, there are five main types of comic productivity which we may broadly classify. Farce stands by itself as marked out by certain definite characteristics. The comedy of humours is the second of decided qualities. Shakespeare's comedy of romance is the third, with possibly the romantic tragi-comedy of his later years as a separate subdivision. The comedy of intrigue is the fourth. The comedy of manners is the fifth, again with perhaps a subdivision in the genteel comedy.

FARCE. Farce we have already considered in general; and we have found that its main characteristics are the dependence in it of character and of dialogue upon mere situation. This situation, moreover, is of the most exaggerated and impossible kind, depending not on clever plot-construction, but upon the coarsest and rudest of improbable incongruities. Except in the very flimsiest of such pieces, of course, it is rare to find a play that depends upon nothing but farcical elements; but we can roughly mark the preponderance of those characteristics in the dramas presented before us under this title. It is quite evident that Farquhar and Vanbrugh are more farcical than Congreve; that *The Taming of the Shrew* and *The Merry Wives of Windsor* are more farcical than *Twelfth Night*. In these plays character is deliberately sacrificed to situation, nearly always of a rough-and-tumble type. Horseplay rouses our laughter in them more than the *comique de caractère* or the *comique de mots*. The situations in them are not subtle. There is, for example, nothing farcical in the famous screen scene of *The School for Scandal*. That situation, because it has been cleverly arranged, and because it is interrelated with the characters of the *dramatis personæ*, is eminently and purely comic in the highest sense of the word. The coarse discoveries and confusions, on the other hand, of any of the lower and minor Restoration comedies are as genuinely farcical. The situations here have usually nothing of poignancy in them; the amusement that is extracted from them depends not upon what we might call the idea of the situation, on its connexion with the characters and with the general atmosphere of the play, but upon the physical characteristics of the situation itself.

THE COMEDY OF ROMANCE (COMEDY OF HUMOUR). Farce, it is to be noted, may approximate in tone to any of the major types of comedy, or, rather, it may appear as a debased form of any of those types. It is thus distinct from each in this one quality of exaggerated situation, while all differ from it in an insistence upon something larger and broader than mere incident. The romantic comedy of Shakespeare, among the higher types, may here be considered first. In this term ' romantic comedy ' are included all the chief comedies of Shakespeare from *A Midsummer Night's Dream* to *Twelfth Night*,[1] the last

[1] With the exception of *Love's Labour's Lost*, *The Taming of the Shrew*, and *The Merry Wives*.

three tragi-comedies being of a slightly different tone and atmosphere. What do we find as the characteristics of these earlier
dramas of Shakespeare? First of all, they are markedly separated from later comedies of other dramatists in their scene.
Nearly all are set in natural surroundings—a wood near
Athens for *A Midsummer Night's Dream*, a sea-coast town
with flowering gardens for *Twelfth Night*, orchards and their
surroundings for *Much Ado about Nothing*, the Forest of Arden
for *As You Like It*. There is not a hint in them of those
localities so dear to the later comic dramatists—' Pall Mall ' or
' St James's Park.' This scene, then, is peculiar in that it is
of nature as opposed to the city, and in that it is set, not in the
surroundings of English country life, but in the surroundings
of a country life in some land remote in distance or in time.
Athens, Illyria, Messina, and France—these carry the mind
beyond even the ordinary city atmosphere of the theatre to a
different age and to a different locality. This choice of district
and of country was, on Shakespeare's part, evidently intentional; he was following, it is true, the example of the romancers
Greene and Lyly, but a theory that would explain those scenes
by mere imitation cannot be pressed too far. In following
them he was perfectly conscious of what he was doing. He was
evidently striving deliberately to conjure up an atmosphere
suitable to the characters and to the emotions of his plays. It
is in these characters that there appears the second noticeable
element in this comedy of romance. Whereas some of the
persons have a slightly more romantic colouring than the others,
the majority are more or less realistically drawn, in the sense
that they reflect the manners and the types of Elizabethan
England. Sir Toby Belch is no more an Illyrian than Bottom
is a citizen of Athens. Abstractly considered, such a sharp
divergence between scene and character might be thought fatal
to the production of any homogeneous work of art, but it is
the triumph of the comedy of romance that it has overcome
the many difficulties in its path. The main methods by which
a unified effect has been secured are the general subduing of
high tones, the utilization of humour rather than of wit, and
the introduction thereby of feeling and of emotion into the
body of the plays. In many ways it would be more correct to

style this drama the comedy of humour; and such a title might have been given to it, if that title had not raised a confusion between Shakespeare's comedy and the satiric comedy of Jonson, to the latter of which, rather erroneously, has been given the name of the comedy of ' humours.' Humour it is that preponderates in the earlier comedies of Shakespeare. Had wit appeared largely in these dramas, in all probability we should have seen markedly the discrepancy between the setting and the persons. Our reasons would have been constantly appealed to; and, as a consequence, that romantic atmosphere of emotion, willing to be deceived and not over-critical, would have been destroyed. The subdued tone of all these pieces, going along with this prevalence of humour, is very noticeable. There is a continual series of half-lights, never brilliant gleams and dark shadows. The comic scenes of *Twelfth Night* may become rollicking at times, but they never grow so pronounced as the situations in *The Merry Wives of Windsor*. There is everywhere an evident desire on Shakespeare's part to keep the colouring soft and uncontrasted. This softening process is marked in a multitude of ways. The wit that occasionally appears in the mouth of a character such as Rosalind is mellowed and chastened. It is never allowed free play; if it begins to become scintillating then of a sudden a turn is made and there is a strong appeal to the feelings. Rosalind, moreover, is not a pure wit herself. Like all the heroes and the heroines of these comedies, she is emotional rather than intellectual. Viola, Olivia, and the Duke in *Twelfth Night* are thus bound together in a circle not of wit, but of love; so even Benedick and Beatrice, who crack their jokes about marriage, have a rich substratum of emotion in their natures, and this emotion prevents their wit developing along alien lines. The humour, however, is the surest medium for securing a spirit which might harmonize scene and character; it is of a peculiarly meditative, fanciful, and kindly sort, romantic in its essence, if we connote by romantic the richer glow of a sentiment that is half poetical and half whimsical. All of these comedies of romance are full of appeals to our meditative faculties and to our emotions. The laughter is subdued into a kind of feeling of contentment, a happiness of spirit rather than an

ebullition of outward merriment. Wherever the laughter is
called forth it is immediately stilled or crushed out of existence
by some other appeal.

In those plays, moreover, the laughter is softened and
chastened by an element, usually carefully subordinated to
the main plot, of evil or of misfortune. All along we know
that this evil will be vanquished and that the misfortune will
be put aside; but it is ever present before us throughout the
greater part of the plot. In *As You Like It* it is the banishment
of a duke and his daughter; in *A Midsummer Night's Dream* it
is the hopeless entangling of the lovers' passions and the threat
of execution that hangs over one of them; in *Twelfth Night* it
is the almost fatal neglect of Viola; in *Much Ado about Nothing*
it is the casting off of Hero. In two of these plays the evil and
the misfortune are softened by the gaiety of spirit on the part
of those ill-fated—Rosalind's happiness and Viola's cheerful-
ness. In the other two it is softened by the mirth of certain
characters connected with, but standing apart from, the
characters who appear to be in painful circumstances—by the
mirth of Puck and of Bottom, of Benedick and Beatrice and
Dogberry. It is here that there arises a distinction between
the two types within this romantic species. We should not
dream of calling *As You Like It* a tragi-comedy, but there has
been considerable doubt in the nomenclature of *Cymbeline*,
The Winter's Tale, and *The Tempest*. In these plays of Shakespeare's last years, closely connected in their spirit with the
cognate dramas of Beaumont and Fletcher, the romantic
element is still more deeply stressed. The scene is carried
even farther than France and Athens and Illyria. It is ancient
Britain, or Bohemia, or an island in the " Bermoothes." At
the same time, the incidents are made still more improbable
and ' romantic ' to accord with the highly improbable nature
of the setting. In *Cymbeline* there is the almost impossible
chamber scene and the later wanderings of the heroine; in
The Winter's Tale there is the sixteen years' concealment of
Hermione; in *The Tempest* there is the atmosphere of magic.
This endeavour thus to intensify the improbable and romantic
notes is again evidently deliberate. It represents partly the
exaggeration of the perfectly natural comedy of romance of

Shakespeare's earlier years, partly an adaptation of that comedy of romance to the newer spirit of the early seventeenth century. The comedy of romance was an approximation or a balance between idealism and reality; in the later romantic comedy there is a loss of the reality altogether in scene and in situation, and partly in character. To harmonize with this, moreover, the tragic or the serious element, which had already appeared in the earlier plays, but always in a subordinate position, is in those later dramas deeply stressed, so that the works cease to be comedies at all, taking on instead the characteristics of a decidedly mixed species. Thus, *Cymbeline* was set by the Folio editors as a tragedy; *The Winter's Tale* hovers on the brink of the unhappy; and the theme of *The Tempest* is a banished duke, involving scenes of serious and almost tragic sentiments. This heightened romantic note and increased tragic element mark out the Beaumont and Fletcher and the later Shakespearian romantic plays from the earlier Elizabethan group. There is also in the later type an added element of intrigue. The intrigue in the earlier plays was complicated, but in the later it is carried to lengths which are to be discovered among the former dramas only in isolated scenes. It is made more involved and takes on forms of evil lacking in the earlier type. The conspiracies of Iachimo and of Sebastian are quite apart in spirit from the complications in *A Midsummer Night's Dream*. Obviously the two groups run together, a play like *Much Ado about Nothing* standing between the one and the other in this respect; but in general they are sharply enough distinguished, and, while deserving treatment together, must be regarded as quite separate sub-species of the one type.

THE COMEDY OF ' HUMOURS ' (COMEDY OF SATIRE). Openly opposed to this general romantic species stands the so-called comedy of ' humours.' This class of comedy, which deals largely with exaggerated types or ' humours,' is one which, adumbrated in the classical comedy, was revived in England in *Gammer Gurton's Needle* and in *Ralph Roister Doister*, and then, after a not very glorious career, was rendered popular by Jonson in *Every Man in his Humour*. Of all the types of comedy this perhaps is one of the most confusing for critical analysis, mainly owing to the fact that all comedy, be it of

' humours ' or of romance or of manners, deals with types of character rather than with personalities, and therefore employs what are, to all intents and purposes, the ' humours ' which are often assumed to be the sole property of Ben Jonson. This being so, it may be inquired what precisely are those elements which particularly distinguish this kind from others wherein the types of characters are likewise heavily marked. In the comedy of ' humours,' of course, the types are possibly more exaggerated than, for example, in the Shakespearian form of early romantic comedy. The fact that they are types is for ever being obtruded upon our notice, whereas, in the Shakespearian comedy, there is rather an attempt to conceal the presence of the types under a semblance of personality. On the other hand, none of the persons of Jonson's comedy is any more a type than is Leontes in *The Winter's Tale*, and pronounced ' humours ' appear frequently in the purest of the comedies of manners. Here, then, is not the prime distinguishing characteristic of the Jonsonian drama; the title which has been given to this drama is seen not to be fully justified. Only one claim can be made for its accuracy. In the comedy of romance as in the comedy of manners there are nearly always one or two characters of an ordinary intelligent kind, not marked by any particular folly or vice; there is in the comedy of ' humours ' a tendency to make every one of the characters an eccentric of some kind or other. This tendency, however, again is seen not to be wholly universal. *Every Man in his Humour* has a fairly normal central figure in Young Knowell, and Shadwell's plays, deliberately modelled on the comedies of Jonson, possess always a couple or a quartette of ordinary *dramatis personæ* around whom move the more purely humorous figures.

The qualities which distinguish the Jonsonian type of comedy must, therefore, be sought for in aspects apart from the ' humours ' themselves. These qualities are, in truth, not hard to discover. The Jonsonian comedy, in the first place, is marked off from the romantic drama by its intense realism. It was Jonson's boast and virtue that he drew comedy down from the improbable realms of romantic colouring to the levels of ordinary existence, where he could utilize

Deeds and language, such as men do use,
And persons, such as comedy would choose,
When she would show an image of the times,
And sport with human follies, not with crimes.

Jonson's great merit lies in the fact, not that he popularized
the ancient comedy of 'humours,' not that he infused into
English literature the spirit of Terence and of Plautus, or that
he used Terence as an inspiration for increased dramatic effect,
but that he drew comedy down to real life, presenting the classes
and the follies of contemporary London at a time when there
was a fear of comedy's vanishing altogether into those fantastic
and impossible realms of make-believe which had been popularized by Shakespeare and by Beaumont and Fletcher. All
of Shakespeare's dramas, except *Love's Labour's Lost*, *The
Taming of the Shrew*, and the comic scenes of the first part of
Henry IV, had dealt either with crude absurdity of accident,
or with the humorous that arises out of natural ignorance, all
coloured with his rich romantic imagination. *The Merry Wives*
is farcical as is *The Taming of the Shrew*, and the Falstaff
scenes of *Henry IV* not only depend largely upon humour for
their effect, but merely form part of a larger history. *Love's
Labour's Lost* has a fanciful theme with nothing in it reminiscent
of Jonson's style. Realism, added to intensified 'humours'
treated in a satirical spirit, was first given to the theatrical
world by Jonson. Here, possibly, a remark might be made
concerning Jonson's matter. He has been called by several
critics the founder of the comedy of manners; it has been said
that he dealt with the manners of mankind, and so stands as
the ancestor of the Restoration comedy. Such statements,
however, go far toward confusing the issue, on the one hand,
between Jonson and Shakespeare, and, on the other, between
Jonson and Congreve. Jonson, in point of fact, deals hardly
at all with manners as such: he is not concerned with the social
affectations of the world, but with the follies of particular men
or of particular groups of men. The comic of *Every Man in
his Humour* rises out of the follies of Bobadil, of Matthew,
of Cob, of Clement, not out of the manners of their class. All
the 'humours' of *Every Man out of his Humour* are based on
genuine traits of character, not on the customs and the ways of

mankind. So in *The Alchemist* it is the gullibility of fools and the cunning of sharpers that is presented: in *Volpone* it is the natural greed of all types of men. So far, indeed, is Jonson from being the founder of the comedy of manners that it might almost be averred that his species of comedy is distinguished from several other types by the fact that it puts its stress not on manners, but on natural idiosyncrasies. It is this fact that he does not reproduce the manners of the age that marks off Shadwell, the literary descendant of Jonson, as being a writer, not only of an inferior genius, but of a class different from that of Etherege. In only two things does Jonson stand connected with the later comedy of manners—in his realism and in his satire; and we shall find that the realism and the satire of Jonson are definitely separated at many points from the similar qualities that occasionally appear in the Restoration dramas.

The comedy of ' humours,' be it noted, habitually disregards humour; it depends occasionally on wit, but more generally on satire. The exaggeration of the types gives ample opportunity for the introduction of this last comic method—indeed, in itself it is partly a manifestation of satirical creativeness. This distinction between the plays of Shakespeare and the plays of Jonson is clearly to be seen when we glance at the development of the dramatic productivity of each. Humour, as it advances, tends to become more mellow, moving either toward increased kindliness or toward excessive meditation of a highly contemplative kind; satire, on the other hand, tends to grow more bitter and more severe. Humour may end in melancholy; satire nearly always ends in pessimism. Whereas in Shakespeare's work we see a continued kindliness and, at the close of his life, a melancholy contemplation of the shadows and of the shows of life, in Jonson we find a regular progression from the comparatively genial atmosphere of *Every Man in his Humour* to the bitterness and the unconcealed contempt of *Volpone*. As is evident, this lack of humour in the so-called comedy of ' humours ' marks one of the many anomalies in our literary nomenclature, due obviously to the rapid alteration in the significance of the terms employed by critical writers. It would be much safer to style Jonson's comedy the comedy of realism or the comedy of satire, differentiating it thus from the romantic comedy with its atmosphere of humour and from the later comedy of manners.

THE COMEDY OF MANNERS (COMEDY OF WIT). The comedy of manners is, as its name suggests, an entirely different species from the comedy of Jonson. There may be ' humours ' in the plays of Etherege, Congreve, Farquhar, and Vanbrugh, but those ' humours ' are not stressed to the same extent as they are in Jonson's work; and there is, moreover, a marked change in their conception. In Jonson, as we have seen, the ' humours ' are exaggerated traits of character. The very names of his *dramatis personæ* display this. Deliro, Sordido, Fungoso, Shift, in *Every Man out of his Humour*; Volpone, Corbaccio, in *The Fox*—these show the tendency of his creative activity. In the comedy of manners, on the other hand, the ' humours ' are rarely such traits of character exaggerated. The ' humours,' if we retain the old term, are derived from the conventions, follies, and usages of social life. Novel and Lord Plausible in *The Plain Dealer*; Lord Froth and Sir Paul Plyant in *The Double Dealer*; Witwoud and Petulant in *The Way of the World*; the Sir Harry Wildairs and the Lady Betty Modishes of the eighteenth century—all of these are figures who take their humorous complexion from the social follies of their day, not from the innate follies of mankind. Greed is not much represented in the comedy of manners, but it is in Jonson's plays, precisely because greed is a trait of character, not a quality derived from social custom.

The title given to this type of drama—the comedy of manners —is, of course, derived ultimately from the manners, the social follies and conventions, presented in the plays of the time; but the word ' manners ' itself has a deeper, and for our purpose a more illuminating significance, a significance which may serve us toward a closer analysis of the characteristics of this species. In the second act of *The Double Dealer* Lady Froth is conversing with Cynthia. " I vow Mellefont's a pretty gentleman," she says, " but methinks he wants a manner." " A manner ! " exclaims Cynthia. " What's that, madam ? " To which Lady Froth's answer is instructive. " Some distinguishing quality," she replies, " as, for example, the *bel air* or *brilliant* of Mr Brisk; the solemnity, yet complaisance of my lord, or some-

thing of his own that should look a little *jene-scay-quoysh*."
This quotation shows to us that we have something more in
the term ' comedy of manners ' than at first sight meets the
eye. Manners may mean simply the ways of men, in which
case it will apply to the Jonsonian comedy as to this of the
Restoration. It may mean the conventions of an artificial
society; and it may mean something brilliant about men and
women, not a ' humour ' derived from natural idiosyncrasy,
but a grace or a habit of refined culture, something that looks
" a little *jene-scay-quoysh*." In these last two senses it is to be
applied only to the comedy of Etherege and of Congreve.

The matter and the characters, therefore, of the Restoration plays differ markedly from the matter and the characters
of the comedy of Jonson. In scene, however, both are alike.
Not a single one of the true Restoration comedies of manners
is set out of the bounds of London. Sedley mixes fanciful
with real names in his *Bellamira*, and seems in so doing to
spoil his play, but the finer dramatists of the time were careful
to avoid any such admixture. They clung firmly to the circle
of London society. So soon as the comedy of manners passed
out of the town into the country, as it did in Farquhar's *Recruiting Officer*, it was doomed to perish. It never could have
travelled to the mythical lands of the Shakespearian Thalia;
it would have withered there, as a hot-house plant in a freer
atmosphere. In places, too, the Restoration comedy shared
the spirit of Jonson, but, in sharing that spirit, altered it.
Jonson's dramas, as we have seen, had been built on satire,
which is an integral part of the comedy of manners. This
satire, however, in its reappearance was totally changed. It
was no longer the satire of the self-opinionated and slightly
pessimistic individual as with Jonson, but the gentle satire of
the fine world at the follies of those who strove to enter into
its elegant circle. It directed its laughter at the hangers-on,
at the fops, and at the would-be wits, at the coxcombs and at
the pedantries of the *virtuosi*. Except in " manly Wycherley,"
who " lashed the crying age," it never grew bitter, never passed
beyond a kind of fastidious contempt. The comedy of manners,
moreover, did not confine itself to satire; it utilized far more
what Jonson barely knew—the power of wit. Jonson's is the

satire of exaggeration; he attains his effect not by means of a fruitful fancy, but by means of crude and heavy blows. The comedy of manners neglected all that. It was airy and delicate; and accordingly preferred to satirize by utilizing that species of *esprit* which depended fundamentally upon the incongruity between two ideas or between an idea and an object. Its method is entirely different from the method of the Elizabethan writer; as different, indeed, as that latter method is from the genial, kindly, and meditative humour of Shakespeare.

In discussing the comedy of manners, it is almost inevitable that there should arise the question of morality. The typical plays of the comedy of manners produced during the time of the Restoration are so full of indecencies of word and thought and situation that this problem must be ever present before us. Already some few words have been said on the subject, and little more need be done here than to point out that these comedies, written in the age of the Restoration, could not fail to be indecent to modern eyes. It is by no means the comedy of manners that has a monopoly of immorality at that time. All the types of comedy produced between 1660 and 1700 are stained by the brush of the evil of their time. Indeed, it may be said categorically that there are far worse elements to be found in the lesser-known non-manners dramas of that period than there are in the more accessible plays of Etherege and of Congreve. It is certainly noticeable that a man like Shadwell, in *The Squire of Alsatia*, where he deliberately adopts the Jonsonian style, is inexpressibly vulgar, while in *Bury Fair*, where he has been undoubtedly influenced by the plays of Etherege, he is comparatively pure and modest, even if judged by modern standards of taste.

Before passing judgment on this comedy of manners for its moral delinquencies, there are several things which must be borne in mind. First of all, the comedy of manners is essentially intellectual; it permits of the introduction and expression of practically no emotion whatsoever. It therefore does not play upon our feelings in any way, but appeals primarily and always to our reason. Its wit is purely intellectual; and the appreciation of it comes from our minds, not from our hearts. This intellectual quality in the works of Etherege and of

Congreve undoubtedly renders their indecencies and their vulgarities comparatively harmless. The truly immoral book is that which plays upon our emotions and leaves the reason severely alone. The indecencies in the Restoration drama rarely, if ever, are introduced except for the purpose of raising a laugh from the wit with which they are presented. There is here a genuine insensibility demanded from the audience, and that insensibility dulls and renders innocuous what might otherwise have been of evil effect.

The comedy of manners, moreover, has stressed deeply that tendency in all high comedy—the artificiality of personality and of theme. This comedy is realistic, but not in the way that Jonson's plays were realistic. In his works there is a decided attempt to display through the ' humours ' or through the types traits of contemporary life; there is a mass of topical allusion, and the subjects are often taken from real aspects of his time. The comedy of manners also reflects real life, but it is a real life artificialized, and, still further, it is the airier, what we might almost call the more spiritual, parts of real life. It is this fact which Lamb seized upon in his essay " On the Artificial Comedy of the Last Century." That essay is exaggerated, and therefore loses some of its effect; but it has captured the truth concerning this particular species of dramatic effort. There is an incessant attempt on the part of Etherege and of Congreve to delineate the more refined aspects of their time— the gaiety, the wit, the delicacy of the age. There is, too, the attempt to artificialize the manners presented, or else to present them in their most etherealized forms. While we may say, then, that this drama is realistic in that it presents a picture of contemporary life in definitely metropolitan surroundings, we must qualify that statement by declaring that it presents a picture only of certain aspects of that contemporary life, and that it treats those aspects in a peculiar way of its own.

There is, finally, another consideration. Comedy, as we have already seen, is largely the laughter of society at certain abnormalities or eccentricities. The society of the Restoration was a peculiarly constituted society unlike that either of our own time or of the age of Elizabeth. What it regarded as an eccentricity, therefore, might not by any means correspond

to our idea of such. If we are to regard this comedy aright
we must as far as possible put ourselves back in the position of
the upper-class life of the late seventeenth century. We must
endeavour to secure the true historical point of view. We
must recognize that for this age and particularly for this society
such a figure as a jealous husband was truly comic, because
abnormal and eccentric. The jealous husband, therefore,
could be presented only as a theme of comic merriment; the
deceiving of him could be introduced only as a jest. What for
us might be a pitiful subject, or even a terrible subject, could
be then only a source, and a genuine source, of laughter.

While, accordingly, we cannot deny that there are for us
to-day many passages in the works of Etherege and of Congreve
which must appear as vulgar and indecent, it behoves us to try
honestly to recapture the spirit of that comedy, and, further,
to relate the laughable in that comedy to the manifestations of
the comic in other times and places.

THE GENTEEL COMEDY. The comedy of manners as such,
to all intents and purposes, was killed in the early eighteenth
century by the passing away of the particular society which
had given it birth. Congreve, its high priest, was truly born
twenty years out of his due time. The comedy of manners,
certainly, endured still in an altered form. In its original shape
it was killed by the inrush of sentimentalism, but it continued
in the guise of what was styled in the eighteenth century
genteel comedy. This genteel comedy is the comedy of manners
adapted to the less natural society of the century that followed
that of Charles II. The term was first used, apparently, by
Addison in the very years that saw the development of the type,
but it is explained nowhere more clearly than in the anonymous
introduction to the third volume of *The Modern British Drama*
(1811). *The Careless Husband* of Cibber is there described as

> the first genteel comedy upon the English stage, and the precursor
> of a numerous class of plays, which did not, as formerly, repre-
> sent the operation of one single passion rushing with impetuosity
> to the accomplishment of its desires. It is not the natural, but
> the artificial state of man, which this species of drama presents;
> exhibiting characters not acting under the predominance of natural
> feeling, but warped from their genuine bent by the habits, rules,
> and ceremonies of high life.

226

COMEDY

There is here, of course, a certain misapprehension, probably due ultimately to Addison, but the characteristics thus diagnosed are the genuine characteristics of the genteel comedy. The age of Anne and the later age of the mid-eighteenth century were both sentimental and less natural than the age of Charles. They were still prevailingly intellectual, but the vast changes which had taken place in the years following the Revolution of 1688 had left their marks on society and on the theatre. The age, too, was more effeminate than it had been before. Affectations ruled the life of the upper-class society, and it is these affectations that are reproduced in the pages of the genteel comedy. All that was virile in the earlier drama was lost, and, if the Restoration plays presented a more artificial state of society than had appeared in the plays of Jonson, this was as much more artificial than the comedies of Etherege and of Congreve. In the genteel comedy most of the indecencies which had, in the eyes of the moral critics, marred the earlier dramas were abandoned. Intrigue there is in plenty, but it is intrigue that is shrouded in the midst of the artificial, and, moreover, it is intrigue that is often highly sentimentalized. By the writer of the preface in *The Modern British Drama* Hoadly's *Suspicious Husband* is singled out as a prime example of the later genteel comedy, and in that drama we find, in spite of the licence of the drinking and love-making scenes, a rich air of the sentimental. The coarser manners are toned down to an atmosphere of decorum, and if there may appear to our eyes a more vicious atmosphere in the hypocrisy of certain situations the cruder elements of licence have been cut away and their place taken by a strictly becoming spirit.

In this genteel comedy, however, there is something more than mere ' moral ' tone that separates it from the earlier type of comic productivity. The wit which had distinguished the plays of Congreve has been in it largely lost. The laughter arises not out of the playful fancies of brilliant and highly intellectual men, but out of the affectations of this mannerized society. Lady Betty Modish and her gallants are not truly clever; they have wit of a kind, but they are laughable not so much by reason of their skill in repartee as by reason of their fine airs and their highly artificial mode of life. The heroes of the earlier comedy of manners are usually ordinary men—Careless and Courtine and Beaugard—who laughed at the follies of too refined affectation on the one hand, and of awkward ignorance on the other. Here the follies have become the central part of the picture, and the ordinary men have vanished.

THE COMEDY OF INTRIGUE. Apart from the comedy of manners and its descendant, the genteel comedy, there is one type of comedy which has preserved an almost perennial existence during the whole period from its inception in the days of Fletcher to the end of the eighteenth century. This type is the comedy of intrigue. It is rarely perhaps that we find a genuine and pure comedy of this class; but there are innumerable plays which have a preponderance of the intrigue element, so that the type may be considered as an entity in itself. In this species of comedy, as the name implies, the laughter arises solely or largely out of the disguises and the intrigues and the complications of the plot. In some of the comedies of Fletcher, in those of Mrs Behn, and in those of Mrs Centlivre, the whole interest lies in the skilful manipulation of a series of situations delicately conceived and leading to innumerable mistakes and amusing *dénouements*. In general, this comedy stands far below those types we have been considering, being in its nature closely allied to farce. It differs from farce, however, in that it does not necessarily or even usually employ horseplay or rough incident in its development. Very often the complications of the comedy of intrigue lead to nothing but merely laughable situations, laughable because of the intellectual incongruity they present. There can be little wit in this type of drama, practically no humour, and not a scrap of satire, but there is the genuine comedy of situation highly and, in the best of the species, interestingly developed. This comedy of situation, as we have seen, has a distinct value of its own, and must be accorded an honourable place in the styles at the disposal of the comic dramatist. The danger in it lies in the fact that it becomes, in an exaggerated form, a trifle monotonous and gradually palls on the senses and on the intellect. It has also the disadvantage that, the novelty of the plot-development worn off, it often ceases to have any great value or interest for us. On the other hand, the comedy of intrigue is more universal than many of the other types. The intrigue that it presents is independent of time and of place; it exists in a world of its own. It does not paint the manners of a particular time; its theme is the sportive merriment of mankind. In studying it we have therefore to beware of falling into one of two extremes. We have to guard against condemnation because of the purely external nature of the interest, and we have to guard against excessive praise because of the skill with which many of these comedies are developed. The comedy of intrigue stands at the opposite pole of dramatic invention from such a play as *The Way of the World*. The one dwells entirely on external sources of laughter; the other is based solely on intellectual mirth. In the highest type of comedy, that which is most successful on the stage as in the study, we shall find in general a union of these two.

Before closing this section a further note might be made concerning nomenclature. It has been plentifully apparent that not only in this last instance have the terms applied regularly by criticism to the types of comedy been misleading and erroneous. A plea might therefore be made for a new set of titles, based not on chance application, but upon a study of the comic methods employed by each species. Shakespeare's comedy might deserve the name of comedy of humour, for that is its predominant characteristic, giving birth to all the laughter in his dramas. Romantic tragi-comedy might serve for the plays of Beaumont and Fletcher, in which a union of the serious and of the laughable is marked. Jonson's comedy would be the comedy of satire, dependent not upon wit, and innocent of humour. The plays of Etherege and of Congreve would, on the same principle, be the comedy of wit, the word ' manners,' unless fully understood in all its bearings, merely causing confusion between the dramas of the Restoration and the dramas of the early seventeenth century. By thus clarifying the nomenclature of comic types and by bearing these titles in mind we might go far toward appreciating the fundamental characteristics of each separate species.

IV

TRAGI-COMEDY

SO far we have considered the main features of those two forms of dramatic expression, the tragic and the comic, which since the days of Aristotle have been recognized as the chief of all, and which at the same time serve as touchstones for a consideration of other types. In Greek days, however, besides these two there existed the satyric drama, a species distinct from comedy and from tragedy alike, while some of the playwrights seem to have indulged either in variations from the usual tragic ending in death or in the introduction of comic elements in plays not otherwise laughable. Still further, at least one Roman dramatist, possibly following the freer traditions of the mime, experimented in the writing of a comic play with characters taken from heroic legend and the tales of the gods. There was thus good classical precedent for a type of drama, or, to be more precise, for types of drama in which the usual concomitants of comedy and tragedy were mingled in one manner or another. When a new theatre arose during the Renascence, and particularly when that theatre came to flourish in England, where the freedom of romantic traditions allowed of still further developments, this tendency toward admixture of the two species was still further emphasized, giving rise to forms so diverse as the comedy of romance, the tragi-comedy of Beaumont and Fletcher, and the tragedy with plentiful comic relief. Still later, under the influence of a change in social outlook, arose the sentimental comedy, where laughter was set aside in favour of moral reflections and sympathetic pathos.

THEORIES REGARDING TRAGI-COMEDY. The question of tragi-comedy and of the kindred happily ending tragedy is one which was much discussed in earlier times. For the most part the Italian critics of the Renascence were prepared to

230

allow a happy ending to plays of a tragic sort. Giraldi Cinthio, Scaliger, and Castelvetro are all agreed as to the permissibility of the form; and they are followed by many of the early French theorists, such as La Taille and Vauquelin. The distinction commonly made was that the happy ending to the serious play consisted simply of the avoidance of impending disaster, whereas in comedy no such disaster is ever really threatened. As has been seen in the discussion of the unity of action, the further question which concerns the advisability or even the possibility of mingling genuine tragic and comic elements was one also much discussed, some endeavouring to defend the newer type by reference to nature. Such a defence must, of course, at once be dismissed. Truth to nature is not the test of drama; there are many things in nature which cannot be satisfactorily dramatized, and the union of the different moods of ordinary life must be carefully harmonized before they can be artistically included in one single play. Drama is based on life, but it is life selected and made harmonious. It presents the moods of our minds and hearts abstracted and placed in an intensified isolation. The drama has not only laws of its own, but characteristics of its own; it is human life and character raised and placed on a new plane of existence, where other laws and other customs rule than those on this earth. We cannot criticize this drama from the ordinary point of view of natural existence.

THE ADMIXTURE OF TRAGEDY AND COMEDY. In turning from the theory to the practice we recognize immediately that, taking first the tragic plays in which a certain element of the comic is permitted to intrude, such comic material may be utilized for three very different purposes in accordance with the main aims of the dramatists. Thus, in the first place, the comic may be used simply as a contrast to the tragic. In this case it seldom raises, or is intended to raise, a laugh. The porter scene in *Macbeth* is comic if we will, but it is a grim sort of comedy that merely serves to make more terrible the events taking place within the castle. Instead of alleviating, it increases the tragic tensity of the action. A similar effect is produced by the jesting of Lear's Fool, which but gives an added poignancy to the terrible scene of madness and tempestuous elements. So, too, the gravediggers' scene in *Hamlet*, although in parts this may provide a moment of respite for the overstrung emotions, emphasizes the tragic despair by the ghastly witticisms spent over dead bones and mouldering skulls. Indeed, it will be found that the majority of these comic scenes in the midst of Shakespeare's tragedy contrast with the tragic and so intensify it rather than, by providing a different mood, alleviate our passions.

Sometimes, however, the object is really one of relief. The servant scenes and the Mercutio scenes in *Romeo and Juliet* are an example of this. Here the comic is genuinely amusing and intended to be amusing, devised to form a breathing space, as it were, in the midst of the tragic action. This relief has not been greatly practised by Shakespeare, although it has been a marked feature of many of the other early seventeenth-century dramas. It is just possible that he realized the difficulty it involves in regard to the final disposition of the humorous figures. Generally these have to be got rid of by death; Mercutio is slain in *Romeo and Juliet*, and Bergetto in Ford's *'Tis Pity* is stabbed by mistake. The end of such characters, however, does not fill us with the genuine mood of tragedy. We feel that there is something wrong in their deaths; an element of doubt is raised, and doubt is fatal to the spirit of tragedy. Thirdly, the comic scenes, bound together by the strands of a regular plot, may be developed along lines of their own, parallel to the main plot and sometimes even largely independent of it. For the most part, plays constructed on this plan are liable to artistic disaster. Where the comedy serves the purpose of contrast, as, for example, in Mr Sean O'Casey's *Silver Tassie* or *Juno and the Paycock*, it can be harmonized perfectly with the tragic matter, however uproarious it may become at certain moments. Laughter that suddenly dies away into a frightened whimper or a cry of pain, laughter that cynically succeeds an action of awe and terror —these are integral parts of a major theme. But the laughter that intrudes by itself often strikes the wrong note and is merely disturbing. Shakespeare can introduce a Falstaff into the history of *Henry IV*, but only by linking the comic material with the serious, and only, too, by subordinating perforce the historical events to the atmosphere of the tavern does he succeed in preserving balance. Of tragi-comedies there are many, but of subtly harmonized artistic specimens of the *genre* there are but few. The true tragic spirit is a jealous muse, and will have none other near her throne.

On the other hand, it must be confessed that the union of diverse elements in a play leads frequently to success in the theatre. The tragedy with a comic undertone of contrast or of relief and the comedy in which pathos is occasionally called for are both familiar to us; while melodrama regularly varies its scenes of stirring serious action with buffoonery of a farcical kind. Regarding these, however, we note that the first type uses the comic for purposes of its own; while neither the pathetic elements in certain comedies nor the serious elements in the melodrama aim at securing the tragic tension of emotion. We thus come back to one of our earliest judgments, that there do exist certain kinds of impression (from which arise corresponding kinds of dramatic art) some of which blend artistically with each other, some of which demand the complete and undivided attention of the audience. The thrill of melodrama may go easily with farce, and sympathetic pathos may move alongside comic humour, but tragedy in itself demands, first, that any comic interfusion should be in spiritual accord with the tragic tone, and, secondly, that such comic matter should be strictly subordinate to the other.

SENTIMENTAL COMEDY. There yet remains, however, the problem raised by an entirely distinct form of dramatic expression to which neither the name of tragedy nor the name of comedy may fittingly be given, although the latter, in the phrase 'sentimental comedy,' is frequently assigned to it. Sentimental drama is not, of course, all of one kind. Arising in the last years of the seventeenth century, it had a long and successful career extending well into the Victorian era, when it merged with other forms and gave rise to a still further development. During all this long period it changed shape and spirit constantly, so that here we have to deal, not with one single and easily defined type, but with several. For ease of critical analysis perhaps three of these forms it assumed may here be chosen.

At the start the sentimental comedy was naught but the comedy of manners warped and altered in the last act by some sudden revulsion of character or by some swift change in the conduct of the plot. Thus, in Cibber's *Love's Last Shift*, which tradition habitually acclaims as the originator of the species, although without due accuracy, the hero is an ordinary hero of the manners school, until in the end comes to him repentance and a new way of life. As Cibber himself in his apologetic epilogue explained to the critics, he was very moral at the close,

> But then again,
> He's lewd for above four Acts, Gentlemen !

In this particular form the type has obviously no special significance, for it presents merely a particular species of ordinary comedy spoilt by an ending artistically out of harmony with the rest and introduced solely for the purpose of agreeing with some moral preconceptions. Those moral preconceptions are, of course, of the crudest, and in the Cibberian comedy repentance truly covers a multitude of sins.

When we move onward into the eighteenth century, however, this particular version of sentimentalized comedy begins to decline, and in its stead appears a proper drama of sentiment which might or might not include matter of a risible sort. Where laughable matter does occur it develops not out of the purely sentimental plot and characters, but out of sections of the play in which an ordinary comic atmosphere is conjured up. A couple of examples may serve to make this clear. In *The Fugitive* of Joseph Richardson there is a distinctly sentimental theme dealing with Sir William Wingrove and his daughter Julia, whom he plans to give to Lord Dartford, but around this main story circles a series of episodes occupied almost entirely with the ' humours ' of Larron, O'Donnel, and Admiral Cleveland. Not for one moment do we smile at the first part of the plot; all the mirth arises from the other scenes, which are conceived fundamentally in the style of the comedy of humours. So in *The Secret* of Edward Morris the sentimental is richly stressed in the rejection of Henry by Rosa because of her poverty, and in the subsequent rejection of Rosa by Henry because the latter has found

234

that his sweetheart's poverty is due to the action of his own father. This is perfectly serious; the mirth in this play, too, is aroused entirely by a purely comic under-plot dealing with the 'humours' of Lizard and his family. These two examples, thoroughly representative as they are, prove at once that there is in reality no such thing as sentimental comedy; what passes under that name is merely a kind of sentimental drama which is allied to, or associated with, episodes of a common comic stamp.

Out of this sentimental drama of the eighteenth century arose the problem drama of later years. We cannot call *A Doll's House* sentimental, nor can we assign that name to such a play as *Candida*, yet historically we are bound to recognize that what *The Fugitive* and *The Secret* were to the earlier Georgian era *Candida* and *A Doll's House* are to this. Both types are based on the same fundamental principles, and only the outlook of the authors makes the one different from the other. This, indeed, shows us that the very term sentimental drama itself is a misleading title. Mr Shaw is decidedly anti-sentimental in outlook, yet in method and aim he joins hands with Morris and Richardson. The moral play, if you will, and the problem play, were phrases better suited to express the purposes common to those stage-pieces of 1781 and of 1931 to which we commonly affix the titles of sentimental comedy and of drama.

THE THEORY OF SENTIMENTAL DRAMA. Concerning the final aim of the dramatist who essays this particular form not much has been written; but particularly from the eighteenth century there come a few passages which serve to throw light on this subject. The first, seemingly, to discuss the theme was Diderot in his essay on dramatic poetry (1758). In this work the French dramatist starts by declaring that we are the slaves of custom, and nowhere more so than in our attitude toward the theatre. Tragedy and comedy, he believes, are not the only two kinds possible in drama, but there are many " gaps " between the one and the other. In general, he finds four main forms—the gay comedy, the serious comedy, domestic tragedy, and the tragedy of the great. Such a division is, of course, not wanting in inexactitude, for there can be no fundamental distinction between a tragedy in which the characters are of humble birth and a tragedy in which the hero is a king; but this is not of real account. The important matter is the recognition of a 'serious comedy' or a 'serious drama' distinct alike from tragedy and from comedy. For Diderot this *drame* is distinguished from both in its aim— from tragedy by its refusal to deal with the gloom and misery of existence, and from comedy by its emphasis, not on ridicule and the chastising of vice, but on the displayal of virtue and the inculcation of the duties of man. That is to say, the whole function of the playwright who essays to write a *drame* is a moral function in the sense that he 'philosophizes,' not about metaphysical matters, as happens frequently in tragedy, but about the ordinary social ideals.

Diderot's remarks were followed, in 1767, by Beaumarchais' *Essai sur le genre dramatique sérieux*. For Beaumarchais the object of the " serious drama " is " to interest a body of persons in the theatre and make it shed tears over a situation which, if it happened in reality . . . would assuredly produce the same effect upon those persons." [1] The first implication here —and it is duly emphasized by the critic—is that drama is a mirror of life. " If the theatre," he says, " is a faithful picture of what happens in the world, our interest aroused thereby must necessarily have a close relationship to our manner of observing reality." [1] The second implication is that sympathy is natural to man:

> The picture of an honest man in misfortune touches our hearts; the spectacle opens our hearts delicately, takes possession of them, and finally forces us to examine our own selves. When I see virtue persecuted, the victim of wickedness, and yet ever beautiful, ever glorious, and preferable to all, even in the midst of misfortune —the effect of the drama in which this is displayed does not remain equivocal; it is virtue alone which holds my interest.[1]

The aim of his essay, then, is to prove that " the Serious Drama exists, that it is a good kind of drama, that it affords a lively interest, a moral appeal direct and profound, and that it can be expressed only in one style, that of nature." [1]

As a third example of critical theory devoted to this type

---

[1] *Essai sur le genre dramatique sérieux* (1767).

we may take Goldsmith's ' opposition ' article, entitled *An Essay on the Theatre; or A Comparison between Laughing and Sentimental Comedy* (1772). Peculiarly enough, Goldsmith here starts off with a classical judgment: tragedy represents the misfortunes of the great, comedy the frailties of the humbler sort. Proceeding from this premise, he decides that our higher pity cannot be aroused for the poorer class of people—a Belisarius we may pity, but for a beggar we can experience only contempt. He notes, however, that a new type of drama has become very popular, the sentimental comedy, in which " the virtues of private life are exhibited, rather than the vices exposed; and the distresses rather than the faults of mankind make our interest in the piece." Such a monstrosity Goldsmith unhesitatingly denounces, and he quotes approvingly the judgment of a friend who, sitting unmoved at one of these sentimental pieces, declared that " as the hero is but a tradesman, it is indifferent to me whether he be turned out of his counting-house on Fish-street Hill, since he will still have enough left to open shop in St Giles's."

THE CHARACTERISTICS OF SENTIMENTAL DRAMA. Goldsmith's foolishly illogical attack, no less than the soulful apologies of Diderot and Beaumarchais, indicate well the difficulties which lie in the way of a truly critical approach to this type of drama. It may be fitting here to pause for a moment to see if we can trace more closely some of its main features. Leaving aside the " bourgeois tragedy," which Goldsmith perversely chooses to confuse with the other, we may say that the sentimental drama shows itself removed from tragedy, not only by the absence of an unhappy ending, but by the presentation of the serious matter in such a way that we are not thrilled and awed by the scenes set before us. This lack of thrill and awe is the prime point of difference between the two. On the other hand, it is distinguished from comedy, not only by the lack of episodes designed simply to amuse, but by the ' serious,' ' philosophic ' or ' moral ' aims of the dramatists. Here we must not allow ourselves to be misled by too great attention paid to the eighteenth-century form. In that an appeal is definitely made to our emotions, particularly to the emotions of pity and sympathy (hence the insistence on

" virtue " in the essays of Goldsmith, Diderot, and Beau-marchais). ' Sympathetic ' tears and ' sentimental ' tears are almost synonymous terms for the eighteenth century. Such an appeal to the emotions, however, is merely a temporary phenomenon, due, we may say, to the romantic necessity of combating the intellectual callousness of the age. No appeal to the emotions is made in Shaw's plays, hardly any even in the plays of Björnson. Just as, for example, the ' sympathetic ' and ' sentimental ' ideas concerning the brotherhood of man which were so popular in the late eighteenth century have given place to the essentially intellectual concepts of present-day social theories, although the two are bound together by fundamental ties, so the sentimentalism of the Georgian era and the Shavian drama are intimately related. The one uses the emotional method, and the other the intellectual : that is all.

What, then, is the element common to both? Here the insistence on the " duties of man " is all-important. Neither in comedy nor in tragedy do we get any real emphasis laid on a ' problem ' as such. You cannot say that there is the problem in *Macbeth* of whether it is better to fly temptation or not; or that there is the problem in *Hamlet* of whether you should listen carefully to your father's ghost or not. Such were mere folly. But in these two eighteenth-century comedies which we chose as representative of their class we find the problem duly stressed. In the one it is the relation between father and daughter, when the former desires to hurry the latter into what will quite evidently be a disastrous marriage; in the other it is the relation between a lover and his *fiancée*, first when she is a poor ward and he the son of a rich father, and again when he discovers that she is poor because his father has cheated her of her money. This is simply a Theatre of Sentimental Ideas written with the same purpose as that Theatre of Ideas of which so much was said at the beginning of the present century. It differs from the other in presenting both a problem and a solution based on belief in natural virtue, whereas the modern Theatre of Ideas tries to look at life ' philosophically ' and often omits the solution; but other-wise their aims are identical.

THE QUESTION OF REALISM. Diderot and Beaumarchais pleaded in defence of this new type that it was based on reality, being thus closely related to man's duties in ordinary life, and here we return full sweep to the time-honoured mirror established by Cicero's judgment. As has already been seen, no argument can logically be used to support the view that any type of drama may exist on a basis of pure naturalism; yet Diderot and Beaumarchais were so far in the right that the sentimental drama they helped to create presented characters which, in spite of artificial conceptions, were nearer to those of ordinary existence than the typical characters of tragedy or of comedy. In tragedy the hero is an exceptional figure, drawn on a scale beyond that of common humanity; in pure comedy the *dramatis personæ* are types only; and in both the action has usually a touch of the extraordinary, for tragedy sees life as something dark and terrible, comedy sees it as a joyous vale of laughter from which death and disaster are formally banished. In the *drame*, however, the characters are generally drawn as individuals; our emotions are aroused or our intellects so quickened as to beget at least rational interest in the fortunes of these characters; while the action is designed in such a way as to make us conscious always of the relationship between the fictional scenes and the progress of life around us. In the hands of many dramatists there is here nothing more than an attempt at securing naturalistic effects, and in so far a complete failure to gain true dramatic impression. There is no need to cover once more the ground already covered; sufficient be it to affirm again the essential truth that drama—of whatsoever sort it may be—cannot rest itself on a foundation of reality imitated. The greatest danger for the sentimental or 'problem' dramatist lies here, it is true; for it is easy to drag this form down to a lower plane and thus lose that universality demanded by the finest art.

THE IMPRESSIONS CREATED BY THE 'DRAME.' We have seen that this type of drama aims fundamentally at the presentation of the "duties of man," that phrase being employed in the widest possible significance, and that in so doing it does move closer to real life than tragedy, which deals with the metaphysical, and comedy, which deals normally with the rational. Put in another way, we might say that, whereas tragedy treats of man in relation to the universe, with death as an eternal problem of terrible significance, and whereas comedy treats of man the rational enjoyer of life's sweets in relation to man, with death cast aside as a thing of no import for the pleasures of to-day and the larger universe forgotten in the delights of the minute, the *drame* attempts to deal with human existence from the standpoint of ordinary civilization, conscious of death, but treating it without reference to metaphysical considerations, more intent on social relationships than on abstract problems, and eager to discuss, not merely transitory joys, but the securing of a happiness which shall at least outlive the passing moment. The *drame* is like a man with a money-box, fully awake to the value of wealth and considering the best ways in which he may save to add to his store; tragedy is like the man to whom wealth is a worthless vision in comparison with a terror of infinity; comedy is like the man for whom this day's joys are the only certainty and this day's wealth the means of securing them.

On these attitudes depend the impressions produced by the three types. Those created by tragedy and by comedy have already been considered, and it is easy to see that the impression aroused by the *drame* is that which truly distinguishes it from the others. That impression is not merely midway between those of tragedy and comedy, as some have thought, although the belief that such it is can easily arise from the fact that it is not so awesome as that of tragedy or so joyous as that of comedy; it is utterly different from both, depending upon a different standard of life. The *drame* is essentially the play of conscious civilization, and its development since 1750 is thus intimately related to the social ideals of the modern period. It is interested in all things appertaining to man as a 'civilized' being. Starting with the fundamental question of law, a thing created by man in opposition to nature, it discusses this first, in Shakespeare's *Measure for Measure*. It then proceeds to other matters of particular importance to the happiness of man as an individual in society ruled by law, and thus comes to the problem of love and marriage and parental law—a theme freely exploited in the mid-eighteenth century. From this, the sphere is extended to deal with social prejudice and the fortunes of classes within the community, such as is treated in Cumberland's *Jew*. Thereafter the scope of the interest is rapidly increased so as to include anything in any way associated with social existence—the position of woman in the home (as in Ibsen's *Doll's House*), the question of pre-nuptial chastity (as in Björnson's *Gauntlet*), the problem of the slums (as in Mr Shaw's *Widowers' Houses*), the relationship of the social classes (as in Robertson's *Caste*), even the fundamentals of political government (as in Mr Shaw's *Apple Cart*). Sometimes the social force looms largest; sometimes the play is cast in such a form as to make an entertaining story overshadow the social atmosphere, as, for example, in Mr Besier's *Barretts of Wimpole Street*, where the emotions, the impression, of the *drame* are no less fully called forth than in such plays as those of Ibsen and his followers.

Through the association of the particular problem presented the *drame* may, if the playwright has the ability of the true dramatist to concentrate and typify, secure the same impression of universality as that which distinguishes tragedy and comedy. A crude attempt at realism will not do this, but when the stage action and the stage characters are, as it were, " brief abstracts " of the time, the relationship with the problems of social life in general will clearly build up that broader impression without which no drama can be considered truly great. The *drame* has thus every right to be regarded as one of the main types of theatrical expression; indeed, because of the fact that the individual man ever more rapidly is becoming a mere part of the social body, it may be said to be the most typical form of the present-day theatre. Perhaps social life tends to limit the mystic contemplation of the universe, for its manifold duties distract and confuse; nor can life be taken so easily and joyously and carelessly as it was by the aristocrats of past times; the *drame*, therefore, because of its insistence on that which perforce must most occupy our attentions, seems the form most fitted to express the ideals of the modern age, and for that reason requires as great attention from the critical student as do the time-honoured tragedy and comedy.

In thus considering it, however, no standard provided by

actuality may be allowed to intrude; the *drame*, no less than the other types, must be judged solely as an art, and, although a nearer approach may be made here to real life, that approach can never be complete. We may, certainly, reject as inartistic any play of this form in which a problem is falsely stated, for it is an assumption of the art itself that here the problems of life are to be dealt with, but otherwise the piece must be judged in accordance with its own aims, and not with the ways of life. Put *Widowers' Houses* on the wheel and we may tear from it what we will; we may say then that the facts as presented by the dramatist could not have occurred in reality exactly as he has made them occur. That, however, does not matter, for the essential problem is stated boldly and with that higher truth which makes it typical. After the stating of the problem in broad outlines the drama, judged as a piece of art, is harmonious in its parts and therefore is to be praised. Mere ' truth to reality ' means nothing to drama at all, unless interpreted on these broader lines.

CONCLUSION. This independence of drama, realized so long ago by Aristotle, must appear one of the strangest peculiarities of this particular type of literature, for the drama, more than the majority of other arts, would seem to take its very life from the actions and the thoughts of mortal men and women. Nevertheless, the fact remains that, however much the theatre may attempt to depict human personalities, it must always show them in an idealized light, moving in a world of their own. This world can be fully understood only when we have endeavoured to investigate those elements which seem to be common to all the great dramatists. Herein, therefore, lies the chief *apologia* for this attempt, tentative and possibly fragmentary, to investigate, analyse and, so far as possible, classify the characteristics of that art which has charmed millions for centuries upon centuries, and has given to the world the profound genius of an Æschylus, a Sophocles, and a Shakespeare, as well as the gaiety, the wit, and the laughter of a Terence, a Molière, and a Congreve.

In this investigation it has become apparent that the ancients were indeed right in their classification by kinds, a method not unlike that practised in Sanscrit criticism. There do truly seem to be certain typical impressions which the playwright endeavours to give to an audience, and, although these impressions may sometimes be mixed, only some of them will blend harmoniously. It is the central impression, after all, which counts for most, and to that all else must be subservient. Of these impressions four seem to predominate, and all four depend upon the philosophic attitude of the playwright toward life. In tragedy man is viewed, not as a mere piece of animal existence, but as a soul *sub specie æternitatis*; in the comedy of humour, too, he is viewed thus, but, whereas in tragedy the poet is serious and awestruck in face of the vastness of the universe, in the comedy of humour he regards everything as a rather pathetic jest—for him life is truly a dream; in ordinary comedy the attitude is entirely different : here life is regarded as a thing of the moment only, a thing of laughter and smiles without a thought for the morrow, a cruel thing perhaps, for sympathy cannot enter here, and he who troubles his head about aught else than his own happiness is merely absurd and a fitting butt for ridicule; while, finally, in the *drame* man is viewed as a social being and as little else, as a person surrounded by laws and conventions, as one whose happiness can be secured only by two things—by the improvement of too harsh social regulations and of evil conditions and by the developing in himself of an adaptability to his circumstances. In the first death is a terrible gate leading between this life and the unknown beyond; in the second death is forgotten in the presence of the dream; in the third death is entirely and rationally rejected as having nothing to do with this minute's joys; and in the last death is merely a thing of convention, a thing of coffins and funerals, an end to an existence dependent wholly on the acceptance of civilization's conventional laws. These four represent the four chief ways of looking at life, and it is not by chance that the majority of plays, ancient and modern, fall easily into one group or another, for the art of the drama, independent as it may be and bowing to none but the laws of its own nature, is, when all has been said, a concentrating mirror in which the essentials of man's thought have, perhaps, been more clearly, more gloriously, more succinctly expressed than in any other sphere of artistic creation.

APPENDIX

I. SUGGESTIONS FOR READING IN DRAMATIC THEORY [1]

(i) GENERAL

IT is impossible to dissociate the study of dramatic theory from the larger study of literary criticism generally. The standard history of the whole subject is Professor Saintsbury's *History of Literary Criticism*. The portions devoted to English criticism have been abstracted from this and issued as a separate volume. As a companion book, the *Loci Critici* of Professor Saintsbury is exceedingly useful. In this work the most important critical passages of writers from Aristotle to Arnold have been collected and annotated. A full bibliography of literary criticism is to be found in Gayley and Scott's *Methods and Materials of Literary Criticism*. Two volumes in the "World's Classics" series present collections of critical essays; the first deals with early critical theory, the second with literary theory of the nineteenth century. For further study Spingarn's *Critical Essays of the Seventeenth Century* and his *History of Literary Criticism in the Renaissance* will be found valuable. The various Elizabethan critical essays have been collected by Gregory Smith. Nichol Smith's *Eighteenth-century Essays on Shakespeare* and the same editor's *Shakespeare Criticism* present the typical pronouncements on our master-dramatist by the neo-classicists and others. Durham's *Critical Essays of the Eighteenth Century* is a valuable detailed study of the ideas of this period. Of modern works I. A. Richards' *The Principles of Literary Criticism* is very suggestive.

(ii) INDIVIDUAL WORKS

CLASSIC CRITICISM. The best translation of the *Poetics* is that by S. H. Butcher. Butcher's notes should be carefully studied.

---

[1] It will be understood that no attempt is made here to provide a 'bibliography' of critical works. The notes presented in this appendix contain only suggestions for further reading, and necessarily omit a great many, even important, studies.

Important also is I. Bywater's *Aristotle on the Art of Poetry*. Naturally, the question of Aristotle's theory of katharsis is discussed in almost all works on dramatic theory, and there are several particular essays on this subject. Among recent studies A. H. Gilbert's "The Aristotelian Catharsis" (*Philosophical Review*, xxxv (July 1926), 301–314), C. Hebler's "Über die Aristotelische Definition der Tragödie" (*Archiv für Geschichte der Philosophie*, x, 1), and M. J. H. Myers' "The Meaning of Katharsis" (*Sewanee Review*, xxxiv (July–September 1926), 278–290) may be mentioned. In reading Aristotle the few remarks on the drama made by Plato should not be disregarded. These are scattered throughout his discourses, although the most important appear in *The Republic* (" Golden Treasury Series "). On Plato's criticism there is a good essay by Pater in *Plato and Platonism*, and an interesting study by W. C. Green—" Plato's View of Poetry "—in *Harvard Studies in Philology*, vol. xxix.

Horace's *The Epistle to the Pisos* is well rendered by Saintsbury in his *Loci Critici*. A useful volume is that by A. S. Cook, *The Art of Poetry : The Poetical Treatises of Horace, Vida, and Boileau*.

MEDIEVAL CRITICISM does not deal largely with drama, owing to the loss of that type of literature after the fall of the Roman Empire. Even Chaucer's definition of tragedy does not strictly refer to dramatic form, but to tragic tales.

RENASCENCE CRITICISM is well dealt with by Spingarn in the work mentioned. Castelvetro is very important, as is Vida. On these the later neo-classic writers of France and of England modelled themselves. A few extracts will be found in *Loci Critici*, and others in Barrett H. Clark's *European Theories of the Drama*.

Sidney's *An Apologie for Poetrie* should be read in the reprint of Professor Arber. In this series also will be found the work of Puttenham, *The Arte of English Poetrie*, and of Webbe, *A Discourse of English Poetrie*, both of which, however, deal rather with poetry in general than with drama in particular.

Jonson wrote no system of criticism, but his ideas are to be seen in his *Timber, or Discoveries*, and in the prologues to his various plays. It should be noted that the judgments given in *Timber* are not wholly original, but, like those of Sidney, are very largely derived, even directly translated, from passages in preceding critics.

Boileau's *L'Art Poétique* should certainly be read before attempting any work on later seventeenth-century English critics. With this might be taken the *Réflexions sur la Poétique* of Rapin. Both of these have been well analysed by Saintsbury.

APPENDIX

Dryden stands out as the first original English writer on literary theory. His essays have been excellently edited by Professor W. P. Ker, and the *Dramatic Essays* have been selected by W. H. Hudson for the " Everyman " series.

AUGUSTAN CRITICISM in England presents little of original material from the point of view of the drama. Rymer should be read to gain an idea of the severer form ; Addison to gain an idea of the more mellowed, refined theories of the age; and Pope (*Essay on Criticism*) to gain an idea of the average rules taken over from the Continent and here laid down with epigrammatic force. Dr Johnson is important because of his defiant personality. Of his work several essays in *The Rambler* ought to be read, as well as his prologue spoken by Garrick at the opening of the Theatre Royal, Drury Lane. Indication of some important French texts is given through the pages of this book. Of particular value are the critical studies devoted to the *drame*, or serious comedy.

ROMANTIC CRITICISM deals almost exclusively with the style or characterization in drama. Hazlitt is one notable exception. His *Lectures on the English Comic Writers* will be found in the " Everyman " series. Coleridge's *Lectures on Shakespeare* (" Everyman ") and Thackeray's *The English Humourists*, should also be consulted.

MODERN CRITICISM has devoted more space to this subject. On comedy there have recently appeared a number of exceedingly important studies. Meredith's *Essay on the Idea of Comedy* is very valuable. Henri Bergson's *Le Rire* (English translation by Brereton and Rothwell) should be read carefully, as well as J. Sully's *An Essay on Laughter*, Herbert Spencer's *The Psychology of Laughter*, and J. Y. T. Greig's *The Psychology of Laughter and Comedy*. In addition to these may be mentioned John Palmer's *Comedy* and A. H. Thorndike's *Comedy* (the latter rather historical than critical). The ideas of the psychologists will be found in Sigmund Freud's *Der Witz und seine Beziehung zum Unbewussten* (English translation by A. A. Brill) and in Max Eastman's *The Sense of Humour*. Interesting matter is presented in L. Cooper's *An Aristotelian Theory of Comedy*. On the relations between comedy and humour there have recently appeared some important studies, notably Theodore Lipps' *Komik und Humor, Beiträge zur Ästhetik*, Tarquinio Vallese's *L'Umorismo nella letteratura inglese*, G. A. Lévi's *Il Comico*, P. Bellezza's *Humour*, and E. Tonini's *L'Umorismo*.

Tragedy too has had many exponents. T. Volkelt's *Die Tragödie* is an important work, and F. Nietsche's *Die Geburt der Tragödie*, in spite of its incoherence, is a powerful study. Among earlier books

W. L. Courtney's *The Idea of Tragedy*, A. H. Thorndike's *Tragedy* (mainly historical), and C. E. Vaughan's *Types of Tragic Drama* are all valuable. More recently there have been published J. S. Smart's *Tragedy* (English Association *Studies*, vol. viii), W. Macneile Dixon's *Tragedy* (in which an effort is made to capture the prime essentials of the tragic spirit—a most suggestive work), and F. L. Lucas' *Tragedy* (which deals critically with Aristotle's ideas). There are, too, several essays on particular aspects of tragic drama, such as A. Beaumont's *The Hero: A Theory of Tragedy*, C. E. Montague's " The Delights of Tragedy " (*Atlantic Monthly*, cxxxviii (September 1926), 362–370), and E. S. Gerhard's " The Differences between Classical Tragedy and Romantic Tragedy " (*Classical Weekly*, xviii (October 20, 1924), 18–22). As stated in the text, Maeterlinck's " The Tragical in Daily Life " (in *The Treasure of the Humble*) is an important piece of criticism. M. Poensgen's *Geschichte der Theorie der Tragödie* is a most useful compilation, and there is much of suggestion in T. Lipps' essay, " Tragik, Tragödie und wissenschaftliche Kritik " (*Zeitschrift für vergleichenden Literatur*, v, 6). M. J. Wolff has also an important study on " Die Theorie der italienischen Tragödie im XVI. Jahrhundert " (*Archiv für das Studium der neueren Sprachen und Literaturen*, cxxviii, 1–2). E. Bertana's *La Tragedia* contains likewise much critical matter.

Besides these, there are numerous more general studies such as Ashley Dukes' *Drama*, W. Archer's *The Old Drama and the New*, D. Clive Stuart's *The Development of Dramatic Art*, H. Bosworth's *Technique in Dramatic Art*, G. J. Nathan's *The Critic and the Drama*, H. A. Jones' *Renascence of the English Drama*, and W. A. Darlington's *Through the Fourth Wall* and *Literature in the Theatre*. Much of value will be discovered also in various ' practical ' books on play-writing. Here may be mentioned W. Archer's *Playmaking*, Clayton Hamilton's *The Theory of the Theatre* and *Problems of the Playwright*, and Brander Matthews' *Playwrights on Playmaking* and *The Principles of Playmaking*. A fairly full list of such works up to the dates of publication is included in Barrett H. Clark's *European Theories of the Drama* (1929), to which I am indebted for some quotations, and his *Study of the Modern Drama* (1925). The " World Drama Series," edited by R. M. Smith, contains useful anthologies of ' types ' of drama, with comments. On dramatic speech Bonamy Dobrée has a subtle essay, entitled *Histriophone*, and the problems of poetic drama are discussed in a ' dialogue ' by T. S. Eliot prefixed to a reprint of Dryden's *Essay* (Etchells and Macdonald).

APPENDIX

II. SUGGESTIONS FOR READING IN DRAMA

(A) GENERAL

There exists quite a number of works which essay to treat the entirety of drama in one general survey. Most of these are necessarily prejudiced and often lack balance, but the conspectus they provide is frequently of great value. One of the best known is J. Klein's *Geschichte des Dramas* (13 vols.); J. Janin's *Histoire de la littérature dramatique* (6 vols.) may also be mentioned. A. W. Schlegel's *A Course of Lectures on Dramatic Art and Literature* (English translation) is important, as is also W. Creizenach's *Geschichte des neuren Dramas* (5 vols.), which, however, does not carry on to modern times.

On theatrical history there are G. Bapst's *Essai sur l'histoire du Théâtre* and the present writer's *The Development of the Theatre*.

(B) GREEK DRAMA

(i) GENERAL

There is an interesting essay on Greek drama in Dent's " Temple Primers " ; a more detailed account will be found in *The Athenian Drama*, by G. C. W. Warr, J. S. Phillimore, and G. C. Murray. The works entitled *Die griechische Tragödie* recently published by E. Howald and M. Pohlenz are both of considerable value. J. Pickard-Cambridge well surveys the origins in *Dithyramb, Tragedy, and Comedy*.

On the Greek stage K. Mantzius' *History of Theatrical Art*, R. Flickinger's *The Greek Theater*, O. Navarre's *Le Théâtre grec*, A. E. Haigh's *The Attic Theatre*, and T. S. Allen's *Stage Antiquities of the Greeks and Romans* might be consulted.

(ii) PARTICULAR WRITERS

ÆSCHYLUS has left seven plays : *Persæ, Seven against Thebes, Prometheus Bound, Suppliants, Agamemnon, Choephoræ, Eumenides*. The last three form a trilogy dealing with the theme of Orestes, and are often classed together as the *Oresteia*. A translation of all, by A. Swanwick, is published in the Bohn Library. Morshead's *House of Atreus* also is a fine translation of the *Oresteia*.

THE THEORY OF DRAMA

SOPHOCLES. Again, seven of this dramatist's plays are extant: *Trachiniæ, Ajax, Electra, Œdipus Tyrannus, Œdipus Coloneus, Antigone, Philoctetes.* There are besides a few scattered fragments of his 130 odd dramas. The translations by Sir R. C. Jebb and by R. Whitelaw are both excellent.

EURIPIDES. Of Euripides' ninety-two dramas eighteen or nineteen have been preserved: *Alcestis, Medea, Hippolytus, Hecuba, Andromache, Ion, Suppliants, Heracleidæ, Heracles Mad, Iphigenia in Tauris, Troades, Helen, Phœnissæ, Electra, Orestes, Iphigenia at Aulis, Bacchæ, Cyclops.* (*Rhesus* is probably spurious.) The best translations are undoubtedly those of Professor Gilbert Murray. An interesting rendering of the *Cyclops* is to be found in Shelley's works. The *Alcestis* appears in part in Browning's *Balaustion's Adventure.*

ARISTOPHANES wrote, it is said, about fifty-five comedies. Of these only eleven have been handed down to us: *Acharnians, Knights, Clouds, Wasps, Peace, Birds, Lysistrata, Thesmophoriazusæ, Frogs, Ecclesiazusæ, Plutus.* There is a translation, in six volumes, by B. B. Rogers.

(C) ROMAN DRAMA

SENECA, the most famous of the Roman tragic poets, has left ten plays: *Agamemnon, Hercules Furens, Hercules Œtæus, Medea, Octavia* (apparently spurious), *Œdipus, Phædra, Phœnissæ, Thyestes, Troades.* These were translated into English in the second half of the sixteenth century, and have seen several renderings since that date. Handy translations are those of E. C. Harris and W. Bradshaw. There is a well-written account of his work by F. L. Lucas, *Seneca and Elizabethan Tragedy.*

TERENCE has six comedies: *Andria, Heauton Timorumenos, Eunuchus, Phormio, Hecyra, Adelphi.* The text and translation are given in the Loeb Classical Library.

PLAUTUS is more plentifully represented than any of the others, there being twenty-one of his plays as well as various fragments extant: *Amphitruo, Asinaria, Aulularia, Bacchides, Captivi, Casina, Cistellaria, Curculio, Epidicus, Menæchmi, Mercator, Miles Gloriosus, Mostellaria, Persa, Pœnulus, Pseudolus, Rudens, Stichus, Trinummus, Truculentus, Vidularia.* Five of these plays have been translated by Sugden.

The series entitled "Our Debt to Greece and Rome" contains useful volumes on the dramatists and their influence.

APPENDIX

(D) ENGLISH DRAMA

(i) GENERAL

There are several general accounts of English drama. The present writer's *British Drama* (with the accompanying volume of selections, *Readings from British Drama*) essays to cover the whole field. Besides these there is B. Brawley's *A Short History of the English Drama*, F. E. Schelling's *English Drama*, and H. F. Rubinstein's brief account in " Benn's Sixpenny Library." The standard history from the beginnings to 1714 is that of A. W. Ward, although that has been superseded by other more detailed studies.

On the theatres H. B. Baker's *History of the London Stage, 1576–1903*, J. Doran's ' *Their Majesties' Servants*,' the present writer's *The English Stage*, and R. Farquharson Sharp's *A Short History of the English Stage* might be consulted.

(ii) MEDIEVAL

On the development of the mysteries see Sir E. K. Chambers, *The Mediæval Stage*; F. E. Schelling, *Elizabethan Drama*; J. A. Symonds, *Shakespere's Predecessors*; F. S. Boas, *Shakspere and his Predecessors*. C. M. Gayley's *Representative English Comedies* contains specimens of this early work, as does *Everyman and other Mysteries* (" Everyman " series). A. W. Pollard's *English Miracle Plays, Moralities, and Interludes* is most useful.

(iii) PRE-SHAKESPEARIAN

Most of the books noted in the preceding section deal also with this period. The standard history of the stage during this time is Sir E. K. Chambers' monumental *The Elizabethan Stage*. The earlier field is also excellently covered by F. Tucker Brooke's *Tudor Drama*, and much detail is entertainingly presented in A. W. Reed's *Early Tudor Drama*. The dramatic literature of the age is also surveyed in F. E. Schelling's *Elizabethan Drama, 1558–1642*. There are besides numbers of special studies, most of which are chronicled in Chambers' work.

The collections of plays edited by J. Q. Adams and W. A. Neilson respectively provide representative texts; two volumes in the " Everyman " series likewise provide a small set of selected plays. There are besides many larger collections of early and Elizabethan dramas (*e.g.*, Dodsley's, Farmer's *Facsimiles*, Malone Society publications). The best edition of Lyly is that edited by R. W.

251

THE THEORY OF DRAMA

Bond. A. H. Bullen has edited Peele's works (Stratford-on-Avon). Greene's plays appear in the " Mermaid Series," and have also been edited by J. Churton Collins. The best edition of Nashe is that of R. B. McKerrow. Marlowe's plays appear in the " Mermaid Series," and are now being re-edited by a group of scholars. Suggested short list for reading :

(i) **Early interludes:** *The Four P's, Johan Johan.* (ii) **Early comedy:** *Gammer Gurton's Needle, Ralph Roister Doister.* (iii) **Romantic comedy:** Lyly's *Endimion,* Greene's *Friar Bacon and Friar Bungay.* (iv) Marlowe's *Tamburlaine* and *Dr Faustus.* (v) **Senecan drama:** Sackville and Norton's *Gorboduc,* Kyd's *Spanish Tragedy.*

A study of some of Shakespeare's originals is also interesting as showing his methods; the anonymous *King Leir* (" Shakespeare Classics ") and *The Taming of the Shrew* (" Shakespeare Classics ") might be suggested in this connexion.

(iv) Shakespearian

The critical work on Shakespeare is so vast that only a few suggestions may here be made. In connexion with this book A. C. Bradley's *Shakespearean Tragedy* ought to be studied, and there are several works specially devoted to Shakespeare's craft which will be found of prime value, notably R. G. Moulton's *Shakespeare as a Dramatic Artist,* J. Brander Matthews' *Shakspere as a Playwright,* T. R. Lounsbury's *Shakespeare as a Dramatic Artist,* G. P. Baker's *The Development of Shakespeare as a Dramatist,* F. Schücking's *Character Problems in Shakespeare's Plays,* and E. E. Stoll's *Shakespeare Studies.* For the life see the biographies by Sir E. K. Chambers and Sir Sidney Lee. Sir Walter Raleigh's volume in the " English Men of Letters Series " and E. Dowden's *Shakespeare: a Critical Study of his Mind and Art* are also exceedingly suggestive. Some of the ideas given in the present book are more fully dealt with in the author's *Studies in Shakespeare.*

(v) Contemporaries of Shakespeare

The collection of Neilson referred to above will be found useful. The " Mermaid Series " and the " Belles Lettres Series " present interesting selections of plays. For one comparatively unacquainted with the plays of the period the following might be taken as a suggested course of reading :

(i) **Domestic tragedy:** *Arden of Feversham*; Heywood's *The English Traveller* and *A Woman Killed with Kindness.* (ii) **Domestic**

252

APPENDIX

comedy: Jonson's *Every Man in his Humour*; Dekker's *The Shoemaker's Holiday*. (iii) **Satiric comedy**: Jonson's *The Alchemist* and *Volpone*. (iv) **Early comedy of wit**: Fletcher's *The Wild Goose-Chase*. (v) **Tragedy of horror**: Marston's *Antonio and Mellida* and *Antonio's Revenge*; Ford's *'Tis Pity* and *The Broken Heart*; Webster's *The White Devil* and *The Duchess of Malfi*. (vi) **Neo-classic tragedy**: Jonson's *Sejanus*. (vii) **Romantic tragedy and tragi-comedy**: Beaumont and Fletcher's *The Maid's Tragedy, Philaster*, and *A King and No King*. (viii) **Burlesque serious drama**: Beaumont and Fletcher's *The Knight of the Burning Pestle*.

It must be noted that this list presents merely a few plays possessing features discussed in the text of this book.

(vi) RESTORATION

The present writer has a general *History of Restoration Drama*, while the period 1642–1780 is covered also in G. H. Nettleton's shorter *English Drama of the Restoration and Eighteenth Century*. On the tragedy of the time see Bonamy Dobrée's *Restoration Tragedy*, and on the comedy the same author's *Restoration Comedy*, K. M. Lynch's *The Social Mode of Restoration Comedy*, H. T. E. Perry's *The Comic Spirit in Restoration Drama*, and J. W. Krutch's *Comedy and Conscience after the Restoration*. Among older essays that of Lamb, " On the Artificial Comedy of the Last Century " and that of Macaulay, on " The Comic Dramatists of the Restoration," are of fundamental importance.

Nearly all the major dramatists have been edited in recent years, and there are some volumes of selections. The " World's Classics " series includes the works of Congreve as well as *Five Restoration Comedies* and *Five Restoration Tragedies*. Still other plays will be found in M. Summers' *Restoration Comedies* and *Shakespeare Adaptations*. The following might be suggested for reading : (i) **Rimed heroic drama**: Settle's *The Empress of Morocco*, Dryden's *The Indian Emperor*, D'Avenant's *The Siege of Rhodes*, Otway's *Don Carlos*. (ii) **Blank verse heroic drama**: Dryden's *All for Love*, Congreve's *The Mourning Bride*, Otway's *Venice Preserv'd*. (iii) **Pathetic drama**: Rowe's *The Fair Penitent* and *Jane Shore*. (iv) **Jonsonian comedy**: Shadwell's *The Sullen Lovers* and *The Virtuoso*. (v) **Dryden type of comedy**: *The Marriage à la Mode* and *The Spanish Fryar*. (vi) **Comedy of manners**: Etherege's *The Man of Mode*, Wycherley's *The Gentleman Dancing Master* and *The Plain Dealer*, Congreve's *The Way of the World*, Vanbrugh's *The Relapse*, Farquhar's *The Beaux' Stratagem*. (vii) **Comedy**

253

of intrigue: Dryden's *Sir Martin Mar-all*. (viii) **Shakespeare** adaptations : Dryden and D'Avenant's *The Tempest*, Dryden's *Troilus and Cressida*. On the last G. C. D. Odell's *Shakespeare from Betterton to Irving* should be consulted.

(vii) EIGHTEENTH CENTURY

The present writer has a history of eighteenth-century drama in two volumes. The standard authority for the theatrical records is J. Genest's *Some Account of the English Stage*. On the sentimental drama of the period see E. Bernbaum's *The Drama of Sensibility*. F. W. Bateson has a volume of essays on particular dramatists. Some of the writers mentioned above (*e.g.*, Vanbrugh, Farquhar, and Rowe) really belong in date to this section. Lillo's *The London Merchant* and *Fatal Curiosity* (" Belles Lettres Series ") should be read, and along with them W. H. Hudson's admirable essay in *Quiet Hours in a Library*. Addison's *Cato* is the typical neo-classic tragedy, Steele's *The Conscious Lovers* one of the typical sentimental dramas, Gay's *The Beggar's Opera* the typical ballad opera. Moore's *The Gamester* is a readable domestic tragedy. Goldsmith's *She Stoops to Conquer* and Sheridan's *The School for Scandal* represent the revival of the comedy of manners. For this period *The British Theatre*, a series of plays collected by Mrs Inchbald and published in 1808, will be found invaluable. It is still fairly easily procured second-hand.

(viii) ROMANTIC

The present writer has *A History of Early Nineteenth Century Drama*. E. B. Watson's *Sheridan to Robertson* is most stimulating, and W. Archer's *English Dramatists of To-day* is a useful volume for the study of the later years of the century. Among other works A. Filon's *The English Stage* and Clement Scott's *Drama of Yesterday and To-day* can be recommended.

A clear distinction is to be made between the legitimate and illegitimate plays during the early period. Fitzball, Dibdin, Colman are fairly typical of the writers of the early period; their works are represented in various series published by Cumberland, Dicks, Richardson, and others. Planché's extravaganzas are important. In the legitimate sphere we meet almost all the poets of the time: Shelly's *The Cenci*, Coleridge's *Remorse*, Byron's *Cain*, *The Two Foscari*, and *Werner* may be taken as indicative of the common qualities. Later there is to be traced the growing realistic element and the influence of Ibsen. Boucicault, Lytton (for *Money*),

APPENDIX

and Robertson are all pioneer workers. Gilbert shows the spirit of the extravaganza at work in a more refined style; while the 'modern' drama is born with the writings of Wilde, Shaw, Pinero, and Jones in the last decade. The journal called *The Theatre* will be found useful as a guide, and G. B. Shaw's *Dramatic Opinions and Essays* are a stimulating commentary on the theatre of the time.

(ix) Modern

The modern period is covered by a number of studies—A. E. Morgan's *Tendencies of Modern English Drama*, W. Archer's *The Old Drama and the New*, T. H. Dickinson's *The Contemporary Drama of England*, Ashley Dukes' *Modern Dramatists* and *The Youngest Drama*. The Irish drama is dealt with in E. Boyd's *Ireland's Literary Renaissance* and *The Contemporary Drama of Ireland*. Much detail is given in Barrett H. Clark's *A Study of the Modern Drama*, of great value as a reference book.

It is, of course, impossible to give suggestions for reading; Clark's volume may well be used as a guide.

(E) FRENCH DRAMA

There are many histories of French dramatic literature; of these that of Petit de Julleville is the most thorough. Gaiffe's work on *Le Drame* is an interesting and detailed history of that particular species of sentimental drama which dominated Europe in the eighteenth century. Some of Racine should be read, for preference *Andromaque*, *Phèdre*, and *Bérénice*. Molière, of course, is of tremendous importance, not only intrinsically, but for his influence on English comedy after 1660. A selection of his plays is issued by Heath; there is an edition of the *Œuvres Complètes* by the Oxford University Press; and John Grant, of Edinburgh, has a full edition with French on one page and translation (by A. R. Waller) on the other. There are many biographies of Molière. The most recent in English is that of J. Palmer. Something of eighteenth-century French drama should be read (*e.g.*, Diderot), and full attention should be paid to the revival of romance after the famous production of *Hernani*. There are many 'problem' plays in modern French literature, such as those of Brieux, plays that take their rise from the Ibsen movement, but present interesting variations. Maeterlinck is exceedingly important.

THE THEORY OF DRAMA

(F) ITALIAN AND SPANISH DRAMA

Some of Calderon's plays have been excellently translated by Fitzgerald, and deserve reading for their peculiar romantic atmosphere. Goldoni's work is vast, and only a very few of his comedies have been rendered into English. There is a beautifully printed selection with designs by Lovat Fraser. Other plays may be found in a collection of *Masterpieces of Foreign Authors* (1890). Alfieri is certainly the greatest tragic poet of Italy. His dramas have been translated into English and published in the Bohn Library.

Some modern Italian plays, such as the earlier dramas of D'Annunzio and those of Pirandello, repay close analytical study. L. Tonelli has a book on *L'Evoluzione del teatro contemporaneo in Italia* (1913). L. MacClintock's *The Contemporary Drama of Italy* (1920) might also be consulted.

(G) GERMAN DRAMA

The earlier history of the German drama is not of fundamental importance for this subject. G. Witkowski has a good survey of *The German Drama of the Nineteenth Century* (translated by L. E. Horning), and A. Stoeckins discusses *Naturalism in Recent German Drama*. A useful pamphlet is P. Loving's *Revolt in German Drama*.

(H) SCANDINAVIAN DRAMA

The appearance of Ibsen, Björnson, and Strindberg has brought the Scandinavian drama well to the fore. G. B. Shaw's *The Quintessence of Ibsenism* is stimulating. A. Farinelli has two important articles on " La Tragedia di Ibsen " in the *Nuova Antologia* (Nos. 1085 and 1089, 1917). H. H. Boyesen's *Essays on Scandinavian Literature* should be read, and the essays of G. Brandes, edited by Archer.

(I) RUSSIAN DRAMA

Several good books have appeared on the recent developments of the theatre and drama in Russia. Leo Wiener's *The Contemporary Drama of Russia* provides a good survey, and the ideals of the Moscow Art Theatre are well outlined in C. Stanislavsky's *My Life in Art*. A. Bakshy's *The Path of the Modern Russian Stage*, O. M. Sayler's *The Russian Theatre*, and *The Russian Theatre*, by R. Fülöp-Miller and J. Gregor, deal more particularly with the theatrical than with the dramatic movements. The works of Turgeniev, Andreev, and Evreinov are of special importance.

256

INDEX

Abraham Lincoln, 155
Accius, 14
Action, importance of, 72
Addison, J., 20, 48, 98, 176, 189, 227
Ælius Donatus, 24, 69
Æschylus, 10, 23, 26, 92, 106, 120, 124, 125, 128, 130, 132, 139, 153, 158, 159, 160, 242
Agamemnon, 106
Aigaliers, P. de Laudun d', 42
Ainley, H., 65
Albertino, 163
Alchemist, The, 212, 221
Aldus, 16
Alfieri, V., 53, 62, 93, 94, 120, 126–128, 130, 153
All for Love, 47, 152
Amphitryon, 176
Andromaque, 94, 150
Antigone, 115
Antony and Cleopatra, 47, 159, 171
Apius and Virginia, 164
Apple Cart, The, 241
Archer, W., 23, 29
Arden of Feversham, 62, 99, 100, 104, 106, 115, 119, 139
Arion, 10
Aristophanes, 11, 13, 24, 26, 30
Aristotle, 9–12, 14, 16, 17, 18, 19, 21, 22, 23, 24, 36, 39, 71–72, 85, 92, 101, 102, 151, 230, 242; his theory of imitation, 26–28; his theory of purgation, 69, 122–123; on the tragic hero, 103–104, 147–148; on pity and terror in tragedy, 119–128; his theory of comedy, 194
Arnold, M., 12
As You Like It, 52, 184, 215, 217
Atheist, The, 147
Athenæus, 13, 134
Audience, importance of, 30–32, 61–62
Aureng-Zebe, 63
Averroës, 16
Aveugles, Les, 72

Back to Methuselah, 32, 37, 48
Bacon, Francis, 30

Bale, J., 164
Banks, J., 157, 158
Barretts of Wimpole Street, The, 38, 241
Barrie, Sir J. M., 107
Beaumarchais, P. A. C. de, 21, 25, 86, 236, 238, 239
Beaumont, F., 183
Beaumont and Fletcher, tragicomedies of, 62, 63, 120, 148, 217, 229, 230
Behn, Mrs A., 228
Bellamira, 223
Bergson, H., 95, 177, 180, 187, 188, 192, 194, 195, 198, 202
Besier, R., 38, 74, 241
Björnson, B., 238, 241
Black, J., 64
Blake, W., 179
Boileau, G., 10
Broken Heart, The, 173
Brunetière, F., 23; his 'law of drama, 28–30
Budd, F. E., 40
Burbage, J., 61
Bury Fair, 224
Butcher, S. H., 101, 119
Byron, Lord, 21, 42, 44, 150

Calderon, P., de la Barca, 139, 140
Cambises, 164
Candida, 37, 48, 235
Cardinal, The, 138
Careless Husband, The, 226
Caste, 187, 241
Castelvetro, L., 18, 34, 66, 85, 150, 231
Catiline, 18, 52
Cenci, The, 147, 149
Centlivre, Mrs S., 228
Cervantes, M., 41, 199
Changeling, The, 187
Chapelain, J., 18, 41, 85–86
Charley's Aunt, 64, 69, 87
Charlton, H. B., 40, 41
Chatterton, W., 21
Chaucer, G., 104, 162
Chaussée, N. de la, 21

Choephoræ, 106, 125
Chorus, functions of the, 158–159
Cibber, C., 96, 226, 234
Cicero, 24, 239
Clarissa, 150
Clark, B. H., 15, 28, 41, 42, 51
Coleridge, S. T., 21–22, 28, 35, 121
Collins, W., 21
Colonna, V., 170
Comedy, 85–88, 175–229; of manners, 54, 55, 222–224; of romance, 214–216; of ' humours,' 218–220; of intrigue, 228–229
Comedy of Errors, The, 177, 204
Comical Revenge, The, 54
Commedia dell' arte, 67, 68
Conflict in drama, 92–98
Congreve, W., 54, 63, 70, 91, 96, 98, 179, 199, 214, 222–224, 226, 227, 242
Conquest of Granada, The, 63, 187
Conscious Lovers, The, 63
Constant Couple, The, 208
Conventions in drama, 38–60
Coriolanus, 171
Corneille, P., 19, 41, 69, 76, 86
Countess Cathleen, 107
Critique de l'école des femmes, La, 65
Cromwell, 27, 44, 50
Cumberland, R., 241
Cupid's Revenge, 107
Custom of the Country, The, 182–183
Cymbeline, 144, 217, 218

D'Avenant, Sir W., 181
Damon and Pithias, 164
Daniello, B., 83, 85
Dante Alighieri, 15, 85, 162
Dark Lady of the Sonnets, The, 37
Deirdre of the Sorrows, 142
Dekker, T., 107
Descartes, R., 52
Dickens, C., 53, 133
Diderot, D., 21, 139, 235, 236, 238, 239
Diomedes, 13
Dr Faustus, 93, 167–170
Doll's House, A, 100, 131, 235, 241
Domestic drama, 174
Dorian mime, 11
Double Dealer, The, 208, 222
Drama, significance of, 24–38
Dramatic criticism, main problems of, 60
Dramatic illusion, 34–35
Drame, 186–189, 190, 233–243
Drinkwater, J., 74, 155–156
Drummer, The, 176

Dryden, J., 11, 19, 20, 43, 47, 49, 54, 55, 63, 70, 94, 101, 124, 139, 140, 152, 176, 181, 190, 196, 205
Duchess of Malfi, The, 89, 174
Dumas, A., *fils*, 66
Dunsany, Lord, 142
Dynasts, The, 116, 141

Eccerinis, 163
École des femmes, L', 179
École des maris, L', 179
Edward II, 93, 167–170
Edwardes, R., 164
Elizabethan tragedy, 161–172
Enemy of the People, An, 115
English Traveller, The, 115, 184, 187
Ennius, 14
Etherege, Sir George, 54, 179, 199, 222–224, 226
Étourdi, L', 146, 196
Eumenides, 106, 107
Eunuchus, 197
Euripides, 10, 13, 19, 92, 107, 128, 139, 149, 159, 160
Every Man in his Humour, 52, 218, 219, 220, 221, 222
Every Man out of his Humour, 220, 222
Exposition in drama, 76

Far-off Hills, The, 197, 203
Farce, 87–88, 213–214
Farquhar, G., 43–44, 66, 70, 91, 176, 208, 214, 222–224
Fatal Curiosity, 148
Fate in tragedy, 109–112
Fausse Antipathie, La, 21
Faust, 116
Fletcher, J., 20, 97, 107, 139, 182, 228
Fontenelle, B. de, 135
Ford, J., 121, 174, 232
Franco, V., 170
Freytag, G., 57
Frogs, 30
Fugitive, The, 234

Galsworthy, J., 37, 118, 154
Gamester, The, 62
Gammer Gurton's Needle, 218
Gauntlet, The, 241
Genteel comedy, 226–228
Gentleman Dancing-master, The, 70
Gervinus, G. G., 151
Getting Married, 48
Ghosts, 69, 70, 118, 131, 186
Gielgud, J., 65
Giraldi Cinthio, 40, 74, 123, 231

INDEX

Gismond of Salerne, 163
Gods of the Mountain, The, 142
Goethe, J. W. von, 22, 28, 44, 71, 116
Goldoni, C., 53, 69
Goldsmith, O., 236–237
Gorboduc, 18, 41, 138, 163
Graves, T. S., 34
Gray, T., 21
Greek drama, 10–11, 158–160; lyrical element in, 137–138
Greene, R., 165, 215
Greig, J. Y. T., 190
Gulliver's Travels, 191

Hamlet, 32, 36, 46, 47, 52, 61, 63, 65, 66, 67, 68, 69, 72, 76, 80–81, 82, 83, 89, 93–94, 97, 99, 100, 108, 114, 116, 117, 119, 121, 123, 133, 140, 144, 146, 151, 153, 159, 171–172, 187, 232, 238
Hardy, T., 30, 116, 140
Hazlitt, W., 22, 194, 195, 198, 211
Heartbreak House, 48
Heauton Timorumenos, 197
Hédelin, F., 18, 27, 58
Hegel, G. W. F., 115
Hermann, 16
Heroic drama, 54, 55, 172–173
Heywood, T., 99, 115, 117
Hippolytus, 149
Hoadly, B., 227
Hobbes, T., 194
Holcroft, T., 130, 139
Horace, 13–14, 16, 19, 53, 59, 82, 163
Horestes, 165
Horror tragedy, 173
Howard, Sir Robert, 43
Hughes, T., 163
Hugo, V., 27, 44, 50
Humour in comedy, 198–200, 210–212
Hurd, R., 21

Ibsen, H., 89, 99, 115, 118, 130, 139, 160, 241
Imitation, theory of, 24–28
Importance of being Earnest, The, 37, 98, 210
Isidore of Seville, 15

Jackson, Sir Barry, 65
Jew, The, 241
Jew of Malta, The, 93, 167, 168
Johnson, S., 20, 50, 86; on the question of dramatic rules, 58
Jones, H. A., 29

Jonson, B., 18, 20, 52, 61, 63, 70, 146, 194, 212, 218–224, 227
Joyce, J., 75
Julius Cæsar, 112
Juno and the Paycock, 232
Justice, 116, 154, 155
Juvenal, 191

Kant, E., 194
King Henry IV, 189, 205, 220, 232
King Johan, 164
King Lear, 46, 54, 83, 89, 94, 99, 113, 123, 130, 146, 153, 154, 157, 159, 171–172
Kingsley, C., 133
Kotzebue, A. F. F. von, 139, 188
Kyd, T., 87, 107

Lamb, C., 22, 225
Lancashire Witches, The, 176
Laughter, sources of, 193–197
Legge, T., 164
Lessing, G. E., 21, 45, 58, 69–70, 123, 139
Lillo, G., 105, 130, 139, 148, 174
Locke, J., 98
Locrine, 165
London Merchant, The, 105, 130, 139, 174
Lost Leader, The, 37
Love for Love, 91, 210, 211
Love *motif* in tragedy, 173
Love's Labour's Lost, 214, 220
Love's Last Shift, 234
Lucas, F. L., 47, 123, 135
Lyly, J., 165, 166, 215

Macaulay, Lord, 189
Macbeth, 46, 47, 78–79, 80, 94, 99, 109, 112, 114, 117, 129, 130, 133, 140, 146, 149, 156, 171–172, 176, 187, 231, 238
Macchiavelli, N., 167–169
Maeterlinck, M., 72, 90, 95, 117, 133, 142
Maggi, 40
Man and Superman, 32, 37
Marlowe, C., 64, 93, 96, 137, 150, 157, 166–170, 171
Mary Queen of Scots, 158
Mary Stuart, 155
Masefield, J., 84, 117, 132
Masse-Mensch, 156
Massinger, P., 20, 107, 182
Matthews, B., 27
Measure for Measure, 188, 240
Medea, 128, 147, 148
Melodrama, 87–88, 233

Menander, 11, 12
Merchant of Venice, The, 113, 184, 187
Meredith, G., 12, 97
Merry Wives of Windsor, The, 83, 187, 189, 200, 214, 216
Mesnardière, H. de la, 18
Middle Ages, drama in the, 14–15, 161–162
Midsummer Night's Dream, A, 63, 72, 89, 146, 176, 178, 180, 196, 205, 214, 215, 217, 218
Milton, J., 41, 161
Minturno, A. S., 40, 59, 85, 134
Misanthrope, Le, 69, 146
Misfortunes of Arthur, The, 163
Moissi, F., 65
Molière, J. B. P., 18, 24, 26, 52, 65, 66, 68, 69, 96, 146, 179, 194, 242
Molina, Tirso de, 42, 51
Moore, E., 62, 139
Moral attitude toward drama, 14–15, 68–70, 224–225
Morris, E., 234, 235
Morris, W., 116
Much Ado about Nothing, 113, 146, 184, 187, 205, 215, 217, 218
Mystery plays, 14, 161

NATURE, idea of, 16, 20
Neo-classical drama, 94–95
Norton, T., 138, 163

O'CASEY, S., 107, 122, 133, 142, 154, 232
O'Neill, E., 122
Œdipus Coloneus, 89, 147
Œdipus Tyrannus, 63, 67, 148, 186
Ogier, F., 11, 18, 19, 42, 43
Old Bachelor, The, 91
Oreste, 126–128
Orphan, The, 89, 99, 145, 148, 154, 158
Othello, 46, 47, 55, 66, 93, 100, 114, 119, 133, 144, 146, 149, 151, 154, 156, 157, 171–172, 185, 186
Otway, T., 61, 89, 99, 145, 146

PACUVIUS, 14
Pamela, 30
Paolo and Francesca, 95
'Pathetic fallacy,' 112–113
Pelléas et Melisande, 91, 95, 117
Père prodigue, Un, 66
Phillips, S., 95
Philoctetes, 89, 113
Phrynichus, 10

Pikeryng, J., 165
Plain Dealer, The, 191, 212, 222
Plato, 12, 52, 123, 194
Plautus, 14, 16
Playboy of the Western World, The, 52
Plot in drama, 71–72
Preston, T., 164
Prometheus Unbound, 140, 161
Provok'd Husband, The, 197
Prynne, J., 14
Przybyszewski, S., 117, 132
Puttenham, G., 162

RACINE, J., 19, 52, 62, 93, 94, 130, 139, 140, 150, 152, 159
Radcliffe, Mrs A., 21
Ralph Roister Doister, 218
Rapin, R., 19
Rasas, theory of, 57
Räuber, Die, 153
Realism in drama, 25–26, 231, 239
Recruiting Officer, The, 223
Remorse, 121
Ricardus Tertius, 164
Richardson, J., 234
Richardson, S., 30, 150
Riders to the Sea, 52, 117
Road to Ruin, The, 130, 187
Robertelli, 40, 122
Robertson, T., 241
Robinson, L., 37, 197
Roman drama, 13–14
Romantic criticism, 21–23
Romeo and Juliet, 82, 110, 111, 138, 151, 171, 177, 232
Ronsard, P., 41
Rosmersholm, 100, 118
Rossi, E., 150
Rousseau, J. J., 136
Rowe, N., 157, 158
Rules in drama, 13, 16–17, 57–59
Rymer, T., 19, 55

SACKVILLE, T., EARL OF DORSET, 138, 163
Saint-Évremond, C. M. de, 19
St Joan, 74
St John, J., 158
Saintsbury, G., 19
Samson Agonistes, 41, 161
Sanscrit criticism, 57
Sarcey, F., 23, 27, 60, 100; theories of, concerning nature of drama, 30–32; on question of realism, 51; on unity of impression, 56
Satire, 190–192, 212–213, 218–220
Savonarola, G., 162

INDEX

Scaliger, J. J., 17, 18, 40, 85, 231
Schiller, F. von, 22, 153, 160
Schlegel, A. W., 22, 64, 134
School for Greybeards, The, 179
School for Scandal, The, 97, 98, 179, 214
School for Wives, The, 179
Schopenhauer, A., 133, 135, 194
Scornful Lady, The, 97
Scott, Sir W., 19
Scribe, E., 66
Second Mrs Tanqueray, The, 121, 131
Secret, The, 234
Secret Love, 54, 187
Sedley, Sir Charles, 223
Segni, B., 40, 136
Sejanus, 18, 52
Selimus, 165
Seneca, 14, 15, 23, 92, 107, 128, 129, 149, 163-164
Sentimental drama, 20, 25, 233-243
Shadwell, T., 176, 179, 199, 224
Shakespeare, W., passim
Shaw, G. B., 26, 32, 33, 37, 48, 68, 73, 74, 78, 235, 238, 241
Shelley, P. B., 53-54, 135, 140, 150, 161
Sheridan, R. B., 96, 179
Shirley, J., 138
Sidney, Sir P., 18, 41, 48, 69, 163, 191-192
Silver Tassie, The, 107, 122, 142, 154, 155, 232
Sir Harry Wildair, 176
Sir Martin Mar-all, 200, 204
Smart, J. S., 110, 115, 132, 150
Snow, 117, 118, 132
Socrates, 52
Sofonisba, 163
Soldier's Fortune, The, 147
Sophocles, 10, 19, 63, 71, 89, 92, 113, 115, 128, 130, 139, 148, 149, 159, 160, 242
Spanish Fryar, The, 181, 187, 200, 205
Spanish Tragedy, The, 87, 108
Spingarn, J. E., 41, 42
Squire of Alsatia, The, 224
Steele, Sir Richard, 63
Strife, 37, 116, 141, 154
Strindberg, A., 139
Style, in drama, 81-84; in tragedy, 137-145
Sully, J., 53, 196, 198, 199
Sunderland, Scott, 65
Supernatural, in tragedy, 106-112; in comedy, 175-177

Suspicious Husband, The, 227
Swift, J., 191, 212
Synge, J. M., 52, 117, 133, 142

TAGORE, S. M., 51
Taille, J. de la, 41, 59, 100, 231
Tamburlaine, 64, 93, 156, 167-170
Tamer Tam'd, The, 97
Taming of the Shrew, The, 54, 65, 97, 201, 211, 214, 220
Tempest, The, 76, 176, 178, 181, 217, 218
Terence, 14, 15, 16, 91, 96, 197, 242
Tess of the D'Urbervilles, 30
Thackeray, W. M., 191
Theatre, influence of, on drama, 61; necessity of appreciating, 64-65
Thérèse Raquin, 25
Thomas, B., 87
Timocles, 134
'Tis Pity, 232
Toller, E., 156
Tragedy, 85-86, 103-174, 242-243
Tragedy of Jane Shore, The, 158
Tragedy of Nan, The, 84, 117, 118, 131, 132
Tragi-comedy, 48-50, 230-243
Tragic hero, the, 145-158
Tragic irony, 111-113
Traitor, The, 138
Trip to the Jubilee, A, 91
Trissino, G. G., 163
Troades, 92
Troilus and Cressida, 55
Trojan Women, The, 69
Tropes, 14
Twain, M., 205
Twelfth Night, 97, 180, 196, 211, 212, 214, 216
Tyr et Sidon, 19

Ulysses, 75
Unities, the three, 39-57
Universality, in drama generally, 98-102; in tragedy, 103-119, 131-132, 143; in comedy, 175-185; in the drame, 241

VALLA, G., 16
Vanbrugh, Sir John, 214, 222-224
Varchi, B., 17
Vaughan, C. E., 62, 89, 92, 115
Vauquelin de la Fresnaye, J., 231
Vega, Lope de, 42, 48
Venice Preserv'd, 61, 100, 147, 154, 158
Vertue Betray'd, 157
Vida, G., 16

Virgin Martyr, The, 107
Vittoria Corombona, 173
Volpone, 63, 69, 146, 187, 188, 190, 211, 212, 221, 222
Voltaire, F. M. A. de, 20, 41, 62, 152

WARTON, T., 21
Way of the World, The, 63, 70, 97, 98, 185, 187, 197, 204, 210, 211, 222, 229
Webster, J., 89, 174
Werner, 21
Widowers' Houses, 37, 241, 242
Wild Gallant, The, 101

Wild-goose Chase, The, 97
Wilde, Oscar, 37
Winter's Tale, The, 47, 182, 186, 187, 217, 218, 219
Wit, 98, 209–210
Wit at Several Weapons, 182
Woman Hater, The, 183, 188
Woman Killed with Kindness, A, 99, 104, 117
Wycherley, W., 70, 212, 222–224

YEATS, W. B., 107

ZOLA, E., 25